FAST TRACK

to

CRUISING

HOW TO GO FROM NOVICE TO
CRUISE READY IN SEVEN DAYS

FAST TRACK
_to_
CRUISING

HOW TO GO FROM NOVICE TO CRUISE READY IN SEVEN DAYS

Steve and Doris Colgate

INTERNATIONAL MARINE / MCGRAW-HILL

Camden, Maine • New York • Chicago • San Francisco • Lisbon •
London • Madrid • Mexico City • Milan • New Delhi • San Juan • Seoul •
Singapore • Sydney • Toronto

The **McGraw·Hill** Companies

1 2 3 4 5 6 7 8 9 QPD QPD 9 8 7 6 5

Library of Congress Cataloging-in-Publication Data
Colgate, Stephen.
Fast track to cruising : how to go from novice to cruise ready in seven days /
Steve and Doris Colgate.
p.   cm.
ISBN 0-07-140672-7 (pbk. : alk. paper)
1. Sailing. I. Colgate, Doris. II. Title.
GV811.C562 2004
797.124—dc22   2004017467

Questions regarding the content of this book should be addressed to
International Marine
P.O. Box 220
Camden, ME 04843
www.internationalmarine.com

Questions regarding the ordering of this book should be addressed to
The McGraw-Hill Companies
Customer Service Department
P.O. Box 547
Blacklick, OH 43004
Retail customers: 1-800-262-4729
Bookstores: 1-800-722-4726

Photography supplied by the authors, Hunter Marine,
The Moorings, Billy Black, Dana Bowden, Jim Raycroft, Patience Wales.
Illustrations by Affinity Design Group. Illustrations on pages 22 (middle), 41,
73 (bottom), 92 (top) by Elayne Sears. Illustration on page 79 by U.S. Coast Guard.

CONTENTS

DAY ONE
GETTING TO KNOW YOUR BOAT

CHAPTER 1
The Language of Sailing 8

CHAPTER 2
Start Sailing 17

CHAPTER 3
The Points of Sail 28

DAY TWO
BUILDING CONFIDENCE AND SKILLS

CHAPTER 4
Wind and Sails:
A Powerful Team 43

DAY FIVE

SETTLING DOWN FOR THE NIGHT

DAY SIX

TECHNIQUES FOR SUCCESSFUL CRUISING

FOREWORD

Four years ago, in 2000, my husband Douglas and I made a radical decision. One day, out of the blue, we decided to look for a boat, quit our jobs, and go cruising. Just like that. We had no experience maintaining the mechanical systems of a cruising boat. We weren't even sure where we might go. We only knew that our lives were moving way too fast, that we were ready to engage ourselves in a pursuit that would test us, push us to live more fully, and hopefully reward us with personal growth and new ideas. Within one year of making that decision, we were waving good-bye to our family and friends on the dock. Within three years we'd sailed throughout the Western Caribbean, Central America, and down to South America.

At first, learning all about the engine and systems aboard our 1992 Shearwater cutter was challenging, but there's nothing like learning by doing. Luckily, the sailing itself, and boat handling, were a nonissue; I'd gotten a strong foundation from Colgate's Offshore Sailing School in Florida 20 years ago. The skills I'd learned there had strengthened my knowledge as a *Cruising World* editor, and they're the same skills I now use every day as we voyage on *Ithaka*. Having that foundation gave me the confidence I needed.

Doris and Steve Colgate are extremely active and passionate cruising and racing sailors, as well as excellent teachers and motivators. They understand that people want to reach their sailing goals as quickly as possible and they've built the excellent Fast Track program to accomplish it. They also understand the importance of motivation by example; their new book is loaded with stories about people like you and me, people who've taken the leap and are now embracing the cruising lifestyle—some by chartering boats in exotic destinations, and others by buying their own boats. Like them, Douglas and I set out cruising on the fast track. It changed our lives. If we can do it, you can do it, too.

—Bernadette Bernon

ACKNOWLEDGMENTS

The inspiration for this book comes from the more than 100,000 adults who chose Offshore Sailing School as their way to embark on a sailing lifestyle. Their stories are illuminating, their profound love for sailing heartening. We thank the many graduates who took the time to answer our questions about the learning experience and their sailing progress since taking a course with Offshore. We are grateful to our dedicated teaching staff for their input and tips. And most of all, we appreciate the efforts and energy of our entire team as they guide the inquisitive adventure seeker along the path that fulfills sailing dreams.

INTRODUCTION

The ultimate goal of many sailors is to go cruising. They begin with a dream of sailing through crystal waters, getting away on a sailboat without a care in the world, and finding relaxation, freedom, and rejuvenation. Many graduates of Offshore Sailing School's Fast Track to Cruising course have gone on to live the cruising lifestyle. If you are a new sailor, you likely want to fulfill your cruising dreams too—and as quickly as possible. That is the reason for this book.

You are about to embark on the *fast track*, moving from a desire to learn how to sail to being ready to cruise in easy, logical steps. When you finish this book, you will have the knowledge to take the helm of a cruising boat and experience the cruising lifestyle—for a day, a week, or months at a time.

If you're not yet ready to own a sailboat, start by renting one near home or sail with friends who own boats. Then hop a plane to the popular cruising grounds of the Caribbean and spend a week living aboard and cruising. When the urge to buy your own boat arises, you can find the right one to fit your cruising plans at a sailboat show or with the help of an experienced dealer. From there, you will embark on the most pleasurable phase of your life.

ABOUT THIS BOOK

This book compiles the core points covered in Offshore Sailing School's Learn to Sail and Live Aboard Cruising courses. The instruction and its methods are designed to give you the insight and understanding that builds confidence and skill. You will learn why you are doing something, and not just how. The text and the illustrations cover what you need to know to be a competent sailor. Throughout the book, you will be encouraged to test what you have learned at the end of each chapter. A final exam with the same questions used to test Offshore students is also an appendix in the back of this book.

Colgate 26 and Hunter 460 sailing together

Fast Track to Cruising is like two books rolled into one. Together, the chapters in both sections of the book will teach you to sail and prepare you to cruise in just seven days.

In the first half of the book you will learn the basics, including the language of sailing and how it applies to maneuvers aboard, and the theory and functions that make handling a sailboat easy. You will then progress from the initial steps of boarding a small to mid-sized sailboat to sailing away from a dock or mooring, understanding how to use the wind to move the boat efficiently, and returning safely and confidently back to the dock or mooring.

You will become skilled at controlling a boat in overpowering conditions and learn the procedure for picking up a hat that has blown overboard or a crew member who inadvertently ended up in the water. Maneuvers such as tacking and jibing will become second nature. You will learn how to stop the boat where and when you want and how to sail backward—all without a motor, of course. You will practice the safe way to handle lines, and the proper way to ease or pull when forces and friction are involved. Learning how to navigate when there are no road signs will become as natural as driving a car on a crowded highway.

Starting with Chapter 9 of the book, you will step aboard a cruising boat 35 to 46 feet in length, with all the amenities of home. The theory and most of the techniques of sailing are the same no matter how large or small the boat. But as skipper of a cruising boat, your vessel has more mass, a different steering mechanism, and mechanical systems such as a diesel engine and an electrical system. The forces on a cruising boat are greater and the reaction of the boat to your actions is slower.

You will also learn to plan a cruising itinerary and chart your course, using age-old methods and modern technology. You will be skilled at adjusting for current and tides. You will be trained in setting your sails for maximum speed and comfort, reading and reacting confidently to weather patterns, and depowering your boat for safety and comfort in heavy-air conditions. You will learn how to care for the engine and use it to come and go from docks and moorings. And you will continue your training in how to tie useful knots.

"The basic principles of sailing are the same; the main difference is primarily one of scale: bigger boat, more complex checklist—and bigger horizons."

**MARGOT JACQZ (45),
NEW YORK, NY**

"The Colgate 26 we used for the basic keelboat course was the right size, and at the end we were able to handle it very well. The next step was the Beneteau 464 [a 46-footer]. I had no idea what this boat would be like, but when we arrived at the marina I couldn't believe my eyes. We would maneuver this boat? It is only a matter of practice. After a few maneuvers in the harbor before leaving—that was it; the fear that I would not learn to handle this boat was gone!"
CLAUDIA LOGOTHETIS (MID-30s), DREIEICH, GERMANY

Claudia Logothetis in St. Barts on a Coastal Passagemaking course

In the end, you will be ready to go on your first real cruise, handling your home-away-from-home with a skill and confidence that puts you head and shoulders above the everyday duffer.

This book serves as your preparation before you start your hands-on training, and it will serve as a refresher for years to come. If you never take a sailing course, *Fast Track to Cruising* provides the information you need to go from learning-to-sail to ready-to-cruise on a mid-sized liveaboard cruising boat. Read this book, start practicing on your own, and you will be ready to live the dream.

WHAT IS CRUISING?

Picture yourself gliding over a placid sea, buoyed by a gentle breeze that fills your sails and teases your hair. Your boat tilts slightly and you adjust your position comfortably, steering toward a distant shore as water rushes past your hull and trails behind in a glimmering trail.

You are sailing a sleek craft whose motor is wind and whose pathway is the water. It will take you to places the ordinary traveler can never see. It will excite you when the wind pipes up and whitecaps form, relax you when quiet zephyrs skim the surface. You are its master. The boat is your soul.

"Hands-on is a must! I discovered the best method of skill development: read the book first; practice on the boat; go home and read more; more practice."
SUZANNE WENDEROTH (34), NORTHPORT, NY

Close to home and in distant ports, the world awaits. You can sail any time of the year, almost anywhere there are sailboats and water. Along the coasts and on most lakes there are sailing and yacht clubs that welcome new sailors. You may want to own a sailboat—large or small—that allows you to

Tim Gapen

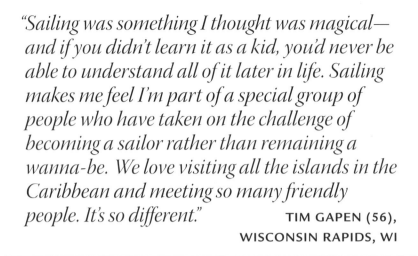

"Sailing was something I thought was magical— and if you didn't learn it as a kid, you'd never be able to understand all of it later in life. Sailing makes me feel I'm part of a special group of people who have taken on the challenge of becoming a sailor rather than remaining a wanna-be. We love visiting all the islands in the Caribbean and meeting so many friendly people. It's so different." TIM GAPEN (56), WISCONSIN RAPIDS, WI

steal a few hours aboard after a busy day, escape with friends on a weekend getaway, or embark on a family adventure. You may just want to rent a sailboat whenever you have the time and desire. Or you may want to join a club that maintains boats for your regular use and enjoy the camaraderie of other sailors. The information you need to start cruising is right here in this book; the rest comes with hands-on experience.

After taking an Offshore Sailing School Fast Track course, Tim Gapen and his wife Suzen bought a 23-foot Hunter to sail on a 13-mile-long lake near their home in central Wisconsin. A year later they chartered a 41-foot yacht with a couple they met while taking the course and sailed around St. Martin, St. Barts, and Anguilla. Each winter, alone or with friends, they cruise somewhere in the Caribbean.

LIVING THE CRUISING LIFESTYLE

While writing this book, we sent a questionnaire to more than seven hundred graduates of the Fast Track to Cruising course. We received an astounding number of responses from former students who described their sailing adventures close to home and far afield since taking the course. Some of their comments lace the pages of this book.

Legendary cruising sailors also have unique tales to share that will inspire and motivate you to start planning your own cruise. Some go to extremes; others live the dream in a very achievable way. Their adventures are charted in the pages of sailing magazines and the books they write.

Captain Bill Pinkney took an Offshore Sailing School course in the late sixties and never stopped dreaming about going around the world. The first African American to circumnavigate all five capes alone, Bill is a hero to the thousands of Chicago youngsters who followed his progress every step of the way. After that odyssey, he spearheaded the building of the slave-ship replica *Amistad* and captained it while touring and promoting sailing in every port he could reach.

Bernadette Bernon, former editorial director of *Cruising World* maga-

Captain Bill Pinkney at the helm of *Amistad*

zine, and her husband Douglas, a successful psychologist, stopped their careers midstream in their early 40s and are still cruising as we write this book. The Bernons' inspiring story is chronicled in the pages of *Cruising World* and *BoatU.S. Magazine*. In the September 2003 issue of *BoatU.S. Magazine*, Bernadette wrote:

> *"Cruising is better in many ways than we'd imagined when we set off, more challenging in others; but pushing ourselves out of our comfort zone has been one prime reward of taking huge risks. When things go wrong, major gear breaks, when the danger of deteriorating weather and killer reefs threaten life and home, cruising exacts a fearsome toll. But when things go right, the hook's set well, dinner is a freshly speared fish, and surroundings are jaw-droppingly beautiful, the feeling of accomplishment makes us feel more alive than ever."*

SAILORS LIKE YOU

We have cruised all over the world, chartering from companies in the business of providing the best boats and first-class vacations. Chartering is an effortless way to see the world under sail. This book is designed to give you a seamless path to successful chartering. Later in the book, we will talk about where and how you can start cruising. First we want to share a few stories told by people like you who took the Fast Track to Cruising course. Perhaps you will be inspired to set your course for cruising—just as they did.

Bernadette and Douglas Bernon

William and Sally Lee took Fast Track to Cruising in the British Virgin Islands in December 2000. William was new to sailing but had always been fascinated with the sport, especially the cruising lifestyle. He ordered his first boat—a brand-new 47-foot sloop—three months before starting the course, which he hoped would prepare him as an owner and a captain. Sally's goal was to learn just enough to give him a hand when needed. "After one short summer season of sailing," said William, "she was able to do a night watch alone going from Nice to Corsica." But we're getting ahead of the story.

In April 2001 the Lees chartered a 55-foot boat in Greece. In June 2001 they took delivery of their Beneteau 473 and sailed it all over New England—Boston, the Cape and surrounding islands, then to Maine. In February 2002 they chartered for two weeks in New Zealand's Bay of Islands and went back to the British Virgin Islands for a week of cruising in March.

William and Sally Lee at the helm of their first boat, a 47-foot Beneteau

"Since taking the course three years ago I am on my second boat. The more I sail, the more I know what I want in a boat. I spent about six months living aboard, sailed over 5,000 miles, and visited over 50 ports. None of these sailing adventures would be possible without Fast Track to Cruising."

WILLIAM LEE (30),
BOSTON, MA

"I had been on several crewed charters and sailed on other people's boats but didn't feel very confident about my abilities to sail alone and/or in command of my own boat. My goal was to build my confidence and knowledge so I could sail my own boat safely and skillfully. Fast Track gave me the confidence to first purchase a boat and then sail it in all conditions."

DOUG DANGERFIELD (60), FAIRFAX, VA

Then they sold their 47-footer and picked up a new Farr 50 Pilothouse in the Netherlands in June 2002.

With three crew, they sailed on an odyssey that took them past the English Channel and across the Bay of Biscay, to northern Spain, then down the coast of Portugal to Costa del Sol. In September they did a shorthanded passage (just the two of them) from Costa del Sol to Mallorca to Nice, circled Corsica, and cruised on to Tuscany and back to Toulon. Along the way they picked up visiting friends to share that cruising adventure. The Lees and their boat are now back in the States, and William has since singlehanded his 50-footer.

Doug Dangerfield of Fairfax, Virginia, is a former military pilot who hadn't done much sailing in the past 10 years and wanted a refresher course before going sailing in his new boat. At age 60, in April 2000, he took the Fast Track to Cruising course in the Florida Keys.

Soon after the course Doug bought a Sabre 35 and is pursuing his plan to cruise from Maine down the Intracoastal Waterway to the Florida Keys and over to the Bahamas. "Apart from lowering my blood pressure about thirty points," says Doug, "sailing helps me relax, develop and improve skills, and enjoy life."

Sailing, and particularly cruising, appeal to people with a wide range of personalities and career backgrounds. Retired scientist Larry Hansen (58) says his life is turning into an exciting retirement because of sailing. In less than two years, he went from novice to taking friends on boats he chartered in the British Virgin Islands. Then he purchased a Beneteau 423 and got his wife and kids to learn to sail so they could go with him. They are now enthusiastically pursuing plans to sail the islands.

Chicago elementary school principal Jeff Hildreth wrote,

"I have found an activity that truly relaxes me—it's the most peaceful thing we do. My wife and I are making plans for our future around sailing. It has brought us together in wonderful ways—and this is after 27 years of a happy marriage."

Jeff Hildreth (49), Dekalb, IL

Sailing is best learned by doing. But you will learn twice as effectively by doing the *right* thing the *first* time. This book is designed to speed up that process, so that when you actually set sail you will feel comfortable with your abilities aboard. You will emerge from this fast track with the knowledge of an experienced sailor. When you combine that knowledge with on-the-water experience, you will possess the skills of a seasoned skipper.

Now it's time to turn the page and embark on the *Fast Track to Cruising*. As sailors say to each other, "See you on the water!"

① THE LANGUAGE OF SAILING

The language of the sea is deeply rooted in the era of square-rigged ships, and today sailors around the world use a kind of shorthand that has evolved from that period. We were reminded of the importance of sailing language when we raced our 54-footer with crew from various countries. We could all communicate easily during those races—even though we didn't share a common tongue.

To the uninitiated, sailor-talk may sound strange. But it's an essential language to learn. There are times on a boat when the correct action must be taken quickly and at the right moment, or problems will result. You can't afford to say, "Let go of that thing over there!" when you really mean, "Free the jibsheet!" Through repetition, you will learn the necessary sailing terms to help you sail well.

Although there are many types and sizes of sailboats, the learn-to-sail sections in the first part of this book are focused on one type of boat—the Colgate 26, a family sport boat designed for training, racing, and family fun. The Colgate 26 is characterized as a sloop-rigged keelboat. The word *sloop* refers to a boat with one mast; the *keel* is a heavy fixed fin beneath the boat that provides stability. What you learn on this boat can be applied to any sailboat.

> *"I was apprehensive about all of the language involved with sailing, but that's all gone."*
> **MARY EAMAN (37), LONGMONT, CO**

IMPORTANT WORDS TO KNOW

This chapter covers some key terms that are important to learn, along with summary lists that will serve as an easy reference.

If you are standing on a sailboat facing forward, you are looking at the *bow*, with the *starboard side* on your right and the *port side* on your left. Conversely, if you are facing the back end of the boat, you are facing *aft* and looking at the *stern*, with the starboard side on your left and port to your right. The widest part of a boat is called the *beam*. Some people confuse stern (the whole back end of the boat) with the word *transom*, which is the vertical or slanted part that goes from the deck to the water.

When identifying a direction, another boat, or something you need to take note of, the words *ahead*, *astern*, and *abeam* come in handy. A buoy you're looking for may be ahead, or forward of the boat. The dinghy you are towing is astern, or behind the boat. A lighthouse ashore might be abeam, at a right angle off the left or right side of the boat. "Abeam" is a word that takes on special importance when you learn to identify the proximity of other boats, especially at night, as you'll learn later.

HOW TO MEASURE A SAILBOAT

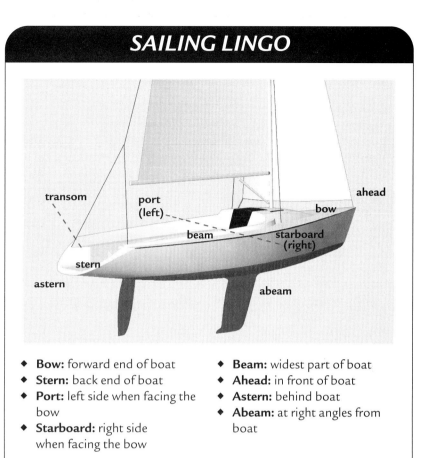

SAILING LINGO

- **Bow:** forward end of boat
- **Stern:** back end of boat
- **Port:** left side when facing the bow
- **Starboard:** right side when facing the bow
- **Beam:** widest part of boat
- **Ahead:** in front of boat
- **Astern:** behind boat
- **Abeam:** at right angles from boat

Open any sailing magazine and you will find a list of dimensions, usually abbreviated, alongside sailboat designs. These are the terms you use in describing the length, depth, and width of a sailboat.

LOA stands for *length overall*. This is the total length of the boat from the bow to the end of the stern in a straight line. LOA does not include the *bowsprit* (if your boat has one), which is a pole that extends beyond the bow of a boat. When you rent or buy a sailboat, LOA is a very common specification—as common as MPG is to a car shopper.

LWL is the *load waterline length*, or simply waterline length. This is the straight-line distance from the point where the bow emerges from the water to the point where the stern emerges from the water. Sailors need to know the LWL when calculating the potential speed of a sailboat.

Draft is the vertical distance from the water surface to the deepest part of the boat (the bottom of the keel). This measurement will tell you where you can and cannot sail. If your boat touches bottom in 3 feet of water, its draft is 3 feet. Stated differently, your boat

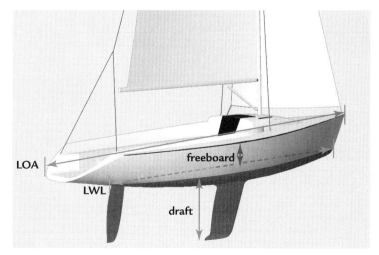

Figure 1-1. Terms that describe a boat's dimensions

draws 3 feet. When you ask a marina for a slip to rent you will probably be asked, "How much does your boat draw?" You will also be asked the LOA of your boat, because slip fees are calculated in dollars per foot.

Instead of a keel, some boats have a *centerboard*—a relatively thin panel made out of wood, fiberglass, or metal that can be raised or lowered to change the draft of the boat. In this case, you might hear someone describe the boat as having two drafts: "My boat draws 6 inches with the board up and 4 feet with the board down."

The *freeboard* of a boat, which is measured vertically from the edge of the deck to the waterline, is an important determinant of its interior space. The more freeboard a boat has, the more headroom there will be in its cabin (assuming the boat has one). Some sailors erroneously use freeboard interchangeably with the *topsides* of the boat, but the latter term actually refers to the sides of the hull above the waterline.

The beam of the boat described earlier is its maximum width, not its width at deck level as one might expect. The topsides on some boats curve outward from the deck and back in at the waterline. In this case, the beam is measured at the widest part of that curve.

HOW TO DESCRIBE A SAILBOAT

Picture yourself standing or sitting in the *cockpit*—where the crew sits to operate the boat. The *hull* is the body of the boat. The *keel*, which you can't see while you're sailing, is the fin under the boat that is loaded with lead to make the boat stable. The Colgate 26 weighs 2,600 pounds and 40 percent of that weight (1,050 pounds) is the lead in its keel. The boat can lean over in the wind, but it will not easily turn over.

In the back of the cockpit is a stick called a *tiller*. The tiller attaches to a post that goes through the hull of the boat to a *rudder*, a fin-shaped blade located underwater, behind the keel. When you move the tiller you are actually moving the rudder, which steers the boat by diverting the water that is moving past it. If the boat is not moving, turning the rudder will not cause the boat to turn.

Aboard a sailboat that has a cabin, you enter the cabin through a *companionway*—a passageway from the cockpit to the interior. The roof and sides of the cabin house comprise the *cabin trunk*.

STANDING RIGGING

Now that you are able to look at a sailboat and describe its parts, the next step is to identify rigging and what it does. *Rigging* is all the wire and rope (called line) on a sailboat and is divided into two major categories: *running rigging* and *standing rigging*. Because there is a lot of force on sails when they are filled with wind, and sails need something to hang from, rigging is required for sail support and shape.

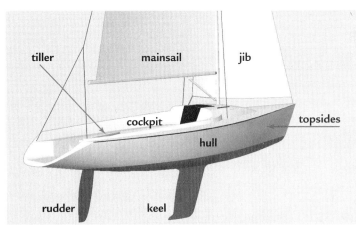

Figure 1-2. Terms that describe the parts of a sailboat

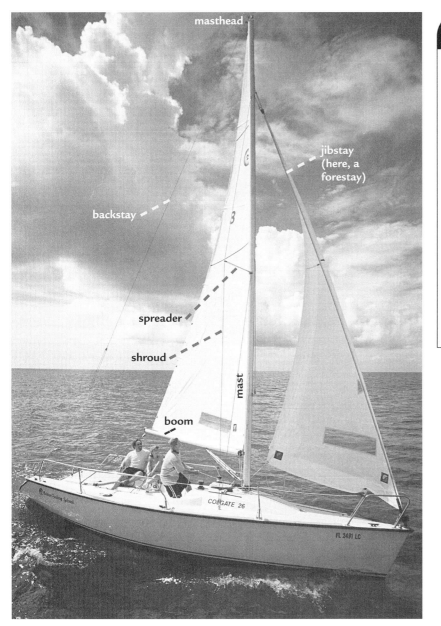

masthead

jibstay
(here, a
forestay)

backstay

spreader

shroud

mast

boom

COLGATE 26

FL 2491 LC

RIGGING LINGO

- ◆ **Mast:** vertical spar
- ◆ **Boom:** horizontal spar, connected to the mast and supporting foot of mainsail
- ◆ **Jibstay:** wire from mast to bow; called a headstay if it goes to top of mast
- ◆ **Backstay:** wire from top of mast to deck at or near stern
- ◆ **Shrouds:** wires from mast to left and right sides of deck
- ◆ **Spreaders:** struts that increase the angle shrouds make with mast

Figure 1-3. Terms that describe standing rigging

The *mast* is the vertical pole (spar) and the *boom* is the horizontal spar. Together, they support the mainsail. Incidentally, the word *boom* is Norwegian for tree. Kevin Wensley, an Offshore Sailing School instructor who hails from England, likes to tell his students that the boom gets its name from the noise it makes when it hits you. As you will learn later, when the boom crosses the boat you always want to stay out of its way.

Standing rigging holds up the masts of a sailboat. Made out of twisted wire on small to mid-sized boats, standing rigging consists of *stays* and *shrouds*. Stays keep the mast from falling forward or—over the bow or the stern. Shrouds keep the mast from falling *athwartships*—over the sides of the boat.

The *backstay* runs from the *head* (top) of the mast down to the deck at the middle of the stern. The *jibstay* runs from the bow of the boat up to the top or near the top of the mast. If it leads to the head of the mast, it is a *headstay*, and the rig is called a *masthead rig*. If it leads to a point partway down the mast, it is a *forestay*, and the rig is called a *fractional rig*. Many sailors use the terms *jibstay*, *headstay*, and *forestay* interchangeably. If a wire leads from partway up the mast to the middle of the *foredeck*, between the mast and the bow, it too is called a *forestay*; but this is a complication that doesn't concern us for the time being.

Because shrouds lead from the deck edges to attachment points on the mast, the angle they make to the mast is more acute than that of the stays. For this reason, the shrouds that lead highest on the mast—the *upper shrouds*—run through the ends of a strut or tube on either side of the mast to make a wider angle. These struts or tubes are called *spreaders*, since they spread the angle the shroud makes with the mast and thus provide better support for the upper section of the mast.

The compression load on the spreaders tends to bend the mast from side to side at the spreader base. To counteract this tendency, most boats have another set of shrouds—*lower shrouds*—on either side of the mast leading from the base of the spreaders to the edge of the deck. Since these originate lower down the mast, the angle they make with the mast is sufficiently wide to eliminate the need for extra spreaders.

RUNNING RIGGING

Running rigging consists of all the lines on a boat that adjust the sails. *Halyards* raise and lower the sails. *Sheets* adjust sails in and out.

Halyards and sheets take the name of the sail to which they are attached. For example, a *main halyard* raises and lowers the mainsail. A *jibsheet* adjusts the trim of the jib.

The trim of the jib or any sail is the angle of that sail to the wind direction at a given time. The word trim is also used as a verb in sailing. For example, the sailor to the left in Figure 1-4 is turning a winch (more on this later), which is moving the corner of the jib in, and he is therefore trimming the sail.

When you trim a jib, you are pulling the sail in with the jibsheet. When you *ease* a jib, you are letting it out.

When you're sailing you adjust the sheets a lot; but halyards are seldom changed after the sails are up. When you're preparing to go sailing, you raise the halyard to

Figure 1-4. Adjusting a jibsheet (running rigging) changes sail shape.

hoist the sail. Actually, you are pulling down on the halyard as the woman on deck is doing in Figure 1-5. When you are finished sailing, you ease the halyard out to lower the sail. (The halyard is actually going up.) The word *halyard* is a derivation of "haul the yardarms," from tall-ship days.

SAILS AND HOW TO DESCRIBE THEM

Today's mid-sized to large sailboats are designed with your precious time in mind, as well as your desire for an easy-to-sail boat. Regardless of size, they usually have a *mainsail* and a *jib*. On a sloop like the Colgate 26, the mainsail (pronounced *mains'l* but more often just called the *main*) is the large sail behind the mast, supported by the mast and the boom. The jib is the sail carried on the headstay or jibstay in the front of the boat.

On the Colgate 26, as on many boats these days, you control the jib with a furling mechanism that allows you to roll the sail up on its headstay when you're not using it. When a jib is on a *roller-furling headstay* like this, the jib halyard is always up. Not long ago, when you were finished sailing for the day you had to lower the halyard to bring the jib down, take the jib completely off the jibstay, fold the sail carefully to avoid wrinkles, and place it in a bag to stow below or ashore. This is still the case on most small boats and many large ones. But on some big boats, even the mainsail can be rolled up inside the mast (as you'll learn later, in the cruising section of this book).

Most mains and jibs are made of Dacron, which doesn't stretch much and, therefore, holds the shape of your sails. A sailmaker cuts and sews a sail to create a desirable contour for maximum speed when the sail is filled with wind. Since it is important the sail retain this shape when wind creates pressure on the cloth, sailmakers choose cloth with a predictable stretch factor, the least amount possible.

When you see a sailboat gliding along the horizon with a dazzling white sail, you're looking at Dacron. More exotic sails that are steely gray, brown-tinged, or even translucent are made of Mylar, Kevlar, or Spectra cloth. With even less stretch than Dacron, these pricey materials are in demand by highly competitive racing sailors to whom "go-fast" ability is more important than cost.

A finished sail is triangular in shape, and each corner has a name. The *head* is the top corner, the *tack* the

Figure 1-5. Raising a sail with the halyard (running rigging)

forward lower corner, and the *clew* the aft lower corner. The *luff* is the leading (front) edge, the *leech* is the trailing (aft) edge, and the *foot* is the bottom edge.

If you draw a line from the head of a mainsail to its clew, you can see that the leech is convex. When the leech of a sail is curved or rounded so as to incorporate more area than the equivalent straight-sided triangle, that extra cloth is called *roach*, and its purpose is to give you more sail area, which results in more power. To remember where the leech and roach are located on a sail,

LINGO FOR DESCRIBING SAILS

- **Mainsail:** large sail attached along mast's after edge
- **Jib:** sail carried on the head-stay or jibstay
- **Head:** top corner of a sail
- **Tack:** forward lower corner of a sail
- **Clew:** aft lower corner of a sail
- **Luff:** front edge of a sail from head to tack
- **Leech:** after edge of a sail from head to clew
- **Foot:** bottom of a sail from tack to clew
- **Battens:** slats inserted in trailing edge (leech) of sail to retain shape
- **Roach:** convex area of extra cloth along mainsail leech

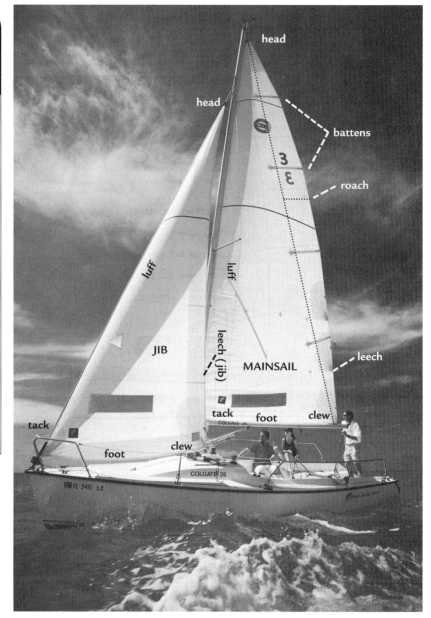

Figure 1-6. Terms that describe the parts of a sail

instructor Kevin Wensley says: *Nasty critters like roaches and leeches hang out at the back of the sail.*

To support this extra cloth and hold its shape in wind, thin pieces of wood or fiberglass called *battens* are inserted in pockets that are evenly spaced along the leech. A typical batten for a 26-foot boat might be 1 inch wide by 24 inches long. Some sails have full-length battens running all the way from leech to luff.

Sails that are furled up when not in use, rather than taken off and folded, don't have battens because they cannot be wound around a headstay or furled up inside a mast. Sails without battens do not have extra cloth (roach) along the leech. When you're out for a lazy afternoon sail or cruising

TEST YOURSELF

Key Sailboat Terms
On the sailboat above, identify the following and then check your answers against the labeled photos and illustrations in this chapter:

1. Cockpit
2. Hull
3. Tiller
4. Bow
5. Stern
6. Port
7. Starboard
8. Beam
9. Ahead
10. Astern
11. Abeam

Describe the following:

1. LOA
2. LWL
3. Freeboard
4. Draft
5. Rudder
6. Keel

Rigging
Identify the rigging, referring to labeled photos in this chapter as necessary:

1. Mast
2. Boom
3. Jibstay
4. Backstay

5. Upper shrouds
6. Lower shrouds
7. Spreaders

The Anatomy of Sails
Identify the sails and their parts, referring to the labeled photographs in this chapter as necessary:

1. Mainsail
2. Jib
3. Battens
4. Head
5. Tack
6. Clew
7. Luff
8. Leech
9. Roach

off to wondrous spots, extra sail area doesn't matter that much. Ease of managing the sails is more important. Roach is most helpful when performance is a priority—either for competitive sailing or for fast passages in light winds.

The only rope on a sailboat that isn't called *line* is the *boltrope*, which is sewn to the sailcloth along the foot and luff of the mainsail for reinforcement. Sometimes *sail slides* are sewn into the boltrope, and the slides literally slide the mainsail onto a track that is screwed to the mast or boom. But sail slides are usually found on larger boats; on a smaller boat, the boltrope is likely to be inserted directly inside a groove in the mast or boom when raising the mainsail.

To keep the leech of a sail from unraveling, the sailmaker sews a strip of doubled-over material—called *tabling*—along the edge. Sometimes a light line—the *leech cord*—is sewn inside the tabling. The leech cord is attached at the head of the sail and can be adjusted at the clew—either eased out to free a curl in the leech and permit smoother air flow, or pulled tighter to reduce the flutter that occasionally occurs along the trailing edge of a sail (especially a jib). Not only is flutter unattractive, it decreases the efficiency of a sail and eventually causes the sail cloth to wear out.

Sails are your boat's driving force. Just as an engine needs care, so do your sails. Sunlight deteriorates cloth. When not in use, sails should be taken off and put away or rolled up under a UV-protective cover. Keeping sails clean is also part of good sail care. If your sails are not washed occasionally with warm water and mild soap, encrusted salt will pick up moisture from the air and the dried salt will make your sails heavy. Dirt particles may also shorten the life of the cloth.

2 *START SAILING*

Weather conditions have a lot of impact on whether you will enjoy sailing. If you are dressed properly and come prepared for the best and worst conditions, you can experience the full range—from flat calm to whitecaps—in comfort.

SAILING COMFORT IS ALL ABOUT PREPARATION

Apprehensions are natural for new sailors, but you'll find that they dissolve quickly as you learn. Here are answers to some questions new sailors often ask:

What should I wear in warm sunny weather? Those who sail a lot are careful to protect skin and eyes from the sun. You might want to shed layers as the day heats up, but whatever you wear should be comfy, dry quickly, and protect you from slipping.

What should I wear if it's cold, wet, and windy? A good suit of foul-weather gear is really important, with layers underneath that breathe and shed moisture. Proper shoes, gloves, and a hat make all the difference. Think about long pants and long underwear with a shirt, sweater, and warm jacket.

What if I can't swim? There are Coast Guard–approved life vests of several types on the market that are very comfortable, and even inflatable versions you can wear like a harness or around your waist. In addition, consider using a sailboat that won't capsize, is easy to control in any condition, and has lifelines around the deck.

What if I'm small and not very strong? Sailing on most boats is more about timing and mechanical advantage than strength. All-women crews sail, race, and win aboard some of the largest, most challenging sailboats out there. When pulling a line, put your whole body into it, not just your arms, and place your hands over (not under) the line as you bring it toward you.

Am I too old? You can learn to sail at any age. A 79-year-old woman took Offshore Sailing School's Learn to Sail course and had a ball. She wanted to try sailing before she reached 80!

Is sailing safe? Sailing is one of the safest pastimes there is if you know how to handle lines, winches, and sails properly. Seasoned sailors say sailing is 90 percent sheer bliss and 10 percent challenge. For the casual cruising sailor, the chances of being caught in extremely bad conditions are remote. Through this book and in hands-on sessions, you learn how to master whatever nature throws at you.

What type of boat should I learn on if my goal is to cruise? Avoid the temptation to start on a large cruising boat. You can learn much faster on a smaller, more maneuverable boat such as the Colgate 26. The process involves two steps: first, learning to sail, and then, learning to cruise. For the learn-to-sail phase, the boat should be a keelboat, unable to capsize, and unsinkable. This type of boat provides an easy transition to the more massive equipment used on a larger cruising boat. For the learn-to-cruise phase, the boat should be a popular style of boat that one might charter from one of the major charter companies or buy for personal ownership.

> *"My wife is a non-swimmer and not very strong. We had a lot of fears she would not be able to handle the courses. She handled everything, including 5-foot seas, with flying colors, and she now loves to sail."*
>
> **TIM GAPEN (56),**
> **WISCONSIN RAPIDS, WI**

GETTING ABOARD

The sailboat you are about to board is a dynamic platform. Whether it is tied to a dock or hanging off a mooring, it will move as you step aboard. The key is to make decisive moves, keeping your safety in mind.

If the boat is at a dock you will be walking aboard from a relatively stationary platform. If it is on a mooring, you will be boarding from a so-called taxi—a small dinghy or motor launch. The smaller the taxi, the tippier it is; when you step aboard, always step into the middle of the boat and not onto the rail or seats on the sides of the boat. The lower you place your weight in the boat, the more stable it will be. Once you're aboard, sit down immediately before someone else attempts to step in. Load the middle of the dinghy first to keep it from tipping to one side.

If any boat (the sailboat or the dinghy) has too much weight forward, which includes the crew and equipment, it is *down by the bow*. Having too much weight aft is called *dragging the stern*. Neither is good for performance, safety, or comfort. Keep the dinghy level or slightly down by the stern, and don't overload it. Remember, freeboard is the distance from the edge of the deck to the water when the boat is level. If the dinghy is so heavily loaded that its freeboard is reduced to only 6 inches or so, any rolling caused by waves or shifting passenger weight could cause the dinghy to *ship water* over its side and fill up.

Whoever is rowing the dinghy or running its outboard may ask you, after you are seated, to *trim the boat*. This means you should ease your weight to port or starboard to keep the dinghy level from side to side. This is called keeping a boat on an *even keel*, and it makes the boat easier to row and safer in choppy water.

Getting aboard a keelboat like a Colgate 26 is easy. Because a keelboat has a fixed fin that adds stability you don't have to be concerned about capsizing the boat if you step on a side while boarding. If your boat has a centerboard, however, and the centerboard is in the up position, be careful to keep your weight low and in the middle of the boat as you board, just as if you were boarding a dinghy.

When you get to your sailboat, whether you board at a dock or at a mooring, the basic rules for boarding are the same:

1. If you are carrying anything, pass it across to someone onboard or throw it in the cockpit before you start to board.
2. Locate the easiest point to board—where there is a shroud you can grab and where the gap between the dock and the boat is narrowest. If the boat isn't close enough to the dock to board comfortably, find a point where you can readily pull the boat closer.
3. Make sure that whatever you grab to support yourself is fixed—not a loose line that will "give." Keep your hands and toes away from areas where they can get pinched, such as between the dock or dinghy and the sailboat.
4. The boat will probably move as you step aboard. Don't pause with one foot on the boat and the other on the dock or taxi, poised over this ever-widening split. Once you commit yourself, be decisive. The instructor in Figure 2-1 is demonstrating how *not* to board.

A good launch driver will have you board a sailboat at its middle or near its stern, where it is easier to grab something and hold the boats close together. Sometimes an eager crew member will board the sailboat near its bow and then let the boats drift apart before other crew can board. If you board first, you can help by holding the launch in close as gear is passed aboard and the rest of your party follows. If the sailboat is high-sided and there is nothing firm to grab, the safest way to board, particu-

Figure 2-1. How not to board a sailboat

larly when the water is rough, is to turn around, sit on the deck, and then swing your legs over.

GETTING READY TO SAIL

Whatever you brought aboard needs to be stowed, so find a safe place in a locker on deck or *down below* (in the cabin) where your gear won't move around or get in the way. If you haven't done so already, make sure there are enough life vests for everyone on board. Now is also a good time to reassess what you are wearing. The list below is a good reminder of the clothing adjustments you should make before you go sailing.

- ◆ Take off any big rings and dangling bracelets or earrings.
- ◆ Tie your hair back if it's long.
- ◆ Put on sunscreen.
- ◆ Secure your hat to a comfortable place on your shirt or jacket with a lanyard.
- ◆ Put on your sailing gloves.
- ◆ Be sure to wear a life vest or have one handy.

Life vests—commonly called personal flotation devices (PFDs)—are approved by the U.S. Coast Guard, if they are manufactured to meet or exceed specifications. Type I PFDs—the large, bulky orange horseshoes typi-

Figure 2-2. Type III PFDs

cally found on ferries and cruise ships—are made to keep an unconscious person face up in the water. A Type II PFD, called a near-shore buoyant vest, is less bulky, less buoyant, and not as likely to keep an unconscious person face up. Type III, the type of vest the sailors are wearing in Figure 2-2, is probably the most popular PFD because it is fairly comfortable to wear; but it will not do much for an unconscious person. Type IV is a throwable flotation device such as a cushion. Type V is inflatable.

Preparing the Boat

Take a few minutes to look around. Try to determine where the wind is coming from, and position the boat with its bow in that direction if you can. If you're at a mooring, the boat should already be pointing into the wind, since that's its natural tendency when tethered from the bow. If you're at a dock and can move to a spot that allows the boat to hang off or lie alongside facing

the wind, that's preferable. If not, you can still get underway, as you will learn later (see Chapter 10).

Check where the dock or mooring lines are tied to the boat. That way, you'll know exactly what lines you need to untie when you are ready to *cast off* (release your lines to get underway). If you have fenders hanging over the side, check to see where they are located too; all of them will have to come off as you get underway. The Colgate 26 in Figure 2-1 has a fender hanging from the boat's rail to protect the hull from contact with the dock or other boats. On some boats the rails are actually wires called *lifelines*. Locate the halyards and sheets you'll be using to pull the sails up and pull the sails in and out; make sure they are not tightly cleated or jammed in a block. Assign jobs to your crew, and position yourself comfortably to execute your jobs.

Preparing the Sails

Since so many sailboats allow you to leave the sails rigged (but not raised) on the boat, this section starts from that premise.

You will typically have a sail cover over the mainsail, which has been folded (or *furled*) on the boom at the sail's foot. The cover will be tied or hooked at intervals beneath the boom. Remove the sail cover by folding it repeatedly, starting at the after end of the boom; then stow it below or in a cockpit locker. You should now see the mainsail neatly folded and tied onto the boom.

You will see a stiffener, or *headboard*, in the head of the mainsail. Attach the main halyard to the grommet hole in the headboard and pull up on the halyard just enough to get a little tension. You should still have three or four sail ties holding the mainsail in place along the boom. Untie these now and stow them.

Before you hoist the sail, look up to make sure the halyard is running free and not wrapped around anything. Make sure your boat is headed directly into the wind. If you try to raise a sail when the wind is at an angle to the boat or coming from behind, you will have a devilish time trying to haul against the pressure of the wind in the sail. And while you're preoccupied with this challenge, your boat will be trying to sail around its mooring.

You're raising the mainsail first because it's nearer the stern and can act like a weather vane to keep the boat headed into the wind. If your boat was attached to a mooring or at anchor and you raised the jib first, the jib would fill with wind and force the bow to turn away. Eventually the boat would swing broadside to the wind and strain at the mooring line, creating a general nuisance. If you were to forge ahead by raising the mainsail, it too would fill with wind and press against the rigging and bind on the mast track. This would make it virtually impossible to raise the sail any farther.

When raising a sail, you want the lines that control the sail to be loose so the boat (and sail) can line up with the wind like a flag. All lines that might be holding the boom down—principally the mainsheet, but also the boom vang and cunningham (if you have these on your boat)—must be eased so nothing can prevent the main from going all the way up (we'll discuss the boom vang and cunningham in good time). A crew member should hold the back end of the boom up in the air to relieve the tension on the leech of the sail.

You will know the sail is all the way up when the luff (the edge attached to the mast track) is taut, with no scallops or horizontal wrinkles. When the main is up, *cleat* (tie off) the halyard so the sail can't slip back down, but leave the mainsheet loose while you get the jib ready. Watch out for the boom swinging back and forth, particularly on a windy day.

Next, *unfurl* (unroll) the jib. Note that the jib halyard is already attached and that the two jibsheets, which lead back to the cockpit on either side of the mast, are wrapped around the rolled sail. The drum at the bottom of the sail has a line leading all the way back to the cockpit, where it is normally cleated; the excess is typically coiled up and hung on a lifeline to keep it out of the way when the jib is not in use. To unfurl the jib, all you have to do is uncleat this furling line and pull on the jibsheet.

If you do not have a roller-furling jib, you must *hank* (attach) the sail on the jibstay with piston hanks or snaps spaced along the luff of the sail. The jib should have been folded starting with the foot, then rolled so the tack is on the outside. After removing the jib from its bag, find the tack and attach it to the fitting in the bow at the bottom of the headstay. Then, straddling the sail with your legs to keep it under control, place each hank on the stay working up the luff to the head of the sail. Then tie port and starboard jibsheets to the clew of the sail with bowlines and *reeve* (pull) them through the jibsheet leads. Attach the halyard and hoist.

Some boats have a *jib foil*—a slotted tube into which the luff slides. In this case, start with the head of the sail, attach the halyard and feed the luff of the jib into the groove of the foil while one crew raises the halyard. Often you'll find a prefeeder, a small device that

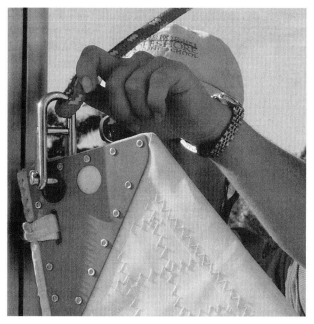

Figure 2-3. Attaching halyard to the head of the sail

jibsheets

furling line

Figure 2-4. Jib furled around the headstay

21

KNOTS TO KNOW

The ends of most sheets have knots in them to keep the sheet from running completely out of the *blocks* (the pulleys that sheets run through) and out of your reach. The two most common *stopper knots* used in the ends of jibsheets and mainsheets are the *figure eight* and the *stop knot*.

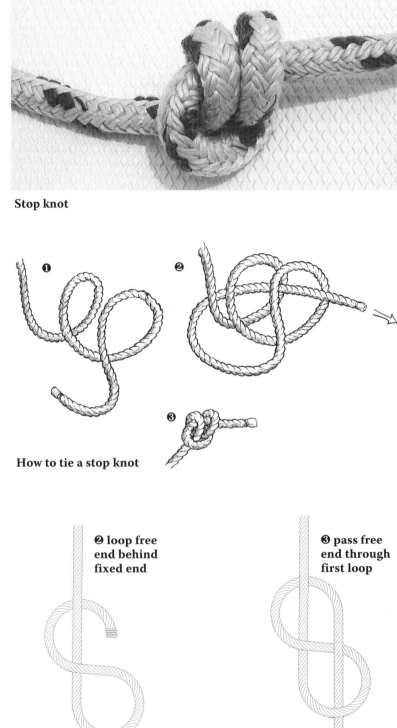

Stop knot

Figure-eight knot

How to tie a stop knot

❶ **cross free end over fixed end**

❷ **loop free end behind fixed end**

❸ **pass free end through first loop**

How to tie a figure-eight knot

automatically feeds the luff into the groove. This is the same process you'll go through when initially raising the jib on a roller-furling jib foil.

Since one jibsheet leads aft along the port side of the boat and the other to starboard, which sheet do you pull on? It really doesn't matter until you get underway, but if you know which side of the boat the wind will be coming over, pull on the jibsheet farthest from the wind (the *leeward* jibsheet), unless you need to *back* the jib as described later in this chapter.

On small boats, where the jib is smaller than the mainsail, you could raise the two sails simultaneously; but it's good protocol to raise the jib last so it won't flail around. Not only does this flogging tangle the jibsheets and cause an awful commotion on a windy day, it also reduces the life of the jib by breaking down the cloth fibers.

GETTING UNDERWAY

Now you're ready to sail away. But since the boat is headed directly into the wind at a mooring and is not moving through the water, how are you going to do this? The boat is dead in the water, or *in irons*. When the bow is headed into the wind like this, you are in the *no-go zone*.

This can happen at other times too. For example, when a boat attempts to change direction by turning into the wind, it can be stopped by a wave and lose *steerage* or *headway*. In order to steer a boat, you need to have water flowing past its rudder. If the boat is *dead in the water*, meaning it's motionless, the rudder is useless. The sails have to be manipulated to get the boat going.

Because the boat is pointing directly into the wind, the sails are *luffing*—flapping in the wind like a flag. To fill the sails, you will have to place the boat at an angle of 45° or more to the wind. When the boat reaches this position the sails will fill with wind and the boat will start moving forward. Until that point, the sails have to be manually forced out against the wind to fill them. This is called *backing* the sail.

If you want to turn the bow of the boat to port (to the left), back the jib out to starboard; if pulling on the starboard-side jibsheet won't accomplish this, you'll have to grab the clew of the jib and literally hold it out to starboard until it backs. Once the wind hits the starboard side of the jib, it will push the bow to port. After the boat is pushed 45° to the wind, release the starboard-side jibsheet and pull in on the sheet on the port side.

Though backing the jib is the fastest and surest method of falling off onto the desired tack, there are other ways. If the boat is drifting backward and you want to change direction and sail forward and to the right, push the tiller to the starboard side of the boat. The rudder turns the stern of the boat to the left and the bow moves to the right.

Figure 2-5. Backing the jib to get underway

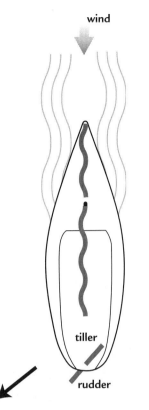

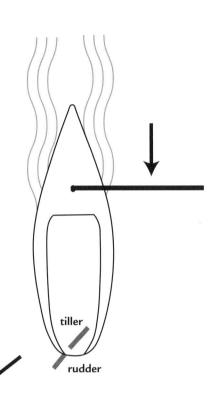

Figure 2-6 (left). How to get going when the boat is drifting backward. Here, the bow will fall off to starboard.

Figure 2-7 (right). Backing the main to get underway

FROM NO-GO TO GO

When a sailboat is motionless:

◆ It is in *irons* or in *stays*
◆ Water is not flowing past the rudder
◆ And the rudder therefore can't steer boat

To get out of irons:

◆ Back the jib to one side
◆ The bow will swing to the opposite side
◆ When the bow is 45 or more degrees off the wind, trim the sails for the wind direction
◆ Steer with the rudder

You might be sailing a small boat that has no jib. In that case you can push the main out against the wind. This starts the boat moving backward and turns the stern to the side opposite the main. If you *back* the main to the starboard side, the stern will go to port. You can abet the turn by putting the tiller to starboard.

The standard procedure when leaving a mooring is for one of the crew to untie the mooring line, but hold onto the end while another crew backs the jib. If possible, pull the boat forward with the mooring line to gain a little forward momentum. Sometimes it helps to *scull* the boat to start the boat moving forward. To scull, move the tiller rapidly back and forth. This causes the rudder to move like a flipper, resulting in forward motion. (On the Colgate 26 you can actually turn the rudder 180° and scull the boat backward out of a slip or away from a dock.) When the bow is definitely swinging in the desired direction, release the mooring line and you are off sailing.

STEERING

Taking command of a sailboat is one of the most delightful things you'll ever do. There's simply nothing like feeling your boat's pulse as it cuts through the water and the way it responds to your slightest moves on the helm.

Most new sailors learn on boats steered with a tiller, often referred to as the *stick* by seasoned sailors. The tiller, positioned in the back of the cockpit

Figure 2-8. Steering with a tiller

where you'll sit if you're steering, is attached to a rudder under the boat. It's the deflection of water against the rudder that determines the boat's direction as it moves. As the rudder's angle to the flow of water changes, so does the sailboat's direction. The extent to which you push or pull the tiller determines how much deflection there will be, which translates into how fast or far you'll turn the boat.

At first, steering with a tiller might seem unnatural; but it's the best way to learn because you can really *sense* how the boat reacts to you. Most boats up to 30 feet in length have tillers, not wheels, so it's appropriate that you start out on a boat with a tiller like the Colgate 26. When you step aboard a cruising boat later on, you will get behind a wheel and drive that boat as you would a car—but you'll have the fingertip control of somebody who learned to steer a sailboat first with a tiller.

A sailboat responds best when you can feel a slight tug as you hold the tiller. The only time you want a *neutral helm*—no pressure at all—is when you are sailing in a straight line with the wind directly behind the boat.

> *"Relax. That's the one thing impressed on us. Don't stress, or you tighten your hold too much on the sheets [and] overturn the tiller."*
> **SHARON MARION (49), SAN JOSE, CA**

TILLER STEERING TIPS

- *Tiller Toward Trouble*—push the tiller *toward* trouble, and the bow turns *away*
- Push the tiller to the right (to starboard) to turn the boat left (to port)
- Push the tiller left (to port) to turn the boat right (to starboard)
- Avoid oversteering—make minimal, smooth moves
- If you are fighting the tiller, consider easing the sails

Figure 2-9. The rudder is visible in the clear waters of BVI; the crew sits to windward for comfort and balance.

When sails are trimmed correctly, you can hold the tiller with a light touch. The rudder is in line with or at a very slight angle to the keel. The resistance you feel is normal and desired. If you find yourself fighting the tiller, your rudder is probably at too great an angle and actually slowing the boat and diminishing its performance.

If you have ever driven a car that needs its wheels aligned, you will remember how hard it was to keep the car in a straight line without a strong pull on the wheel. This causes you to oversteer, and that's what you are doing when you have too much tug on the tiller. Adjusting the sails usually cures this. In Chapter 6 you will learn more about helm balance.

A sailboat pivots as it turns, with the stern going one way and the bow the other. If you are sitting to the left of the tiller, holding it with your right hand, and you want the boat to turn to the right—to *starboard*—pull the tiller toward you, to the left. Water pushes against the right side of the rudder, which moves the stern to the left and pivots the bow to the right. If you want the boat to turn to the left—to *port*—push the tiller away from you, to the right. Water pushes against the left side of the rudder, which moves the stern to the right and pivots the bow to the left. At first you might have to think about which way to push the tiller, but eventually, steering with a tiller will become automatic.

Note in Figure 2-9 that the sails are over the port side of the boat and everyone is sitting on the starboard side. Not only are they having fun, they are using crew weight to balance the boat. Picture yourself steering and turn the tiller to starboard, in this case toward you. The rudder turns to port, and so does the boat. Now push the tiller away from you, to port. The rudder turns to starboard, and so does the boat.

The keel is heavy, carrying a lot of weight down low. As wind fills the sail and tries to heel the boat over, the keel counteracts this force and keeps the boat moving forward without tipping over or sliding sideways. As you sail along, always watch for other boats and obstacles that might cause trouble.

MAKE YOURSELF COMFORTABLE

When you're learning to sail, you'll probably sail with two to three other crew and rotate positions as you go through maneuvers. Since comfort is key to handling yourself and the boat well, here are a few tips:

1. When steering, sit on the high (windward) side of the boat if it's heeling (tilting or leaning to one side or the other), so you can see the luff of the jib.
2. Ask the crew to join you on the high side when they are finished with their jobs—for their own comfort and to help counteract the heeling effect and better balance the boat.
3. Assign someone to go down to the lower side periodically to look to leeward and make sure you're clear of other boats and obstructions.
4. Always sit so that you can move the tiller freely from side to side without it hitting your body. Usually this means sitting slightly forward of the end of the tiller.
5. To maximize the arc through which the tiller can move, and to give yourself maximum leverage, hold the tiller at or close to its free end.
6. Avoid white-knuckle syndrome—relax and hold the tiller tenderly. A tight fist around the tiller tightens your forearm and puts stress on your upper body, and you end up steering from your shoulder with jerky results, and not comfortably with your wrist.
7. When moving from one side of the boat to the other while steering, always pass in front of the tiller and look forward for better control. This allows you to see your crew and other boats in the vicinity.
8. Before changing course, give your crewmates plenty of warning so that they can position themselves to trim the sails comfortably.
9. When *tacking* (see Chapter 3), work at the same pace as the crew and slow your turn as the sail comes across, giving the crew time to complete their jobs and then move to a comfortable position.
10. When *jibing* (Chapter 3), give your crewmates plenty of time to get the mainsail under control before you turn, and make sure everyone is aware of the pending maneuver and out of the way of the swinging boom.
11. If the winds are very light, you and your crew should sit on the low side (leeward) to induce a heel to leeward, thus encouraging the sails to hold their shape and capture what little wind there is (see more on this in Chapter 6). If you can't see the jib from this position, however, sit elsewhere and let your crew heel the boat.

TEST YOURSELF

Steering Basics
To test what you now know about steering, answer the questions below. Refer back to the steering section in this chapter if you need to review these concepts.

1. What does the rudder do?
2. What does the tiller do?
3. Where is the no-go zone?
4. If you are dead in the water, how do you start moving the boat forward?
5. If you move the tiller to port, where does the bow go?
6. If you move the tiller to starboard, what direction does the rudder go?

3 THE POINTS OF SAIL

Sailing is a lot like riding a bicycle. When you finally catch on, you never lose the knack. Just as balance is the most important skill in bicycling, feeling the relationship between the wind and the sails is the key to sailing.

The *points of sail* describe the boat when it is sailing at various angles to the wind direction. Diagrams that illustrate the points of sail (like the ones that follow) show the wind as nice clear arrows. This may be easy to illustrate on paper; but on the water, it may be hard to relate the boat's heading to the wind direction.

FINDING WIND DIRECTION

Sails are a sailboat's engine, and the wind is that engine's fuel. Until you know where the wind is coming from, you won't be able to fully utilize the wind's power. However, once you become sensitive to wind direction, you never lose that capability.

Since you can't see the wind, you have to use other tricks to detect its direction. Look at ripples on the water. Feel the wind on your face: when you look directly into the wind, you can feel it evenly on both sides of your face; turn even slightly and you know right away you are no longer looking at the source of the wind. You can also look for smoke or flags on land. Sailors use many other aids to find wind direction, including electronic instrumentation. The simplest aids are *telltales* and a *masthead fly.*

Telltales are pieces of wool, thin strips of plastic, or other light materials tied to the shrouds; they show the wind direction by the way they flow away from the shroud. A masthead fly is a swiveling weather vane at the top of the mast with an arrow on one end and a split tail on the other. To find the wind, look up and follow the direction the arrow is pointing. The masthead fly is very light to avoid extra weight at the top of the mast; extra weight aloft will contribute to how far your boat *heels,* or leans over. The masthead fly's light weight is also important because it makes this aid more sensitive to the wind in very light breezes. In most conditions, it will turn easily to a new wind direction and settle down quickly—rather than swinging past the new direction, due to inertia.

YOUR BOAT IS ALWAYS ON A TACK

To describe the direction of the wind with respect to the sails, sailors use the word *tack*. A boat is always *on a tack* unless it is in the process of changing tacks (changing the boat's direction from one side of the wind to the other, while sailing toward the wind). The word tack also has other meanings: as you learned earlier, the word *tack* is also used to describe the forward, lower corner of a sail.

One way to remember which tack you are on is to identify the wind's direction as it comes across the boat. If the wind comes over the port side of the boat, you are on a *port tack*. If it comes over the starboard side, you are on a *starboard tack*.

This method of determining what tack you are on works well unless the wind is directly behind your boat. In this case you are sailing *downwind* and the wind is coming over the back, or stern, of your boat. When sailing downwind, you need to look at where your main boom is located to determine what tack you are on.

Your main boom is either over the port side of the boat or the starboard side. The rule to remember is: a boat is on the tack *opposite* to the side its main boom is on. For example, if your mainsail is over the starboard side of the boat, you are on port tack. If your mainsail is over the port side of the boat, you are on starboard tack. If your boom is pulled in tight and very close to the

Figure 3-1. A sailboat on port tack

Figure 3-2. A sailboat on starboard tack

Figure 3-3. A sailboat on port tack on a run

TACK: A WORD WITH SEVERAL MEANINGS

1. Tack *n* **1** : forward lower corner of a sail **2** : boat's heading in relation to the wind <on a starboard ~> **3** : a course <when the boat is underway it's on a ~>
2. Tack *vb* : to change direction from one side of wind to the other while sailing toward the wind

center of the boat, making it difficult for you to determine which side the boom is on, simply picture which side the boom will be on if you ease the sail out.

Figure 3-3 helps to better illustrate how to determine the tack you are on when sailing downwind. In the photo, the wind is blowing toward the boat's stern and the boat is on a *run*—sailing away from the wind. Note that the boom is over the starboard side of the boat. Remember, the tack the boat is on is the *opposite* side of the boat the boom is on. This boat is on *port tack*.

Another way to determine which tack you are on is to look at how the wind is filling the mainsail. If the wind is filling the port side of the mainsail, you are on port tack. If it is filling the starboard side of the mainsail, you are on starboard tack.

Just like cars on the road, sailboats on the water also have their own right-of-way rules. Knowing what tack you are on is important because it determines which boat has the right-of-way. (You'll learn what these rules are and when to observe them in Chapter 8.)

CYCLING THROUGH THE POINTS OF SAIL

To get to your destination, you have to ease and trim your sails in relation to the direction of the wind. The relationship between your boat's *heading* (the direction it's going) and the wind direction represents a point of sail and determines how you set your sails. To easily see the relationship between a boat's heading and the wind direction, each point of sail is marked on the circle in Figure 3-4.

These points of sail start with the no-go zone where the boat cannot sail directly into the wind and must *tack* (change from port to starboard tack, or vice versa). When the sails are trimmed in as tight as possible, the boat is *close-hauled*. Sometimes they will be as far out as they can go as you sail downwind on this point of sail, the wind is pushing you from behind. As the boat sails from a close-hauled course, the closest it can possibly sail toward the wind, to a downwind run, the farthest it can sail off the wind, the boat is *falling off*—sailing away from the wind.

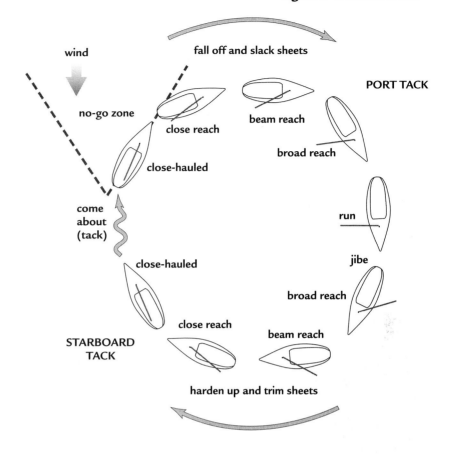

Figure 3-4. Points of sail

As you see on the diagram, as the boat falls off from a close-hauled course and heads downwind, it cycles through a point of sail called a *reach*. There are several different types of reaches. Here is an exercise to help you understand the relationship between the wind direction and your heading on a reach.

Point the bow of the boat close to the direction of the wind, but not quite to the no-go zone. Then point your arm at the wind direction and start falling off, turning your bow away from the wind direction. Keep your arm pointed at the wind direction.

When the angle between your arm and your heading is about 60°, you are on a *close-reach*—a point between sailing as close to the wind as possible and when the wind is at a right angle, or 90°, to your boat.

Keep falling off until the wind until your arm is at a 90° angle to your heading. You are now sailing with the wind *abeam* on a *beam reach*.

The easiest point of sail to practice on is a reach. This is a good point of sail for getting comfortable with steering. The boat won't heel excessively and you can wander off course without the boom accidentally flying across the boat, or *jibing* (which we will cover soon).

Figure 3-5. A close reach

Figure 3-6. A beam reach

TO TRIM FOR EFFICIENT SAILING

- *Ease* sheet until sail starts to *luff.*
- *Trim* the sheet until luffing stops.
- When in doubt, let it out.

On a beam reach your telltales should be streaming right across the boat. Now point your arm at the wind and turn the boat slightly toward the direction you are pointing. This takes you back onto a close reach. As you continue to turn toward the wind, your sails start to luff (flutter) and you need to pull them in to keep them full of wind. When you adjust your sails for wind direction and strength, you are *trimming* your sails.

Picture the sail like a flag waving in the breeze. If you grab the tail of the flag and pull it toward the wind it will fill with air and stop flapping. In essence, you are trimming it by pulling it in. As you let the flag go slowly (like easing a sail) it will start to flutter where it first lines up with the wind. So, as you sail along on a reach, make little adjustments to determine whether your sails are trimmed properly. Ease the sail until it starts to luff at the leading edge (naturally called the *luff* of the sail), and then trim it back until the luffing stops.

Instructor Michelle Boggs uses another tip for trimming sails: *When in doubt, let it out.* This is a good one to remember when reaching. The sail may look perfectly fine; but it may actually be trimmed too tight, which makes the boat heel more and sail slower than it should.

Figure 3-7. A broad reach

Figure 3-8. Close-hauled

Now that you have the feel of sailing on a close reach and a beam reach, the next step is to experience a *broad reach*—the point between a *beam reach* and sailing dead downwind. The wind is on your quarter (aft of abeam) and you have to concentrate a little more on your steering because, at this point, it is easy to go off course without realizing it. If you turn the boat so the wind ends up directly behind you, the mainsail looks perfectly fine but you are no longer on a broad reach. You are now on a run.

Turn the boat back toward the direction of the wind—from a broad reach to a beam reach. If you point your arm at the wind again and continue turning the boat in that direction, you will have to continue trimming the sails to keep them from luffing. When you can't trim the sails any tighter because they are almost in the middle of the boat, you are back to sailing close-hauled—which again is sailing as close to the wind as possible without actually luffing. Most sailboats sail an average of 45° to the wind on a close-hauled course.

When you are on a reach, the crew is responsible for keeping the sails full by adjusting them in or out while you steer a straight course. When you are close-hauled, it is up to the person steering to keep the sails full. If you are steering a close-hauled course and the sails start to flutter or go soft along the leading edge, you are probably *sailing too high,* too close to the direction of the wind. This is also called *pinching.* To fill the sails properly, head away (fall off) from the wind just enough to stop the luffing. Continually test your course by heading up slightly until the jib (or mainsail if you only have one sail) starts to luff, and then head off just a bit until the sail looks firm.

Sailors use many terms to describe a boat's course in relation to the wind, but those that have the connotation of *up* or *high* imply you are sailing too close to the wind. *Down* or *low* imply being away or too far from the wind—more broadside to it. If someone says, "You're too high," you are too close to the wind and your sails are either luffing slightly or will soon start to luff.

We have already learned the term *falling off.* Again, when you fall off from a close-hauled position to a reach, you are sailing away from the wind. Your crew might also say to you, "Head down," to indicate you are sailing too high and need to fall off. The opposite is to *harden up.* When you harden up from a reach to a close-hauled course, you are sailing more toward the wind.

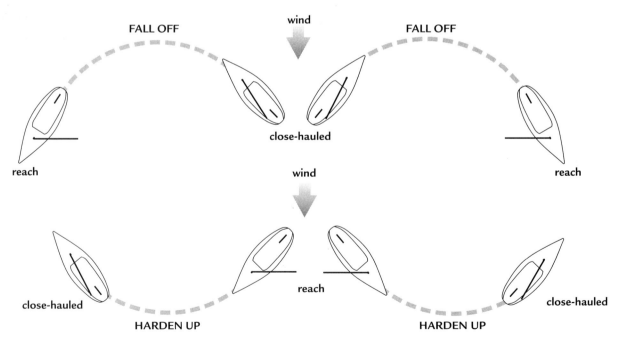

Figure 3-9. Falling off and hardening up

If you are sailing too far away from the wind and your crew wants you to harden up, they might also tell you to "come up."

CHANGING COURSE DOWNWIND

A *run* or *running free* is essentially sailing with the wind pushing the boat from behind. When you fall off from close-hauled to reaching, you ease the sails to maintain a consistent angle to the wind. As you fall off to a run, however, you reach a point when you can't ease the sail out any farther because the boom is against the shrouds that hold up the mast. If you want to turn farther, you will have to *jibe* and bring the boom over to the other side of the boat.

When the boom crosses the centerline of the boat—an imaginary line from the bow to the middle of the stern—you have changed tacks. Any change of tack from port to starboard or vice versa while sailing downwind is called a *jibe*. When sailing downwind, the bow turns away from the source of the wind and the wind comes over the stern. Just changing course downwind is not jibing. Until the boom crosses the centerline, you are simply falling off—turning away from the wind while staying on the same tack.

You will give your crew specific commands during a jibe. On the command, "Prepare to jibe," the crew's job is to start pulling in the mainsheet. It is safer and easier to bring the boom toward the center of the boat as the person steering starts the jibe; this way, the boom has a shorter distance to travel when it swings across. When the wind starts to fill the back side of the mainsail, the boom will come across with fury—and woe to anyone who gets in its path. By trimming it in first, the crew keeps the swing of the boom to a minimum. When you see the boom near the middle of the boat, give the command, "Jibe ho!" and turn the boat. As soon as the boom crosses the boat's centerline, the crew should let out the mainsheet quickly on the other side to keep the boat from heeling excessively.

Don't be alarmed if you start to turn the boat the wrong way in a jibe. New sailors often do this, but it can be corrected easily. The proper direction jibes the boat. The wrong direction causes the boat to *round up* on the same tack toward the wind. Just remember to turn the bow toward the end of the boom when jibing and you will be fine.

Because of the distance the boom has to travel across the boat when jibing, a major concern is that the boom might swing across unexpectedly. This is called an *accidental jibe,* and it can happen when the skipper unintentionally veers off course or a windshift occurs. The wind ends up on the same side of the boat as the main boom and pushes the boom across.

The process of jibing varies with different sailboats. Some sailors throw the boom over to the other side rather than trim it in. But until you know the capabilities of your boat, the safest way to jibe is the prudent way—as described above.

A run is a "warm" point of sail, as

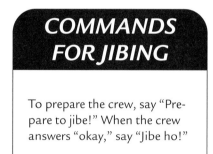

wind

starboard
tack run

shrouds

boom unable
to be eased
farther

shrouds

port
tack run

boom swings
over to same
angle with the
wind as in top
boat

shrouds

Figure 3-10. Jibing is changing tacks downwind.

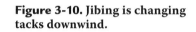

COMMANDS FOR JIBING

To prepare the crew, say "Prepare to jibe!" When the crew answers "okay," say "Jibe ho!"

INSTRUCTOR TIP

"To avoid an accidental jibe: Tiller to the boom to avoid doom."
MIKE HUFFER, MANAGER OF OFFSHORE SAILING SCHOOL—CAPTIVA ISLAND, FL

Figure 3-11. Sailing on a run

the wind is from behind, going with you. In Figure 3-11, all the boats are on a run, sailing downwind. The wind is coming from behind; the sails are all the way out. What tack are they on?

When the wind gets on the wrong side of the sails on a boat like a Colgate 26, which has a main and jib, the jib starts to dance and an accidental jibe can occur. In Figure 3-12, Boat A is sailing with the wind on the opposite side of the boat from the boom, the jib is full, and there is no fear of an accidental jibe. Boat B is sailing dead (directly) downwind, and the jib is looking soft because the main is blocking the wind; but this boat is in no danger of jibing unless you steer sloppily or a wave throws the stern to one side.

Boat C is sailing *by the lee*, with the wind on the same side of the boat as the boom. Though dangerous, a boat can sail along like this with the wind coming over the *leeward* side of the boat. You might think this would make it the windward side because the wind is now hitting that side first; to avoid confusion, right-of-way rules define the *leeward side* as the side over which the main boom is carried.

Boat D has sailed too far by the lee. The wind will catch the other side of the mainsail and throw it across the boat in what is often called a *flying*, or accidental, jibe. The boom rises up in the air unless held down by a *boom vang*, and the wind fills the other side of the sail and causes an accidental jibe. Note that the jib is already crossing to the other side of the boat: this is your first

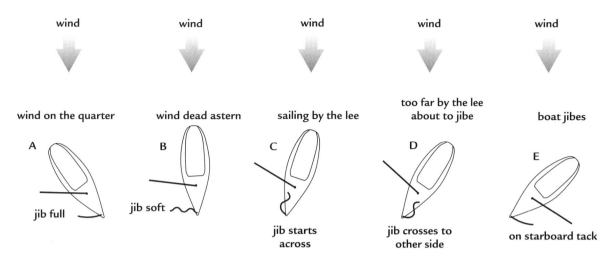

Figure 3-12. How an accidental jibe occurs

warning of an accidental jibe. When the jib crosses to the other side, the main isn't far behind—so watch out! To avoid this, head slightly higher. Boat E has jibed and is now on starboard tack. After jibing, you can steer any course on starboard tack all the way up to close-hauled just by hardening up. Try this often. It's a great exercise in learning the feel of different points of sail.

We knew a grand lady everyone called Aunt Nan, who, well before it was accepted, almost always sailed with an all-women crew. She often invited complete novices to crew. When she was in her 70s, one of her beginner crew was assigned the job of trimming in the mainsail for the jibe around a racing mark. The rest of the crew, who were more experienced, took care of the difficult tasks. Before the race, Aunt Nan carefully described the new sailor's job: "Trim the mainsail with the mainsheet, but don't make it fast," which meant don't cleat the mainsheet or secure it to something. Just before the mark she gave the command, "Prepare to jibe!" The new crew member started pulling in the mainsheet hand over hand at a snail's pace. Terribly agitated because they were barreling down on the mark with boats at close quarters all around them, Aunt Nan cried, "Hurry up!" She then received an extremely haughty reply: "But you said, don't make it fast!"

Sailing terms may seem confusing at first, but proper communication on a boat not only makes sailing more fun, it is an absolute necessity when swift action is required.

SAILING TOWARD THE WIND

You want to reach a destination that is directly upwind of your boat. But when your destination is a point that makes you sail toward the wind, you won't go anywhere but backward if you sail directly into the wind (remember the no-go zone). Therefore, you have to *tack* back and forth to get to your destination.

You know by now that you can't sail closer to the wind than 45°. So to get to that upwind point, you sail a zig-zag course—first on one tack and then on the other, until you reach your destination. Each turn you make from port to starboard and then starboard to port is a *tack*. As you maneuver

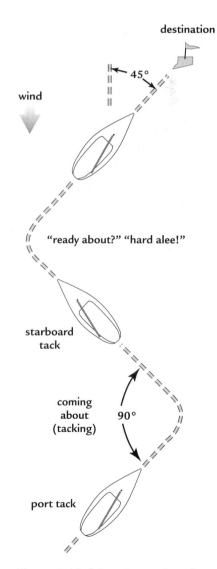

Figure 3-13. A beat is a series of tacks.

UNDERSTANDING WINDWARD AND LEEWARD

The *windward* side of anything is the side from which the wind arrives. The *leeward* side (pronounced *looward*) is the side from which the wind departs. If a wind-propelled beachball hit your boat on the starboard side, that side would be the windward side and the other side the leeward side. If the beachball went on to hit another boat after yours, your boat is the windward boat and the next boat is the leeward boat. The same holds true for windward or leeward islands, marks, or other objects on the water.

upwind each change from one tack to the other is called *coming about*. A series of tacks is called a *beat* or *beating to windward.*

Once again, you will give specific commands to prepare the crew for a successful change of course. Alert the crew first by saying, "Stand by to come about," or "Ready about!" The crew's main job now is to get the jib ready for the tack by uncleating it—but not yet releasing it—and preparing to pull on the opposite jibsheet. As long as you are in open water with no other boats or obstructions around, the mainsail, which is near the middle of the boat when close-hauled, can be left to travel the short distance on its own. There is usually no need to adjust it. However, a crew member should always be prepared to release the mainsheet.

When your crew responds "Ready!", start turning while giving the command "Hard alee!" Now you push the tiller to leeward (away from the wind) for the tack, and the bow turns toward the wind. When you point to the wind and turn the bow in that direction, you are tacking. Remember the two "Ts"—Tack Toward the wind. The command for tacking—"hard alee!"—is an Americanization of the old "helm's alee!" which meant the helm was put to the leeward side of the boat.

When you are sailing close-hauled, figure out where you want to end up before you tack. If you are on port tack and want to change to starboard tack, look directly out (abeam) to port. Find a landmark in that vicinity and plan to end up with your bow pointing at that landmark when you complete the tack.

WHEN TACKS DON'T GO AS PLANNED

The good news is that you now understand the theory of tacking upwind; the bad news is that tacks don't always go according to plan. That is, until

> ### COMMANDS FOR TACKING
>
> To prepare crew ask, "Ready about?" When they answer yes, say "Hard alee!"

Figure 3-14. The lead boat is head to wind, and its sails are luffing; the boat behind has trimmed sails.

REDUCE HEELING AND HEELING FEARS

If someone on your boat is afraid of heeling, which is not uncommon at first, let that person handle the mainsheet so they can control the amount of heel themselves. In a short time, a fearful crew will understand they are truly in control and start to enjoy sailing in strong winds with great confidence.

Another way to reduce heeling is to reduce the wind's force on your sails by heading into the wind and allowing the sails to luff slightly. In small doses this is called *feathering* the boat to windward; but in response to a strong gust it is simply luffing.

you understand the mechanics of changing tacks. (If other boats are close by, always be prepared to release the mainsheet quickly. If you do not release or ease the mainsheet when you fall off to avoid a collision, your boat will heel excessively, rendering the rudder ineffective because so much of it will be out of the water. In short, falling off will be difficult.)

For example, you might fail to complete a tack and your boat ends up dead in the water, or *head to wind*. The bow is pointed into the wind and the boat is motionless. Without motion there is no water flowing past the rudder. Remember that when you were leaving a mooring, the rudder had to deflect water in order to turn the boat. If you aren't moving, your boat has no *steerageway*. Turning the rudder doesn't turn the boat. You are *in irons*.

You know if your boat is about to stop when the sails start to luff and stream aft like a flag. Usually this happens when you allow the boat to slow up too much before attempting to tack. A wave can stop the boat in the middle of the tack leaving you with no *way on,* a temporary condition. The boat will shortly fall off to one tack or the other, but you may not end up on the desired tack.

If, for instance, the reason for the tack was a moored boat dead ahead, it could be very embarrassing (and costly) to get in irons and then fall back on the same tack. Since your boat can't gain any steerageway until it gains speed, by the time you are moving enough to try to tack again, you may collide with the moored boat after all.

If you are steering, you may not be totally at fault. When the crew doesn't get the jib trimmed in on the new tack fast enough, the mainsail may force the boat up into the wind again if its sheet remains cleated. By this time the boat has lost so much forward momentum you end up in irons once more.

> *"I always feared that the boat would turn over in a strong breeze but found out that it wouldn't— and letting out my mainsail would right me again."*
>
> **SANDRA HARRISON (40),**
> **PALMER, TX**

While the main does not regularly need to be uncleated when tacking, as we said earlier, someone (even the person steering) should hold the mainsheet when sailing among moored boats or near obstructions. If a gust of wind hits the boat, or the tack is not completed well (as described above), you can then release the mainsheet quickly to spill wind out of the main. This lets the boat straighten up so you can change course. In a lot of wind, you will surely be heeled over, making it more difficult to maintain your course or turn away from the wind and away from another boat or object, unless the mainsheet is released.

ANOTHER MUST-KNOW KNOT

A bowline

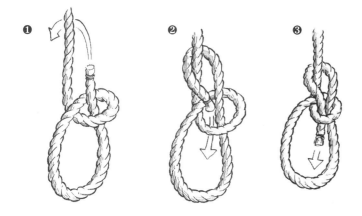

Steps for tying a bowline

One of the most useful knots is the *bowline* (pronounced *bolin*). As a nonslip knot for towing, docking, and a multitude of other purposes, the bowline's major attribute is that no matter how great the strain, the knot won't jam and can easily be untied—unlike many knots that become impossible to loosen when strain is applied.

There are many ways to learn this knot, but the time-honored method is to pretend the end of the line is a rabbit coming out of a hole (the loop) in step 1. Then the rabbit runs around a tree (the standing part of the line) in step 2, and goes back down the hole in step 3. The object is to get the rabbit at the end of the line back through the loop parallel to the way it came out. When you can tie this one in pitch darkness, on a heaving deck, with one hand, you're an old salt!

TEST YOURSELF

On a Tack
Look at the accompanying photo (*right*) to answer the questions below.

1. What tack is this boat on?
2. What side of the boat is the boom over?
3. Where is the wind coming from?

Cycling Through the Points of Sail
Look at the accompanying photos and answer the questions below.

1. What point of sail is depicted in each of the five scenarios pictured?
2. Describe the no-go zone and what happens when a boat sails into it.
3. What is sailing by the lee?
4. What are the commands for tacking? For jibing?

BUILDING CONFIDENCE AND SKILLS

4 WIND AND SAILS
A POWERFUL TEAM

In recent years, a great deal has been learned about the relationship between wind and sails. For a long time sailors thought wind simply pushed sails. When sailing toward the wind, the wind's force is sideways; but the theory was that the wedge shape of the keel kept the boat moving forward. Though not entirely accurate, that theory isn't too far off. Wind exerts both a sideways force and a forward pull on sails. In simplest terms, the keel keeps the boat from slipping sideways—so all that is left is the forward pull.

WIND CREATES LIFT

Forward pull on a sail is caused by air flowing over its surface. To understand this concept, compare your sails to the wings of an airplane. Lift is required to keep a plane in the air, and lift is required to keep a sailboat moving forward.

On an airplane, air splits and passes on either side of its wings. The air on the upper side of a wing has greater velocity than the air on the lower side—because of the *angle of attack* and an airflow phenomenon called *circulation effect*. The angle of attack is defined as the angle between the *chord* (a line from the leading edge to the trailing edge) of an airfoil, and a line representing the undisturbed relative airflow. The circulation effect causes a circular flow that affects velocity and reinforces and accelerates airflow on the upper side of the wing (the leeward side of the sail), while the velocity of flow over the under side of the wing (the windward side of the sail) is opposed and decreased.

Unlike an airplane's wing, all lifting surfaces of a sailboat—the keel, hull, centerboard, and rudder—are symmetrical. Yet they can still develop lift because water hits them at an angle. As air flows past a sail, the sail's curve causes the flow to bend. On the back side of the sail—the leeward side—this results in a greater distance for the wind to travel. In 1738, Daniel Bernoulli discovered that as velocity increases pressure decreases, creating a lift that acts at right angles to the surface. When velocity on both sides of

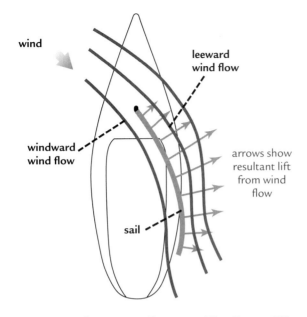

Figure 4-1. Air flow over sails creates lift—Bernoulli's Principle.

the sail and the difference in velocity between the sides of the sail both increase, so does lift.

Deflection of flow is an action that causes an equal and opposite reaction according to Newton's third law of motion. Do you remember, as a child, what happened when you stuck your hand out a car window and then tilted it upward? Because of this deflection and circulation flow, a flat surface or even a thin membrane such as a sail can create lift.

The air, however, has to flow over the surface smoothly and evenly. Once the air starts to separate from the surface it becomes turbulent. Instead of even flow, burbles develop that reduce suction. Much of the turbulence is caused by the angle that the airfoil makes with the airflow. This too is called the *angle of attack* or *angle of incidence.*

If the angle is small, the airflow remains *attached* to the surface for quite a distance back toward the leech of the sail, or the trailing edge of an airplane's wing. When the angle is increased, the airflow detaches earlier and turbulence starts to occur in the forward part of the sail. At a certain angle and speed there is so much separation of flow that the wing or sail no longer develops enough *lift* and a stall occurs. In an airplane the result is dramatic, since the aircraft drops suddenly. A sailboat, however, will just heel over more and slow down.

A sail stalls if it is trimmed in too tight. But a stalled sail can look the same as a sail operating at maximum efficiency. You can easily learn to trim sails properly, by easing them to the point just before they luff. A

luff is easy to see because the leading edge of the sail flaps or flutters. So when trimming your sails, follow this basic rule: ease the sail until it luffs, then trim it just enough to stop the luff.

Like everything else in this world, there are some exceptions. After you have sailed for a while you may find, especially on reaches, the need to trim a little past this point to get maximum drive from the sail. This judgment depends a great deal on wind strength. In lighter winds you can trim tighter before separation and turbulence occur. But the tighter you trim, the more sideways the driving force will be; this can result in detrimental heeling rather than greater forward motion.

TWO SAILS ARE MORE EFFICIENT THAN ONE

Boats with jibs have added advantages over those without. First, the jib is a very efficient sail since there is no

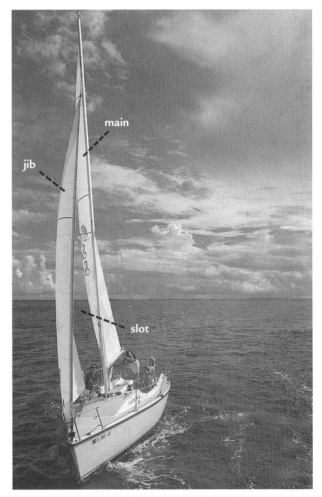

Figure 4-2. The slot between the jib and mainsail improves the wind flow and increases boat speed.

mast in front of it to disrupt airflow. Second, it bends and funnels the air on the leeward side of the main. This funneling action increases the speed of air flowing past the lee side of the main.

The space, or *slot,* between the jib and the mainsail affects the efficiency of airflow when your sails are set properly. The jib not only speeds up this air, but also bends it aft so it can easily follow the curve of the main. Remember, the faster air travels, the less it can bend around the sail. The velocity is substantially faster in the slot between the main and jib, increasing suction and making the mainsail more efficient than it would be without the jib.

> *"Handling the sails and understanding how the wind moves the boat . . . was much easier than we expected."*
>
> **TIM GAPEN (56),**
> **WISCONSIN RAPIDS, WI**

With an accurate handheld windspeed indicator, you can measure the difference in the velocity of airflow on the lee side of the mainsail with and without a jib. You can also feel wind velocity without any instruments. When you are sailing close-hauled, before you unfurl the jib, crouch under the boom with arms on either side of the mainsail, as if you are surrendering. Then ask someone to unroll the jib and trim it in. You will immediately feel more wind pressure on the leeward side of the main than on the windward side.

Without a jib, the efficiency of the mainsail is greatly reduced. Air is not funneled along the main, flow becomes detached, and turbulence occurs. Remember that attached airflow creates lift. When sailing close-hauled, it is important to keep the slot open. For example, if you ease the main before easing the jib, you can close this slot and create *backwind* on the mainsail. Although the main looks like it is luffing, the air is no longer flowing smoothly through the slot. Always make sure the jib is properly trimmed be-

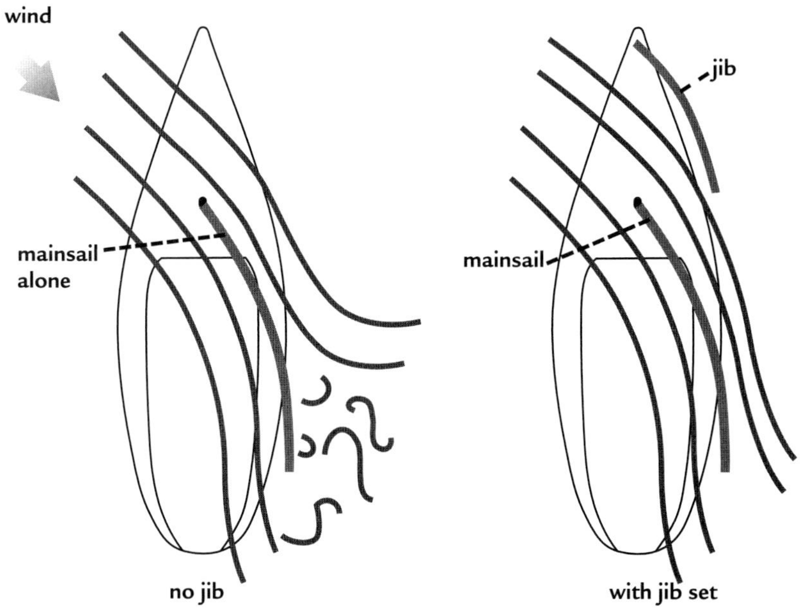

Figure 4-3. Airflow detaches early and turbulence occurs when there is no jib. When the jib is set, air flows across the width of the mainsail and creates better lift.

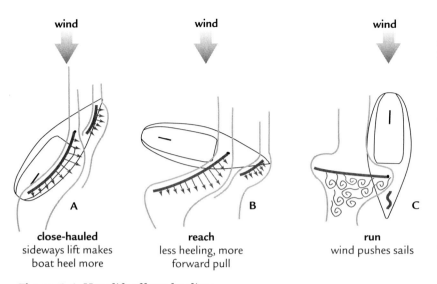

close-hauled
sideways lift makes
boat heel more

reach
less heeling, more
forward pull

run
wind pushes sails

Figure 4-4. How lift affects heeling

fore adjusting the mainsail. As you can now understand, a boat can sail with just a mainsail or jib; but the combination of main and jib makes your sails more efficient.

THE EFFECT OF HEELING

Heeling is a mixed bag for sailors. Until you learn why a boat heels, you might feel uncomfortable with the sensation of being at an angle to the horizon. Some macho, experienced sailors love the challenge of sailing with the rail in the water. But for many reasons, which we'll cover later, that is not a very efficient way to sail.

When a boat is close-hauled with sails trimmed in tight, a large sideways push on the sails makes your boat heel. In Figure 4-4, note that many of the force arrows point sideways on Boat A, which is sailing close-hauled. As the sail is eased out to a reach (Boat B) the arrows start to line up more with the course of the boat, which results in less heeling and more forward pull. A reach, therefore, is usually the fastest point of sailing.

It may appear that you're sailing faster when you are close-hauled because there's a great deal of commotion, the boat is heeling over and plowing through the seas, and the wind seems stronger because you are moving toward it. When you fall off to a reach, however, the commotion quiets down. You are sailing across the wind and water and neither seem to be as powerful. The boat is more upright because the pull of the sails is more forward.

Carrying this one step further, you might think that a run would be even faster because the wind and the boat are both going in the same direction. But on a run, the wind is just pushing the boat and can't flow over both sides of the sail. Lift cannot develop on the leeward side of the sail, and (as you see in Boat C), there is pure turbulence behind the sail downwind. If a jib is set on this point of sail, no wind can reach it because the main is blocking the wind from reaching the jib; in this case, the jib is *blanketed* by the main.

Again, there can be exceptions. When the wind velocity increases to the point where a boat on a reach is *overpowered* and heeling excessively in comparison to forward drive, a run can then be the faster point of sail.

USING TELLTALES

To sail efficiently, you need to maintain the optimum drive angle of the wind on your sails. You can do this by steering well and trimming your sails properly. To help visualize proper sail trim, imagine air flowing past your sails as smoke. Many wind tunnel tests, called *smoke visualization tests,* actually use smoke to see the difference between smooth and turbulent flow. Obviously you can't create a smokescreen in front of your sailboat, but you can do the next best thing: attach telltales to the sails to show whether the flow past the sail is turbulent or smooth. Normally, these telltales are attached at three levels on the jib as described in Chapter 14.

On the boat in Figure 4-5 you can see three sets of telltales on the jib and another set on each shroud. You have already learned that telltales are placed on the shrouds to show *wind direction.* The telltales on your sail show *wind flow* on the leeward and windward sides of the sail.

These telltales on your sail are like a mine canary. They warn you when you are about to lose your jib's efficiency before you can actually see the sail flutter. When the telltale on one side of the sail isn't flowing nicely aft, that telltale is telling you airflow is disrupted. But when the telltales on both the leeward and windward side of the sail stream aft, airflow is smooth and even.

telltales on shrouds

telltales on sails

Figure 4-5. Telltales on the sail help you see airflow. Telltales on the shrouds help you see wind direction.

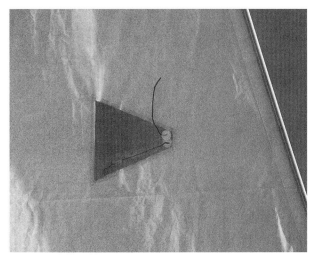

Figure 4-6. Telltales show when the jib is eased too much. This windward telltale is fluttering.

telltales

Figure 4-7. When both telltales stream aft, airflow is smooth and even.

On the sail in Figure 4-6, the windward telltale is pointing up and the leeward telltale is flowing aft. Airflow on the windward side of the sail is not smooth. Either the jib is eased too much and needs to be trimmed in, or the person steering is *pinching*—sailing too high and too close to the wind. When the windward telltale is flowing properly and the leeward telltale is fluttering, the jib is trimmed too tight or the person steering is sailing too far off the wind (too low).

When steering close-hauled, watch the telltales and keep them in line by moving the tiller slightly until you get the desired results. If you are sailing on a reach, the crew should make subtle adjustments to the jib (ease out slightly, pull in a little) until both telltales are streaming aft. Telltales on the mainsail, placed on the leech end of batten pockets, are not important for

recreational sailing. Racing sailors, however, do use them.

You can test how well you are steering or how well the sails are trimmed in a couple of simple exercises. Watch the middle set of telltales on the jib as you change your heading without varying your jib trim. As the boat heads up toward the wind, the windward telltale starts to flutter. Conversely, when the boat heads too far off the wind, the leeward telltale flutters because the angle of attack becomes so great the wind hits

TILLER TOWARD FLUTTERING TELLTALE

- Leeward telltale flutters, sailing too low
- Windward telltale flutters, sailing too high

mostly on the windward side of the sail. This disrupts flow over the lee side and turbulence results.

If turbulence occurs on the lee side, the jib stalls and no longer produces the desired drive. As explained earlier, an impending luff is easy to see because the sail starts to flutter along the luff; but a stall is virtually invisible. So, ease the jib until the windward telltales start to flutter; then trim again until telltales on both sides of the jib stream aft. The difference between a luff and a stall is usually no more than a slight (5°–10°) change in heading.

Telltales are very helpful for the new sailor, and they are also used to advantage by the expert. Dr. Reinhorn, a 1967 Offshore Sailing School graduate, came up with a simple rule for steering to windward that we have used ever since. Dubbed Reinhorn's Law, this little phrase will always keep you out of trouble: *Point the tiller at the fluttering telltale.*

For example, if the leeward telltale is fluttering you are sailing too low, too far away from the wind for the desired close-hauled course. You need to point closer to the wind, so move the tiller to leeward to cure this. If the windward telltale is fluttering, you are sailing too close to the wind and you are on the verge of a luff. To solve this problem, move the tiller to windward and the boat will fall off. As you move the tiller, make slight course adjustments. It doesn't take much to get those telltales streaming together again.

When trying to reach a destination, use your telltales to find the fastest way to get there. If you are on course, adjust the jib (pull in or ease out) to make the telltales stream aft together. If you are sailing close-hauled and can't trim the sails any tighter, steer the boat to make the telltales stream aft.

As usual, there are exceptions when telltales should not be flowing on both sides. In a strong wind and smooth sea you may be able to *pinch* (carry a very slight luff in the jib) and still maintain your speed or even go faster. In this case it is okay for the windward telltale to flutter. If you fall off until both sides flow evenly, the boat will heel a lot, reducing your speed. Experienced sailors steer the fastest course for existing conditions.

Jib telltales help you gain speed on a reach, but you need to *play* (trim and ease) the jib constantly to use them effectively. This means easing when the jib stalls and trimming when it luffs. Racing crew keep their eyes glued to the telltales near the luff of the sail, with the jibsheet in hand—whether they are sailing on a small boat or on a large yacht. Without those telltales on the jib, it is very, very difficult to determine if the sail is stalled.

WIND FLOW ON A RUN

When a reach becomes very broad and approaches a run, the force of the wind changes from a *pull* to a *push.* Instead of flow over the lee side of the sail you end up with *drag* (the force that slows movement of the boat through the air or water). The sail that creates the most drag will push the boat fastest. Though you want to retain aerodynamic flow over the lee side as long as possible, at some point near a run the curve of the sail is no longer helpful and the amount of sail area exposed to the wind is now the most important factor.

Just as a large parachute will lower you more gently than a small one, a large sail will push the boat faster than a small one downwind. As you reach the point where sail area projected to the wind is more important, the leeward telltales (which were flowing aft) start to flutter and easing the sail more doesn't seem to help much. In fact, it will hurt your speed because you start to lose sail area. In practicality, if your boat is rigged to carry a spinnaker (a large parachute-looking sail), you would have probably set one before you reach this point. If you only have a jib and no spinnaker, you might *wing* your jib out to the other side of the boat.

When you sail *wing and wing,* you sail downwind with the mainsail on one side and the jib on the other. This helps move the boat more efficiently downwind because you are exposing more sail area. Sometimes you can just hold the jib out over the side opposite the mainsail. Other times you may want to rig a pole from the clew of the sail back to the mast. When sailing wing and wing with a pole, you will lose one of your early-warning signals for an accidental jibe. The jib may want to move across from one side to the other, but the pole won't let it; you could be on the verge of an accidental jibe, so you need to keep a close eye on the wind direction and your boom.

In Figure 4-9, the jib on the second boat cannot fill because it is blanketed behind its mainsail. The lead boat is sailing more efficiently, with the jib winged out on the side opposite of the main where it can catch more wind.

JIB LEADS

Telltales are also an important aid when determining how jibsheets should lead from the clew of the sail to a winch in the cockpit. On almost all sailboats, jibsheets are led through blocks on tracks on the starboard and port sides of the deck. These adjustable leads determine the shape of the jib. When the block is too far forward the foot of the jib is too loose and the leech is too tight, because most of the pull on the jib sheet is downward. When the block is too far aft, the foot is stretched too tight and the leech is too loose because of the backward pull.

What you want is a compromise between the two extremes to avoid distorting the sail. There should be an even flow of air on both sides of the sail at all levels along the luff. If

Figure 4-8. Sailing wing and wing with jib and main on opposite sides of the boat

Figure 4-9. The jib on the boat behind is blanketed by its main, while the lead boat sails wing and wing.

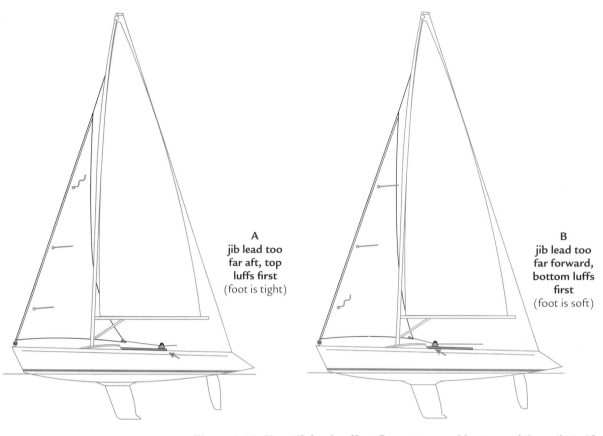

A
jib lead too
far aft, top
luffs first
(foot is tight)

B
jib lead too
far forward,
bottom luffs
first
(foot is soft)

Figure 4-10. How jib leads affect flow at top and bottom of the sail. A. If top of jib luffs first, move jib lead forward. B. If bottom of jib luffs first, move jib lead aft.

the lead is too far forward, the bottom of the sail will have a big curve in it and the lower part of the sail will luff first. Conversely, if the lead is too far aft, the leech will be loose and tend to fall off at the top of the sail, causing that part to luff first. So the test to determine proper jib lead placement is to head the boat up slowly until the jib begins to luff. If it luffs at the top first, the lead is too far aft. If it luffs at the bottom first, the lead is too far forward. But if it luffs the full length of the sail all at the same time, the lead is set in the right spot.

Telltales also allow you to determine if any part of your jib is stalled. If the bottom leeward telltale flutters first, the bottom of the sail is stalled. The sail is too flat at the bottom because the jib lead is too far aft.

HOW SAILS ARE MADE

Sails are your sailboat's engine, their driving force. The shape of your sails allows you to change gears and throttling power. Full sails are like low gear in a car; flat sails are like high gear. Full sails can be likened to flaps down on an airplane, giving power to get up into the air. At cruising altitude, pilots bring the flaps back in to maintain speed going forward. You will adjust sails in much the same way.

TESTING PROPER JIB LEADS

◆ Head up slowly until the jib begins to luff
◆ If the jib luffs at the top first, the lead is too far aft
◆ If the jib luffs at bottom first, the lead is too far forward
◆ If the jib luffs along full length of the sail, the leads are set correctly

Figure 4-11. Chord, camber, and draft define sail shape.

The distance from luff to leech in a straight line at any level in the sail is the chord. If three people, one at each corner, pick up a sail lying flat on the ground, a belly will form as they hold it level. This belly is called the *camber*. The distance from the deepest point of the camber to the chord is the *draft*.

A deep draft sail is considered a *full* sail and is used like first gear in a car—for slow speeds (light winds) and for power in choppy seas (similar to climbing a steep hill). A shallow-draft sail is called a *flat* sail and is used like high gear in a car—not much power but appropriate for high winds and flat seas.

The threads that run across a strip of sailcoth are called *filling threads*, otherwise known as the *weft* or the *fill*. The threads that run lengthwise are

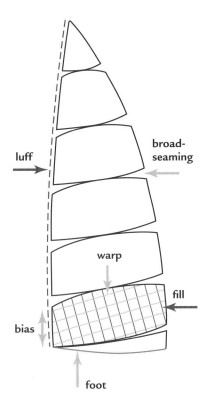

Figure 4-12. Warp, fill, and bias define how sail cloth stretches.

called the *warp*. Warp stretches more than fill, but the greatest stretch comes in a diagonal direction, called the *bias*.

Most sails are designed with this stretch in mind. The mainsheet will exert the greatest force on a mainsail and most of it will fall on the leech. Consequently, the panels of cloth are sewn together so the crosswise threads, or filling threads, lie parallel to the leech of the sail. Thus all the panels of the luff along the mast, where stretch is greatest, are cut on the bias. If you could blow up a small section of the sail along the mast, you would see that the threads look like a whole bunch of little diamonds on the bias. As you pull down on the luff and increase the tension, each diamond elongates and pulls material in from the center of the sail.

As a result, if you pull down hard on the luff when there isn't enough wind, vertical creases will appear that run parallel to the mast. You can simulate this effect by taking a handkerchief and pulling it at two diagonally opposite corners. The same creases will appear just as they will when there is too much tension on a sail. Note that the panels are curved. When the panels are sewn together by the sailmaker a curve, which allows for draft, is created in the sail. This process is called *broadseaming*.

There is a hole in the luff of the mainsail a foot or so above the tack with a line running through it. Strengthened by a metal grommet, this assembly has become known as the *cunningham* and is now commonplace on most sailboats. In heavy winds, sailcloth can stretch and the sail becomes full just when you want it to be flat. Pulling down on the cunningham moves the draft forward in the sail and cures this effect. Some wrinkles will appear along the tack below the grommet when the cunningham is in use, but they don't seem to make an appreciable difference in the efficiency of the sail, so ignore them. You will learn more about draft in Chapter 14.

SAIL CONTROLS

As the velocity of the wind increases or decreases, you need to adjust the draft of your sails for the best efficiency. For instance, you set sail in a 10-knot wind and the shape of your sails looks good. Soon the wind increases to 20 knots and now you are overpowered. With older Dacron sails, the draft of your mainsail may have moved aft with stretch. The leech of the mainsail is tight and becomes a rudder in the air, steering you to windward. So, you need to flatten your sails and bring the draft of your mainsail back to its original position. The *outhaul* stretches and flattens the lower part of the mainsail along the boom. The *backstay* bends the mast forward in the middle when tightened. This frees the leech, reduces weather helm, and makes a flatter sail. The *cunningham* tightens the lower luff of the sail, which keeps the

"Sail trim and shape were difficult concepts to grasp at first, but they proved to be worthwhile lessons. We soon realized there's a better, faster way to sail."

**JON NELSON (50),
DOWNINGTOWN, PA**

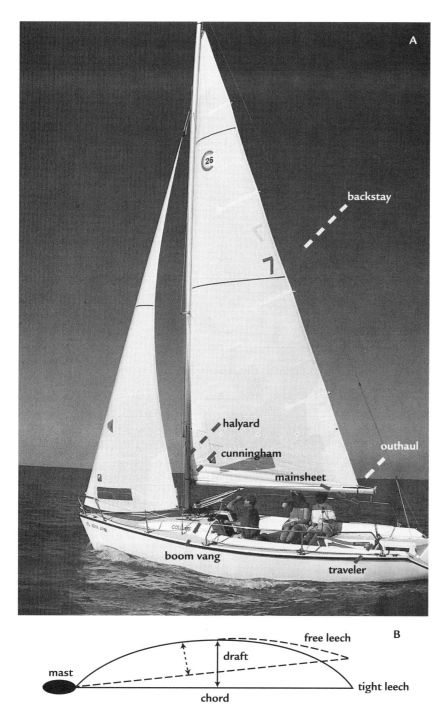

Figure 4-13. A. Sail controls that adjust draft and ultimately sail shape. B. Terms that define a sail's shape.

draft forward. The halyard stretches the whole luff, particularly higher up.

Mainsheet tension pulls the end of the boom down, tightens the leech, increases draft, and increases weather helm. Be careful in light air about trimming the mainsail too tight. Remember: *when in doubt, let it out.*

The *traveler* and *boom vang* also control tension along the leech of the sail. The traveler is a track that's mounted behind the cockpit (sometimes behind the tiller, sometimes in front). A sliding block with a part of the mainsheet reeved through it runs along the traveler and allows you to change the mainsail's angle to the wind. The boom vang is an angled block and tackle arrangement or adjustable rod that runs from a tang or block on the boom to another fitting near the base of the mast or to a rail on the side of the boat. The boom vang keeps the boom from rising and keeps the leech tight. A tight leech cocks to windward and causes a full sail because the chord line moves away from the belly of the sail, increasing the draft as shown as solid lines in the diagram (Figure 4-13B). A loose leech falls off to leeward and flattens the sail (dotted lines).

READING AND USING THE WIND

For the best efficiency, you'll need to adjust your sails according to your boat's precise angle to the wind. However, wind is constantly changing direction, so sails require constant fine tuning.

Before you go sailing, check weather maps in local newspapers, the forecasts put out by the National Oceanic and Atmospheric Administration (NOAA), or any other source that gives you some credible wind and weather predictions. Remember that local topography and large buildings can bend and deflect the wind, so you need to take this into consideration when you hear reports of wind direction and strength.

You cannot see the wind, but you can see how it affects the surface of the water. So as you sail, watch the water all around you. You will see *puffs*, or gusts of wind, which indicate greater wind velocity; these move across the water in patches of ripples. The ripples also show you where a new wind is coming from, especially on a light-air day. If you are sailing close-hauled on starboard tack and see ripples approaching from abeam, you should anticipate a new wind direction, which may be temporary. *Lulls* indicate reduced wind velocity and manifest themselves as smoother areas on the water. As puffs move and lulls form, you can detect changes in wind direction and strength.

"I love the challenge of making a boat go by working with nature. It's calming and invigorating at the same time. One must stay focused on the wind and the water to keep going. . . . It's amazing how an activity can be so relaxing yet can require so much attention. I really believe one's understanding and awe of nature and our universe is heightened by sailing and wish everyone could have this experience. Hearing the wind and the water all around your boat and knowing I can use it to get someplace is nirvana to me."

LEANN SMITH (46), KANSAS CITY, MO

Headers and Lifts

Sailors talk about *true wind* and *apparent wind.* True wind is the actual wind. Apparent wind is the wind you feel as the boat moves,

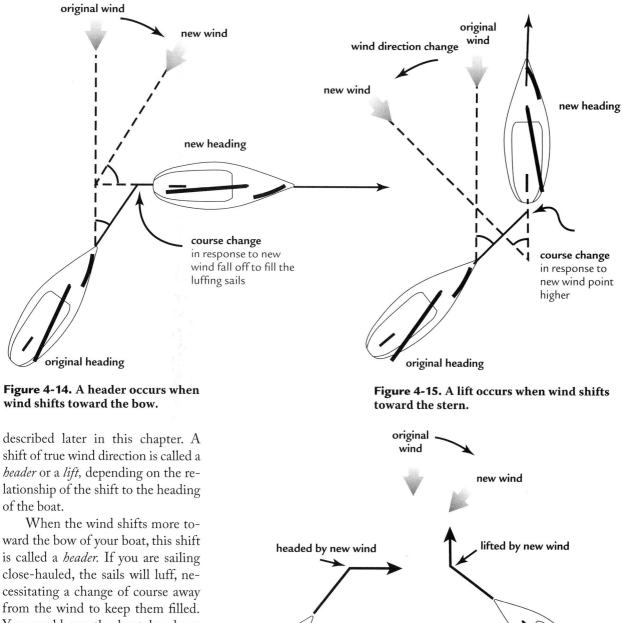

Figure 4-14. A header occurs when wind shifts toward the bow.

Figure 4-15. A lift occurs when wind shifts toward the stern.

Figure 4-16. To get to an upwind destination faster, tack on headers.

described later in this chapter. A shift of true wind direction is called a *header* or a *lift*, depending on the relationship of the shift to the heading of the boat.

When the wind shifts more toward the bow of your boat, this shift is called a *header*. If you are sailing close-hauled, the sails will luff, necessitating a change of course away from the wind to keep them filled. You would say the boat has been *headed* or has *sailed into a header*. When the wind shifts more toward the stern of your boat, allowing you to *steer higher* than before, the boat has been *lifted* or is sailing *in a lift*.

When a header or a lift occurs on a reach, a corresponding sail adjustment is required to maintain your course. So on a reach, trim for a header, ease for a lift. A wind shift that is a header for a boat on port tack is a lift for a boat on starboard

Figure 4-17. A backing wind heads this boat while a veering wind is a lift.

tack. A boat sailing on a lift will reach its desired upwind destination faster than one sailing in a header, since the lifted boat can sail a closer course to its upwind destination. So if you are headed and want to continue sailing upwind toward your destination in the shortest distance possible, you should tack.

When a wind shift is described in relation to the course you are sailing, it's described as a *header* or a *lift*. But when a wind shift is described in relation to a compass direction, it is said to be *veering* or *backing*.

Wind that shifts clockwise—from north to northeast, for example—is *veering*. Wind that shifts counterclockwise—from east to northeast, for example—is *backing*. A north wind is one that blows *from* the north. (Don't confuse these with currents, which are named for the direction to which they flow. For instance, a current that comes from the south, flowing northward, is a northerly current.)

Wind shifts are changes in the direction of the actual (true) wind blowing over the water. Picture yourself steering the boat in Figure 4-17. Your destination is roughly in the middle of the shoreline. If the wind veers (shifts clockwise), you will be in a lift; you'll then be able to point higher and sail closer toward your destination on land without tacking. If the wind backs (shifts counterclockwise), you will be headed; you'll then end up sailing at a broad angle away from your destination. But if you tack, you might be headed directly home.

Apparent Wind

Another type of shift, which also causes the need for sail adjustment, is a change in the *apparent* wind direction. While true wind is what your masthead fly and telltales show when your boat is not moving through the water (at anchor or docked), apparent wind is what you *feel* and what you see in your telltales and masthead fly when the boat is underway.

Apparent wind is derived from the combination of wind produced by the boat moving through the air and wind produced by nature (true wind). Cigarette smoke, telltales, and electronic wind-direction indicators all indicate apparent wind direction when you are moving.

Imagine that you are standing up in a convertible on a windless day. As the convertible starts forward, you begin to feel a breeze on your face that increases as the speed of the car increases. This is like boat-speed wind. At 10 mph, you feel a 10-mph breeze on your face. This is *apparent* wind.

Now imagine yourself in the same parked car, pointing north with an easterly wind (true wind) of 10 mph. You feel that wind hitting the right side of your face. As the car starts forward you don't feel two different winds—one on the side and one on the front of your face. You feel a resultant wind coming from an angle forward of the true wind. This is *apparent* wind.

Figure 4-18 shows apparent wind when towing a boat at 6 knots on a dead-calm day. Since there is no true wind, a resultant angle is not produced and the apparent wind is coming from dead ahead at the same

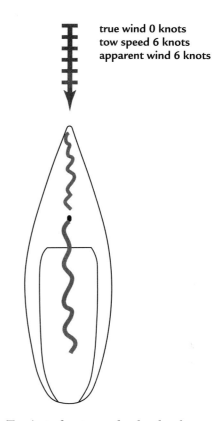

true wind 0 knots
tow speed 6 knots
apparent wind 6 knots

Figure 4-18. Towing a boat on a dead-calm day creates apparent wind dead ahead.

speed as the boat: 6 knots. On your first day out on a close-hauled course, you may wonder why the telltales on the shrouds indicate you are almost sailing directly into the wind, while you are technically sailing around 45° off the wind. The telltales are indicating your apparent wind—the resultant angle of your boat's forward motion and the true wind.

You can demonstrate the force and direction of apparent wind by drawing a parallelogram on graph paper, keeping your boat's speed and the true wind in the same scale. Figure 4-19 shows a boat close-hauled, sailing at 6 knots in a 12-knot true wind. Suppose you know your boat tacks in an 80° arc (the distance it will travel when moving from one tack to another). Therefore, the true wind direction is at half of your tacking range, or 40° off your bow. To find the strength and direction of the wind you feel—the apparent wind—draw a parallelogram on the graph paper using your boat speed (6 knots) and the true wind (12 knots). Then draw a diagonal line through the parallelogram. The diagonal line measures 17 knots of apparent wind by your scale. Now, using a protractor, the apparent wind reads 27° from your heading (versus 40° for the true wind).

APPARENT WIND DOWNWIND

- Apparent wind is *less* than true wind.
- Wind coming from behind feels like the wind has died—because true wind and boat speed counteract each other.
- When changing course, apparent wind can swing wildly.
- A boat is sometimes sailing by the lee—apparent wind is on the same side of boat as the boom.
- Beware of an accidental jibe.

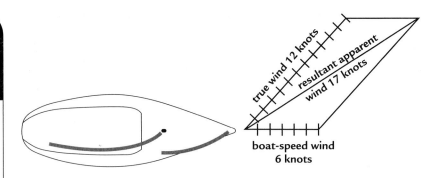

Figure 4-19. When close-hauled, apparent wind is both stronger and more forward of true wind.

This demonstrates that on a close-hauled course, the apparent wind is greater than true wind strength.

There are four points to remember about apparent wind:

1. The strength of apparent wind lessens as true wind comes aft.
2. Apparent wind is always forward of true wind, unless true wind is dead ahead or astern.
3. When true wind is well aft, a small change in true wind direction makes a large change in apparent wind direction.
4. When on a beam reach or close-hauled, apparent wind is of greater velocity than true wind.

The first point states that as true wind comes aft, the apparent wind speed lessens. This is obvious if you have ever seen powerboats head directly downwind. Sometimes they cruise along at the same speed and direction as the true wind. This is when apparent wind and true wind line up and cancel each other out. Their engine exhaust hangs around the boat in an enveloping cloud, and the apparent wind is just about zero (yet another reason why sailing is so much more fun!).

On a reach, as you can see in Figure 4-20, the wind speed lessens—even though the boat speed wind and true wind are pretty much the same as when you were close-hauled. The decrease in wind speed you feel on the boat can lull you into forgetting that the wind will be stronger when you change direction and head up to a beat. You may have started sailing on a run and had no idea what the apparent wind strength would be on a beat. Or the wind may have increased during the run. Either way, if the wind is blowing hard, you must consider the possibility that you may want less sail area when you go to a close-hauled course.

The second point states that apparent wind is always forward of

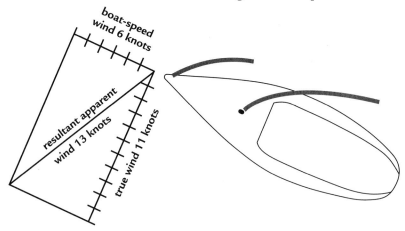

Figure 4-20. On a reach the apparent wind is less than when close-hauled. Compare this diagram with Figure 4-19.

true wind, unless true wind is dead ahead or astern. This is important when you are sailing downwind and need to consider when to jibe. For better speed, it is desirable to sail at a slight angle to the wind rather than dead (directly) downwind; but this means you may have to jibe to reach your destination. It is therefore important to determine the direction of the true wind and the angle your heading is making with it.

For example, if you know you are steering 20° from dead downwind on one tack, then you will be on the same point of sail when you are 20° from dead downwind on the other tack. The right time to jibe is when your destination bears 40° off your bow from your present heading. To find the true wind direction, head off momentarily until you are dead downwind, allowing the apparent wind and true wind to line up. The difference between the new heading and your former heading (20° in the example above; 40° when doubled) is the number of degrees in which you will jibe.

In Figure 4-22, your boat is going 6 knots in a 12-knot breeze. If you are sailing dead downwind, the apparent wind is true wind minus boat speed, or just 6 knots. This doesn't feel like much wind, and the force on your sails is relatively light. But when you start beating at 6 knots, the apparent wind increases to almost 17 knots.

You might assume that since the apparent wind is now about three times greater than the downwind velocity, it exerts three times as much force against the sails. But that assumption would be wrong. The force of the wind *quadruples* as the velocity doubles (the square of the velocity), so the wind force is *nine times greater* on a close-hauled course than on a run in this case. Couple this with a lot of heeling, and the boat may very well be overpowered. The lesson here is to consider shortening sail before you turn to go upwind.

The third point states that when true wind is well aft, a small change in the true wind direction makes a large change in apparent wind direction. This is one factor, among others, that makes steering dead downwind so dif-

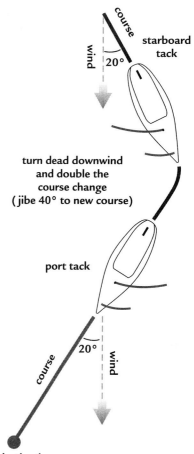

Figure 4-21. How to determine new course after jibing

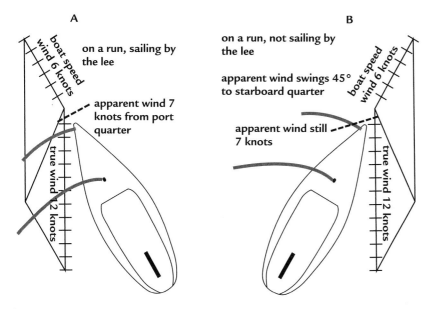

Figure 4-22. When changing course downwind, apparent wind swings wildly.

Figure 4-23. Sailing by the lee, with the wind on the same side as the boom, this boat is in danger of jibing.

ficult. If you have a lot of wave action when steering downwind, the boat's stern and rudder can be pushed to one side or the other by the waves. This complicates staying on course because you must anticipate wave action as well as wind shifts.

If your stern is pushed by a wave the effect is the same as a change in wind direction. When the wind gets on the same side as the boom (by the lee) either because of wave action or a wind shift, you are in danger of a jibe. As you try to get back on course, wind direction swings from one side of the boat to the other. Inexperienced sailors tend to oversteer in this situation, causing repetitive swings (oscillation), because they are late in compensating for the turn of the boat and often move the tiller too far.

In Figure 4-23, the lead boat is sailing by the lee. In this case, the wind is on the same side as the boom and the mainsail looks like it might accidentally jibe. The first sign of an accidental jibe is when the jib starts to come across. When this occurs, heed the instructor's warning: *Turn tiller to boom to avoid doom.* Another sign of that doom is when the shroud telltales on the windward side point away from the boat.

The last point about apparent wind states that when a boat is reaching or beating, the apparent wind is of greater velocity than the true wind. This means you are, in effect, making your own wind. For example, ice boats can attain very high speeds; some easily reach speeds that are five to six times the speed of the wind, because they experience very little surface friction. Boat speeds of 120 knots in 24 knots of wind are not unusual!

The faster the boat goes, the higher the wind velocity it creates. But a normal sailboat is limited in speed by hull resistance, skin friction, and wave-making drag—so it cannot take full advantage of the increased apparent wind velocity. Even so, the faster a boat is to windward, the more *close-winded* (able to sail close to the wind) it will be.

Lulls and Puffs

As you sail along you may suddenly feel a dramatic drop in wind strength. You have sailed into a *lull,* and the apparent wind has gone forward and decreased because your boat speed is now a greater factor than the wind speed, until the boat slows down. Conversely, you might also see a *puff*—a big patch of ripples approaching you—the apparent wind moves aft and increases, and you suddenly feel a strong increase in wind strength because the wind speed is a greater factor than boat speed.

In Figures 4-19, 4-20, and 4-22, everything remained constant except the direction of the true wind, which moved farther aft in each subsequent diagram. What happens if you change wind velocity, keeping the true wind direction at 45° off the bow?

In Figure 4-24, initially the wind speed was 10 knots and the boat speed was 4 knots. The extension of the true wind line indicates a *puff* with a 4-knot increase. The apparent wind moves aft as the puff hits; but by the time your boat picks up speed, the puff has usually passed.

When a puff is very strong, it causes your boat to heel dramatically if you don't make any adjustments. To reduce heeling when hit by a powerful gust, point the boat higher toward the wind. As the gust hits, apparent wind goes aft, causing more heeling and less drive. This changes the angle of attack—the angle the apparent wind makes with the sails. Now your sails are improperly trimmed until you head up or ease sheets or the traveler.

This change in apparent wind direction is important to remember even on light days. On days when you have a 3-knot breeze, the wind velocity in a puff is apt to be more than double the regular breeze. When it is blowing 15 knots, gusts may get to only 20 to 22 knots—or about a third higher. Thus, the change in apparent wind direction aft is often greater on light days than on heavy ones. But if the wind dies suddenly, apparent wind goes forward. In Figure 4-24, boat speed remains constant; when the wind velocity lowers to 6 knots, the apparent wind goes forward.

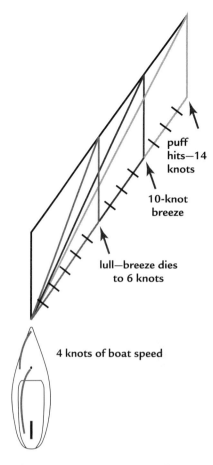

puff hits—14 knots

10-knot breeze

lull—breeze dies to 6 knots

4 knots of boat speed

Figure 4-24. Apparent wind moves aft and increases in a puff; goes forward and decreases in a lull.

LULLS AND PUFFS

- In a lull, apparent wind goes forward and decreases.
- In a puff, apparent wind goes aft and increases.

TEST YOURSELF

Telltales and Sail Trim
Picture yourself sailing the boat in the photo above.

1. What point of sail are you on?
2. If the windward telltale flutters, should you ease or trim the jib?
3. If the leeward telltale flutters, are you steering too low or too high?
4. If you are on course and heading home, do you turn the boat or trim the sails to get there?
5. How does a jib enhance sailing efficiency?
6. What do telltales on the shrouds tell you?
7. What do telltales on the jib tell you?

Sail Controls
1. Find the outhaul, backstay, cunningham, mainsheet traveler, and boom vang on the boat in the accompanying photo.
2. Describe draft in a sail.
3. Does deep draft cause more or less heeling?
4. How does shallow draft affect sail power?

TEST YOURSELF

Wind Shifts and Direction
Answer the questions below on wind shifts and wind direction, based on what you have learned in this chapter.

1. Describe true wind.
2. Explain the difference between veering and backing winds.
3. What is a lift?
4. What is a header?
5. Describe apparent wind.
6. When you are close-hauled, is apparent wind stronger or lighter than true wind?
7. Describe a boat sailing by the lee.
8. How do you know when you are sailing by the lee?

5 *BALANCE AND STABILITY*

In order to sail properly, and certainly in order to race successfully, you must understand the *balance* and *stability* of your boat. A well-balanced boat will tend to maintain its heading when you release the tiller, and a stable boat can absorb more force of wind in its sails without heeling excessively. The greater the ability of a boat to stay upright, all else being equal, the faster it will go. A stable boat is sometimes called a *powerful* boat.

HOW WEATHER AND LEE HELM AFFECT BALANCE

If you release the tiller and the boat turns away from the wind (to leeward) you are experiencing *lee helm*. Conversely, if the boat turns to windward you are experiencing *weather helm*. If the boat sails straight ahead, it is perfectly balanced. When sailing to windward, however, a little weather helm is desirable, for reasons we'll examine shortly.

There are many reasons for weather or lee helm, but foremost is the relationship between the *center of effort* (CE) of the sails (called, collectively, the *sail plan*) and the *center of lateral resistance* (CLR) of the hull.

Imagine a sailboat viewed in profile—this includes the hull underbody, keel, and rudder. Now imagine balancing the boat on your fingertip. When you find that balance point, you've found the center of lateral resistance, or CLR.

To find the center of effort (CE) of a sloop-rigged sailboat, you would find the geometric center of the jib, and then of the main, and finally the combined geometric center of the two sails together. In practice, the overall CE will be closer to the center of the mainsail than the jib, since the main is usually the larger sail. The CE is the focal point of the wind forces acting to push the boat sideways against the resistance of the hull underbody and underwater appendages, which is focused at the CLR. If you add or move

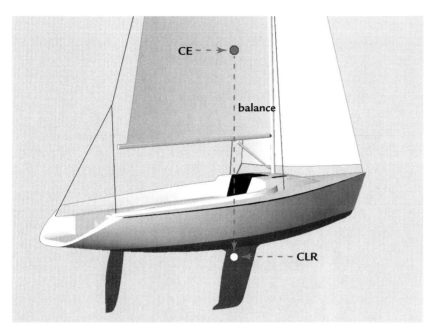

Figure 5-1. When the center of effort (CE) is directly above the center of lateral resistance (CLR), a boat is usually in balance.

CHANGING THE CLR

Although the center of lateral resistance is difficult to change underway, it can be altered by:

◆ Adding weight to immerse the bow more deeply—CLR moves forward
◆ Adding weight to immerse the stern more deeply—CLR moves aft

weight toward the bow, the CLR moves forward. If you add or move weight toward the stern, the CLR moves aft. If you sail a centerboard boat, the CLR moves aft when the board is raised partway (assuming it pivots aft when raised).

Now picture a model sailboat complete with sails, like a weather vane on top of a roof pivoting on its CLR. When the CE is directly above the CLR, the boat is in balance and won't pivot in the wind. However, if you place more sail area toward the bow of the boat, the CE moves forward of the CLR, and the bow of the boat tends to pivot to leeward, away from the wind. If you move the CE behind the CLR by placing more sail area near the stern of the boat, the bow pivots to windward, toward the wind.

HOW SAILS AFFECT BALANCE

The easiest way to change the balance of your boat, at least while sailing, is to move your effective sail area forward or aft. In theory, if you move the mast aft (and with it the main and jib), weather helm increases (CE is aft of CLR). Conversely, if you move the mast and sails forward, weather helm is reduced and a lee helm, if present, increases (CE is forward of CLR). Since most boats have varying amounts of weather helm and rarely have lee helm, the most likely result would be a reduction in weather helm.

In practice, however, moving the whole rig forward or aft is time-consuming on a small boat and close to impossible on a large one without extensive carpentry. An alternative solution is to change either the amount of sail forward or aft or the trim of those sails. The design of the Colgate 26 makes it quite easy to sail, without excessive weather or lee helm, with just the main or jib alone. But on many boats, if you sail without a jib your boat may have strong weather helm produced by the mainsail, and under jib alone

CHANGING THE CENTER OF EFFORT

The center of effort is easy to change underway:

◆ Reduce or add sail area forward or aft
◆ Luff the mainsail to move the CE forward; luff the jib to move it aft
◆ Move or tilt the mast forward or aft

WEATHER HELM

- Weather helm is the tendency of a boat to turn *toward* the wind
- It is caused by a CE that is *aft* of the CLR
- A boat with weather helm *heads up* in gusts, which is what you want it to do
- Weather helm also gives *lift* to the rudder, and this too is good

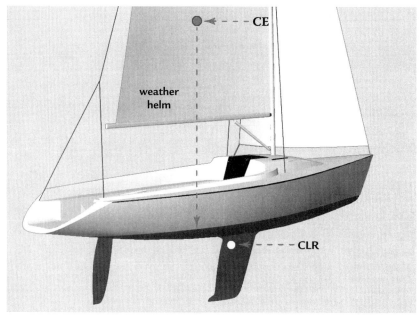

Figure 5-2. Weather helm occurs when CE moves aft of CLR.

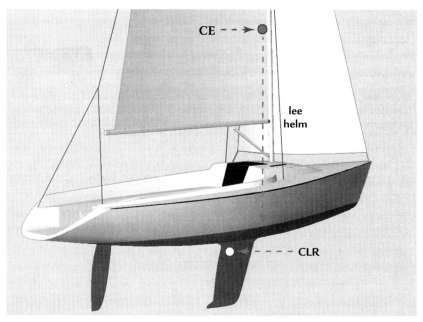

Figure 5-3. Lee helm is caused when CE moves forward of CLR.

the boat may have strong lee helm. In such a case, if you luff the mainsail, you should reduce its efficiency enough to move the CE forward with a corresponding reduction in weather helm. If you luff the jib, the weather helm should increase.

A boat with too much weather helm is harder to turn away from the wind. You may feel it *rounding up* toward the wind in puffs, and in this case you should have someone ready to ease the mainsheet if you are sailing in the vicinity of other boats or having trouble controlling where you want to go.

A boat with lee helm, on the other hand, tries to turn away from the wind. There really are no benefits to having lee helm, and a boat that is constantly trying to turn downwind will get you into trouble sooner or later. A little weather helm, as stated earlier, is best.

If you carefully adjust your main and jib, you can steer a fairly straight course without even touching the tiller. This is good practice—because one never knows when a rudder might fall off or when a tiller might break, as it did for us in the middle of a transatlantic race. With no rudder, we steered the last 1,000 miles just by trimming and easing our sails.

To practice sailing without a rudder on a close-hauled course, trim the jib fairly flat and then play the mainsheet—luffing the main to head off, trimming it to head up. On a reach you can balance the boat by easing the main to reduce weather helm. On a run, ease the main way out and ask a crew member to sit to windward to heel the boat. You may need to take the mainsail down if your boat keeps rounding up, then sail with the jib alone. To tack, ask crew members to move to the leeward side of the boat, then luff the jib completely and trim the main (more on this below).

HOW WEIGHT AFFECTS BALANCE

On a small boat the distribution of crew weight can change your boat's balance. Note the bow wave on the lee side of the boat in Figure 5-4. When a boat heels, the bow wave on the lee side becomes larger and tends to shove the bow to windward, and heeling puts the center of effort out over the water.

Imagine your sailboat in a flat calm with the mainsail and boom hanging way out over the water as if you were on a run. Someone comes alongside in a small powerboat and pushes the end of your boom in the direction your boat is pointing. In response, your bow turns away from the powerboat (into the imaginary wind), because the push at the end of a lever arm (your boom) has caused your boat to pivot around its keel. This in effect is what happens when you are reaching, running, or heeling: more weather helm develops because your boom and sails—and therefore your CE—are out over the water, not over the deck.

In a light breeze, a small sailboat can be steered without using the rudder by shifting crew weight from one side of the boat to the other. Lee helm results when the crew *hikes out*—sits on the high side of the boat with as much weight outboard as is comfortable and safe. This is generally done to flatten the boat and keep it from heeling excessively. To produce weather helm, ask the crew to sit to leeward. If you are steering and you don't feel the helm or the boat isn't gaining any forward momentum, you should try to sit on the low side, too.

Figure 5-4. As a boat heels, the leeward bow wave pushes the bow to windward.

HOW TO STEER WITHOUT USE OF TILLER OR RUDDER

- Close-hauled course—trim jib reasonably flat, luff main to fall off, trim main to head up
- Reaching course—ease main to reduce weather helm in order to sail straight
- Running course—heel boat to windward with main eased out in order to sail straight

Figure 5-5. In light air, create heeling by sitting to leeward.

Even in the lightest wind, a near flat calm, a light boat like a Colgate 26 will move if everyone sits to leeward and the sails gain a little shape.

Sail shape also affects a sailboat's balance. If the mainsail has a tight leech, weather helm will be increased. You will see this if the batten ends are pulled slightly inboard, to windward. To cure a tight leech, ease the mainsheet, then the boom vang, or tighten the backstay, which bends the mast.

CE can be moved in a few other subtle ways. If a mast is *raked* (tilted) aft, the sail area is moved aft. Raking a mast means leaning, not bending it. To lean it aft, ease the headstay. Another way to change the balance of the boat is to leave the center of effort in one place and move the center of lateral resistance forward or aft. Since CLR is the center of the underwater lateral plane of the boat, the only way to move it (without a centerboard) is to submerge less or more of the boat. You can push the bow down by moving crew or equipment forward, which results in increased weather helm as CLR moves forward. The opposite results if you push the stern down, allowing the bow to lift higher out of the water. As a memory aid, think of the bow being blown to leeward by wind as more of it is exposed (because you have too much weight in the stern).

A well-designed sailboat has slight weather helm, which increases as the wind velocity increases. The weather helm creates lift for the rudder and lets you feel the boat as you steer it. That feeling is a slight tug that allows you to ease pressure on the tiller and let the boat come up closer to the wind. It is hard to sail a boat with no feel because you constantly have to steer up toward the wind as well as away from the wind.

TO CORRECT TOO MUCH WEATHER HELM

- Ease mainsheet or traveler
- Reduce heeling by hiking
- Reduce mainsail area or effectiveness by carrying a slight luff, freeing the leech, or reefing
- Put up a jib (if none up) or a larger jib
- Reduce mast rake
- Move crew or equipment aft

You also want some weather helm because this allows the boat to automatically head up in puffs. Remember that apparent wind comes aft in puffs; when a boat with some weather helm naturally heads up in a puff, its heeling is reduced and the angle the wind originally made with the sails is maintained.

HOW THE KEEL AND HULL SHAPE AFFECT STABILITY

If you put a heavier keel on your boat to keep it more upright, the gain in stability might be offset by the increased weight of the boat. Although the boat might be able to stand up to more forces, the hull will sink deeper in the water, which results in greater water volume pushed aside. All this adds up to increased resistance because the weight of the boat displaces more water.

Weight in the keel is not the only thing that keeps the boat upright. The shape of your hull is also a factor. A wide, flat hull will have more stability than a narrow one. Imagine a raft that is 6 feet wide and one that is 12 feet wide. The wider raft will be able to carry more people standing on its edge without tipping over than the narrower one. As the side with all the weight sinks, the other side lifts out of the water; the wider it is, the more area there is to be lifted out of the water.

There is a difference, however, between *initial stability* and *ultimate stability*. A flat raft has high initial stability because it takes a lot of weight to tip it just a little bit. But the deeper the weighted side sinks into the water, the less additional weight is needed to sink it farther. The raft will tip over very easily after it gets to a steep angle, and it therefore has poor ultimate stability.

A deep, narrow boat with a heavy keel may tip the first few degrees very easily, but as the heel angle lifts the keel higher and higher, the more effective it becomes. So the deep keelboat may have poor initial stability but excellent ultimate stability.

HOW TO CONTROL STABILITY

Stability is essentially controlled by the relationship between the *center of gravity* (CG) and the *center of buoyancy* (CB). The boat's CG is the center of the earth's gravitational pull on that particular boat. If the boat were suspended from a wire attached to its exact center of gravity, it would remain perfectly level. The CB of the boat is the center of gravity of all the water that the hull displaces—the center of all the buoyant forces pushing up on the hull.

While CG remains in one spot because hull shape

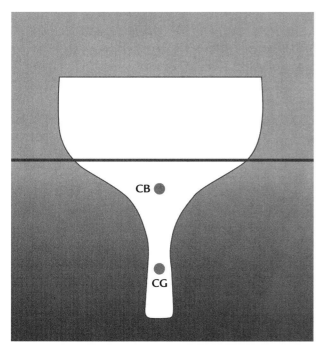

Figure 5-6. A keelboat at rest; center of gravity (CG) and center of buoyancy (CB) are in line.

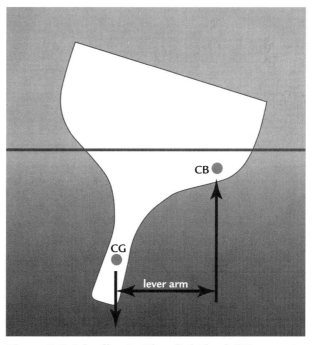

Figure 5-7. A keelboat with a slight heel; CB moves to submerged side, CG swings laterally away.

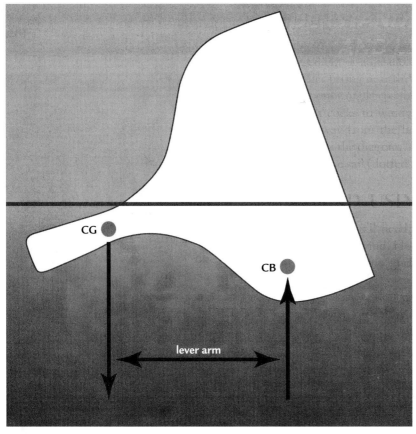

Figure 5-8. A keelboat after a knockdown; righting moment is at its greatest.

doesn't change, CB shifts to whatever part of the hull is most submerged. As the boat heels, one side submerges and the other side comes out of the water causing CB to move farther to the submerged side.

When a keelboat is at rest, sitting perfectly upright, CB and CG are in line, one above another, and CG is very low. As it heels, CB moves over to the submerged side to leeward and CG swings laterally to windward, creating a righting moment or lever arm. As the two move apart, stability produced by the lever-arm increases, with gravitational forces pulling downward at CG and buoyant forces pushing upward at CB.

Sometimes a keelboat can heel over until the spreaders are in the water and the keel and rudder are near the surface of the water. This is called a *knockdown*. Though this is a rare occurrence, you should know why it happens. The distance between CB and CG is now the greatest it has been and the righting moment is greatest too. The lever arm is longest, the sails are angled away from the wind, and the wind has lost its ability to heel the boat farther.

If you take your sails down or luff them completely, the keel's weight should eventually right the boat. But if the boat tips farther (and provided water can't get inside) the boat will go over. First it *turns turtle* (goes upside down) then continues turning until it is right side up again and the CG returns to its lowest point.

A boat that can always right itself is said to have *positive stability*. Instructors have tried to knock the Colgate 26 flat, but the boat has always come back to an upright position without turning over because it has positive stability. Even if a freak wave flipped it over, it would turn upright again.

DETERMINING SPEED

Generally, the larger the boat, the faster it can go. For a displacement boat, which is a heavy, deep-keeled boat, the maximum speed a given hull can attain from wind power is called *hull speed* and is largely dependent on the waterline length of the boat.

Hull speed is expressed as $1.34 \sqrt{LWL}$. A Colgate 26 has a waterline length of 20 feet, so it should be able to sail 1.34×4.47 or approximately 6 knots.

Figure 5-9. *Left:* **Boat is traveling below hull speed (note small waves along hull).**   *Right:* **Hull speed is shown in one long wave between the bow and stern.**

Figure 5-10. When sailboats surf, hull speed is exceeded.

A keelboat cannot travel faster than the wave it creates. The speed of a wave is $1.34 \sqrt{l}$, where l is the distance between the crests. This distance increases proportionally as the height of the wave increases. So the higher the wave, the greater the distance between crests and the faster it travels.

As boat speed increases, the greater the volume of water the bow has to push aside, and the larger the bow wave becomes. As the bow wave increases in height, the distance between its crest and that of the wave following it (the quarter wave) increases until it approaches the waterline length of the boat itself. At first there are numerous small *transverse* waves while the boat travels slowly, as shown in the left panel of Figure 5-9. These spread out as the bow wave increases in height until hull speed is attained and there are only two waves along the hull—the bow wave and the quarter, as shown in the right panel. To push a heavy displacement boat past its theoretical hull speed, though possible, would take more power in wind and sails than most boats can withstand.

Many sailboats, like a Colgate 26, really don't have a hull speed. They are technically *planing* boats, able to skim along the surface of the water like a skipping stone rather than plow the water aside. A boat that planes usually has a V-shaped hull near the bow and a fairly flat bottom aft. As speed increases the bow rides up on the bow wave and finally the boat levels off at planing speed with the bow wave well aft.

Most powerboats act this way. At lower speeds the boat plows through the water. Then as the speed increases and the bow wave moves aft, the bow rises up in the air. At a certain speed the unsupported bow, with the bow wave well aft, levels off as the boat breaks into a high-speed plane. For a sailboat, its ability to plane or not depends on its length/weight ratio. If it is too heavy for its length, it will never be able to plane.

A displacement boat can exceed its theoretical hull speed by *surfing*. The boat in Figure 5-10 is being carried by a wave just the way surfers ride a wave on a surfboard. In large wave conditions, when running downwind, a sailboat can get on the front side of a wave and carry it for quite a number of seconds with a tremendous burst of speed. It takes practice and concentration to get on the wave just right and reap the greatest benefits and thrill. When this happens, you get a real high. Though light planing boats tend to surf more easily, displacement boats are perfectly capable of surfing—and these boats can far exceed their theoretical hull speed when they do.

SAILING DINGHIES

Although this book focuses largely on sailboats with keels, you will probably have an opportunity to sail on a dinghy. Perhaps you'll find a Laser, 420, Optimist, or Sunfish at a resort or near home. Since they capsize easily, the cardinal rule is to *stay with the boat*. You should also wear a life vest, sail with a companion or tell someone about your plans, and wear a wetsuit or warm clothing if the water is cold.

SAILING DINGHIES

To get back aboard a dinghy after a capsize:

1. Free the mainsheet.
2. Rotate the bow into the wind.
3. Put all your weight on the daggerboard or centerboard.
4. Climb in as the boat comes upright.

MORE MUST-KNOW KNOTS

The *clove hitch* is a great knot for securing fenders to lifelines or stanchions or for fastening a rope around a post, because it is held in place by friction. It is even more effective when you add a *half hitch* or two for safety. To practice this knot, find a horizontal bar, like the rung of a chair. Hold one end of the line in your left hand as if it were the line already tied to the boat. With your right hand (1) take the line over the horizontal bar and back across the fixed end (in the left hand). Then (2) go over the bar to the left of the first loop and (3) bring the end up under the left loop and pull tight.

Two half hitches

Clove hitch

How to tie a clove hitch

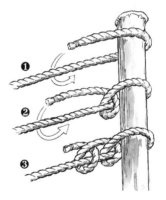

How to tie two half hitches

You use two half hitches when securing a line to a post because it is easy to tie, adjust, and untie. To practice, place the bar in a vertical position and hold one end as before, as if the line were tied to something on the boat. (1) Loop the free end around the stick and (2) go under the line and back through as if you were going to make a knot. (3) Then go around the line again in the same way. The two half hitches will hold tight against each other.

TEST YOURSELF

Balance and Stability
1. Identify which dots represent CLR and CE.
2. What is weather helm?
3. What is lee helm?
4. Does this boat have weather or lee helm?

Center of Gravity, Center of Buoyancy
To test your understanding of the relationship between center of gravity and center of buoyancy, answer the questions below.

1. When a keelboat is at rest (upright), where is the center of gravity (CG) in relation to the center of buoyancy (CB)?
2. What happens to CG and CB when a keelboat heels slightly?
3. What happens to CG and CB when a keelboat is knocked flat?

6 HANDLING HEAVY WEATHER AND RESCUING CREW

Many sailors describe their sailing experiences as 90 percent pure bliss—and 10 percent confrontation with the water devil. A nice day on the water can include a stop at a beautiful anchorage for lunch or a swim and end with a peaceful sunset. But you may also find yourself out on the water when an ominous storm approaches. This chapter will teach you how to reduce sail area in heavier conditions and handle emergencies like crew overboard.

SAILING IN HEAVY WEATHER

You won't always be able to control your sailing conditions. A beautiful morning could turn into a heavy squall in the afternoon, so knowing how to handle a sailboat in changing weather is important. And once you learn how to sail in heavier conditions, you will enjoy it—sailing in heavy weather is usually an adrenaline rush. If you know how to make your boat and everyone aboard comfortable, you will enjoy the exhilaration when the wind pipes up.

When you start taking lessons, what you might consider lousy weather ashore is a great learning experience for the new sailor. We know a cruising-boat owner who likes to race. Every spring he picks the windiest day he can find to go out and practice. This helps him gain complete confidence in his boat, his equipment, and his crew. He believes when everyone is comfortable in a lot of wind—both with the boat and with each other—sailing on a calmer day is a breeze.

Sailing in heavier conditions is a valuable experience. Until you've sailed in a great deal of wind or been caught in a passing squall, you haven't tested your ability to handle the boat in a heavy wind situation. But if the prospect of sailing in heavier conditions is worrisome to you, think about the worst that can happen and then learn how to handle your boat and your crew in that situation.

Your main concern might be losing someone overboard. After you study the techniques covered later in this chapter, you should practice recoveries by throwing a cushion or floatable object overboard. Do this until your reactions become second nature. Time how fast you retrieve the object after it hits the water, bringing the boat to a complete stop when you get alongside. Practice in all kinds of weather—in a flat calm, on a moderately windy day, in a squall.

Heavy weather also puts a lot of stress on your rigging. In very severe conditions, the mast can break. Though you can't practice loss of a mast, you can be prepared for that eventuality. If your mast breaks on a small boat, you should anchor as quickly as possible and sort out all the mess without drifting farther offshore. Once you've cleaned up the failed mast and rigging, a paddle will help you get back to shore if you don't have a motor. When you start cruising on larger boats, where everything is so much bigger, there is more to consider. You will learn more about sailing larger boats in heavy air in the cruising section of this book.

"I wanted confidence. My husband knows it all—and if something happens I want to know how to handle the boat. We sail weekends on Chesapeake Bay and plan to retire and go cruising within 18 months." **CINDY SMITH (50), ANNAPOLIS, MD**

When you are confident that there is nothing that can happen to you or your boat that you can't handle, then all the rest is just sound and fury. It is natural to be a bit apprehensive or frightened of big winds at first; but soon you will find that you actually enjoy the heavy stuff and look forward to that occasional confrontation with nature.

WHAT TO DO IN A SQUALL

When you get caught in a squall, first reduce the amount of sail area you are carrying. On a Colgate 26, you can do this by *reefing* the mainsail and furling the jib. Why should you reduce sail area? Remember, your sails are the boat's power and make the boat heel. Sail area at the top of the mast heels the boat more than sail area lower down. Reefing lowers the sail area (and the CE) and heeling is, therefore, reduced. In Figure 6-1, the boat in front has not reefed its mainsail yet; notice how the unreefed boat is sailing at a slightly greater angle of heel than the boat behind, which has reefed its mainsail. Though the wind is not overbearing, it is strong enough to give the boat behind a little more comfort and control.

As soon as you see a squall approaching, take action before it gets to you. In the end, the squall may not be that bad—sometimes a nasty looking sky turns out to be only dark clouds and rain, not more wind. If you decide not to reduce sail as the squall approaches, you should at least be prepared to do so at a moment's notice. When a bad squall hits, the wind can go from 10 knots to 40 or 50 knots in seconds.

Halyards should be neatly coiled and ready to run (see Chapter 10). Crew members should be briefed on their responsibilities; if the squall is a

HEAVY WEATHER PREPARATION

- Check weather forecasts before you go out (visit www.weather.com or www.nws.noaa.gov).
- Take warm clothing and foul-weather gear.
- Make sure you have a lot of line, an anchor, and distress signals aboard.
- Take a way to communicate with shore—a VHF radio (see Chapter 17) or a cell phone (if you are close to shore).
- Learn to read clouds while sailing.
- Be prepared to reduce sail area or change sails.
- Then, enjoy!

Figure 6-1. The difference between a reefed mainsail (right) and a full mainsail

bad one, everyone on board should know the procedure so not a second is lost to giving orders. This kind of preparation also has a secondary advantage: it can decrease the chance of panic. When the first blast of wind hits, the boat will probably heel over dramatically. That is when the brain process of even some experienced crew tends to go awry. Let everyone know what they are expected to do well in advance so they don't have to think.

On a small boat, the mainsail has greater sail area than the jib, so reef it before furling the jib. If you are still overpowered, furl the jib too. As the wind increases ease the mainsheet to reduce heeling. If you were sailing close-hauled before the squall hit, you will find you are steering more of a close reach in heavier winds because of the strength and weight of the wind and sea.

If you reefed your sails but you are still having difficulty maintaining control, lower all your sails and run before the wind *under bare poles* (without any sails up)—unless there is a chance of running aground. In this case, your best safety aid may be your anchor. If visibility is down to a few feet and you can't be sure of your position and are afraid you may be blown ashore, get your anchor over the side anyway. You may not have enough line to reach bottom in your current location, but you can be fairly sure that the anchor will hook before you get into water shallow enough for your boat to go aground.

Figure 6-2. Sailing with reefed main and no jib

JIFFY REEFING

A. To reef main, lower halyard enough to hook luff cringle

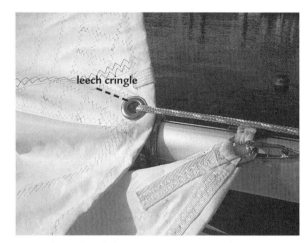

B. Tighten leech line to stretch foot of sail along boom

C. When settled down, tie a safety line

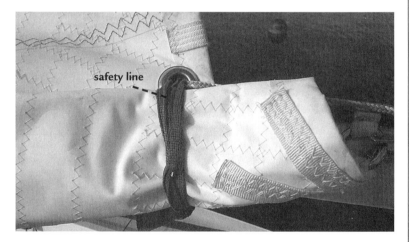

Many sailboats have jiffy reefing. Reef points and the control lines for reefing are all built into the mainsail and rigging, which makes reefing your main a quick and easy job. Below is the procedure for jiffy reefing your mainsail.

1. Ease the mainsheet and vang.
2. Lower the main halyard just enough to place the *luff cringle* on a hook at the *gooseneck*—where the boom is attached to the mast (A).
3. Winch the main halyard up tight before you do anything else (note tight luff along mast above cringle in photo above).
4. Ignore any flapping sail material for the time being.
5. Tighten the line that runs through the *leech cringle* until the foot of sail is stretched tight (B).
6. Trim the mainsheet and vang so you can start sailing comfortably.
7. When you're settled down and sailing comfortably, tie the safety line through the leech cringle and around the boom in case the reef line breaks (C).
8. Tie excess sail along the boom at the reef points as in Figure 6-2.
9. To shake out the reef, follow the above steps in reverse order closely. Make sure you untie the excess sail along foot first, to avoid ripping the sail where you originally tied it at the reef points along the boom.

DISTRESS SIGNALS

In all the years we have been sailing, we can't remember a single time when we had to use distress signals to seek help. Nevertheless, you should know how to use distress signals and be able to recognize the 16 official signals yourself. You should also have one or more of these aboard. Some, like flares, have a shelf life and need to be checked periodically for replacement. Of these 16 signals, only the 8 listed here are practical for small sailboats.

- Red star shells (flares)
- Fog horn
- Orange and black flag
- SOS sounds
- Mayday on radio
- Code flags N and C (November and Charlie)
- Wave arms up and down
- Smoke flare

CREW OVERBOARD!

When a person falls overboard, immediately throw them a flotation device. At the same time shout, "Crew overboard!" and designate one of your crew as the *spotter*. The spotter should keep a constant eye on the overboard crew and continually point at them.

The surest way to recover your crew in the water is to stop the boat immediately. This is called the *Quick Stop Recovery Method*. Tack the boat with the jib cleated, no matter what point of sail you are on. This will backwind the jib and slow the boat almost to a stop as in position 2 in Figure 6-3. The boat can then be maneuvered back to the person overboard to make the recovery. Without changing your sail trim, circle back to the person in the water. When you are able to turn into the wind on your last approach to come alongside that person (6), let your sails luff to come to a stop. If you are running downwind and someone falls overboard, do a quick tack and trim your sails to get back to the person in the water, as shown in Figure 6-3. If a spinnaker is set, someone should release its halyard as you tack, which causes it to fall on the foredeck and not in the water.

Every circumstance in recovering crew overboard has its own idiosyncrasies. You could be in heavy wind and steep seas, you might be in low visibility, it can happen when there's hardly any wind and the seas are flat calm. So it's very important to practice often in a variety of conditions and on different points of sail: while sailing close-hauled, on a reach, or a run.

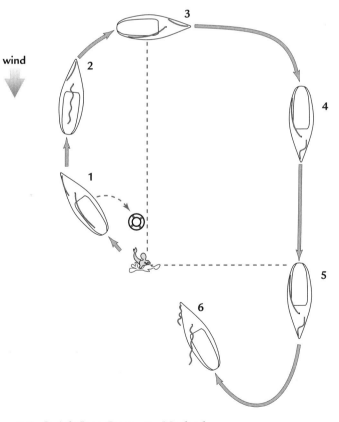

Figure 6-3. Quick Stop Recovery Method

The *LifeSling Method* is best used on larger boats when there are only two of you aboard and one falls overboard, leaving the other crew alone. It is also a good technique in bad conditions when it is hard to maneuver alongside the person. A LifeSling is a floating lifting sling attached to the boat by a long floating line. You can buy LifeSlings in most boat supply stores. Immediately throw the sling over (3) and circle the person until they can grab the circling line and get to the sling (7). Stop the boat with the quick stop procedure outlined above, pull the person to you, attach a tackle arrangement to a halyard and the sling, and hoist the person aboard.

On small, maneuverable boats the *Mooring Pickup Method* is as fast as the Quick Stop Recovery Method and gets the boat closer to the person during the entire maneuver. Regardless, toss a floating cushion just in case. When you are close-hauled or reaching, jibe around immediately and shoot into the wind alongside the person. On a run, don't jibe! Harden up, tack, and shoot into the wind. The only difference between this and picking up a mooring is the time span. You need to do it fast!

A variation on this method is called the *Quick Turn Recovery Method*, which may be easier to use in heavy weather since it does not include a jibe. As soon as someone goes overboard, sail on a beam reach a maximum of four boat lengths, tack rather than jibe, and sail on a broad reach until you are to leeward of the person. Then turn into the wind as if picking up a

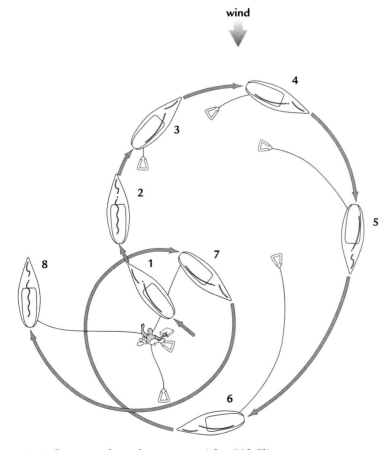

Figure 6-4. Crew overboard recovery with a LifeSling

mooring. Stop alongside by luffing or backing the sails. Heave a line to the crew, attach him to the boat, then get him or her aboard.

These four methods of picking up a crew member who has gone overboard are all different but achieve the same goal. Which one you use depends on the wind and wave conditions, type and size of your boat, number of crew you have aboard to help you, and your lifesaving equipment. Some things common to all four procedures are: shout "crew overboard" immediately; designate a spotter; toss a lifesaving flotation device overboard; stay close; stop the boat alongside the person in the water.

TEST YOURSELF

Handling Heavy Weather and Crew Overboard Techniques
To test your knowledge of heavy weather and how to rescue someone who goes overboard, answer the questions below.

1. How should you prepare for heavy weather?
2. What should you check before you set out?
3. If a squall hits and your boat is overpowered, what should you do?
4. Name three things you do immediately if someone goes overboard.
5. Describe the Quick Stop Recovery Method.
6. What is a LifeSling?
7. When should you use the the LifeSling method?

7 MOORING, DOCKING, AND ANCHORING UNDER SAIL

When your day of sailing is over, you may be dropping the anchor or picking up a mooring in a peaceful anchorage or you may end up comfortably tied to a dock in a quiet marina. This chapter will give you the knowledge to pick up a mooring, and anchor or dock under sail, without the assist of an engine. In Chapters 12 and 13 you will learn how to use an engine in these maneuvers; but the true test of a good sailor is the ability to get around without the use of an "iron genny" (sailor-talk for motor) under any circumstances.

MOORING PICKUP WITHOUT A MOTOR

Unfortunately, a sailboat without an engine doesn't have the brakes of a car or the reverse gear of a propeller to help it stop. The only way a sailboat, using only the sails, can stop is by heading into the wind. Sure, you can luff your sails and this will slow you down; but you won't come to a complete stop unless you head directly into the wind. Even if you point the boat (called *shooting* the boat) directly into the no-go zone, your boat will gradually slow down—not come to an immediate stop.

In order to stop with your bow at a mooring buoy, you must judge how far the boat will shoot. Pick an imaginary spot as your *shooting point*—the spot where you will turn toward the buoy—that is downwind of where you want to stop. The distance between this point and your stopping point will vary greatly with different wind and wave conditions, and with different hull types.

The stronger the wind, the shorter the distance you can shoot. The boat stops faster because of great resistance made by the flapping sails and rigging facing the wind, and because waves are usually higher in heavy winds. As you turn your bow into heavy wind, it tends to slam into the waves created

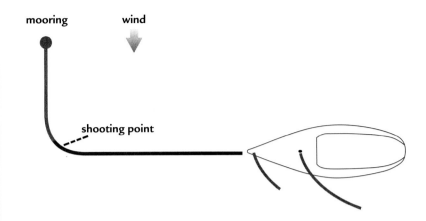

Figure 7-1. Approaching a mooring on a reach

APPROACH A MOORING ON A REACH

- It is easy to reduce or accelerate speed
- It is easy to fall off or head up
- No tack or jibe is necessary
- In heavy winds and choppy seas, the boat stops quickly and makes the shooting point closer
- In a light breeze and flat seas the boat shoots farther and is slower to stop, making the shooting point farther downwind

TO SAIL BACKWARD

- Back the main
- Push the tiller toward the main
- At 45° to the true wind, trim the main, center the rudder (bring the tiller to midship), trim the jib and the boat will go forward

by the wind. In lighter air it will take longer for the boat to stop, even though it is going slower. Make sure you allow for more room in these conditions.

The approach to the shooting point that allows the most flexibility is a reach. If you approach your turning point on a close-hauled course and experience a wind shift, you may have to tack to get there. If you approach on a run, you will find it difficult to judge the turning point accurately or reduce speed easily. Also, with the mainsail set so far out for the run, you cannot slow down by easing the mainsail farther as you spin into the wind. On a reach, however, you have both speed control and directional control. You can luff or trim the sails for less or more speed, and you can head up or fall off to adjust your approach to the shooting point.

As you round up into the wind, free the sheets and let the sails luff completely. If you don't release the jib, it might back (wind will be on the leeward side), forcing the bow away from the wind and the buoy. As you travel from the shooting point to the buoy, you may want to stay at a position pointing 10° to 20° toward the desired tack with your sails luffing. That way, if you miss the buoy, you can just trim in the sails and fall off slightly to get moving again. Though you probably won't come to a complete stop, there is no chance of falling off accidentally onto the wrong tack toward other moored boats with this method.

If you find you misjudged the turning point and are approaching too fast, back the main—push the mainsail out against the wind—to slow the boat quickly. Keep your bow headed into the wind and push the boom out at right angles to the boat. If you continue to hold the boom out after the boat has stopped, the boat will start sailing backward.

Practice stopping the boat by backing the main as often as you can. To sail well is to have complete control at all times. It's important to learn how to sail the boat backward because quite often, when you leave a mooring, the boat starts drifting backward naturally. Your sails are luffing (the boat is in irons) and moving the tiller doesn't have any effect. To get underway and gain control, back the main by pushing it out against the wind and turn the rudder to fall off on the desired tack. When you are about 45° from the true wind direction, you can trim your sails and go forward.

HOW TO ANCHOR UNDER SAIL

Proper anchoring technique is a skill you will use in both fair and foul weather. When heavy weather hits, anchoring in a protected harbor may be your best way of avoiding the worst of the storm. When the weather is fair, a night in a serene anchorage may be part of your planned itinerary. Anchors and techniques are discussed at length in Chapter 13. This section covers the proper technique for anchoring under sail.

When you are ready to anchor, several decisions come into play. Look for sheltered, calm water where there isn't much wind or current. Never anchor in a channel. Check the chart to make sure there will be enough water under your keel at low tide. Then choose a spot with enough room to swing without hitting other anchored boats, obstructions such as submerged rocks and shallow areas, or swinging too close to shore.

Your anchor is either kept in an anchor locker on the bow or stored in a lazarette in the cockpit. Bring it out on the foredeck, coil the anchor line so it will run free, and secure the *bitter end*—the end of the anchor line not attached to the anchor—to a cleat on the boat. You may think this is a silly, unneeded directive, but many anchors are lost because someone forgot to tie it to the boat.

Since you will be sailing right up to the point where you want to anchor, your halyards should be ready to drop and crew members should know they will need to ease the main and the jib as soon as you head into the wind. It is actually preferable to roll up the jib completely or (if you don't have roller furling) lower and clear it off the foredeck so you have a clear area to work with the anchor.

Look around and decide where you want the bow of the boat to be when you are finally anchored. Check the depth of the water in the vicinity of that spot to determine how much *anchor rode*—the line attached to the anchor—you should use. You may eventually let out enough rode to equal seven times that depth of water. The ratio of anchor line length used to the depth of water where you are anchoring is called *scope*.

Head into the wind when you reach the spot where you want to anchor and allow the boat to coast to a complete stop before the anchor is lowered. It is always good practice to lower the anchor over the side, as

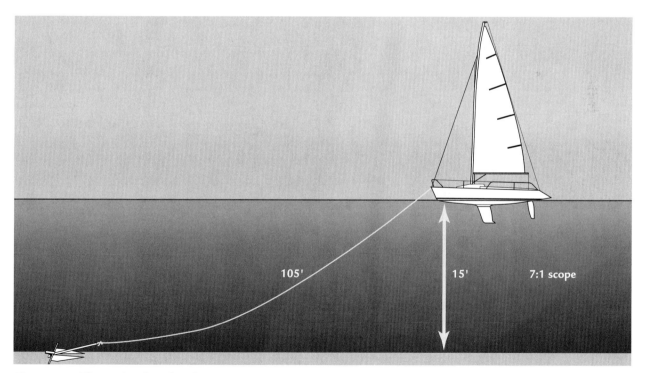

105'   15'   7:1 scope

Figure 7-2. The ratio of anchor line to depth is called *scope*.

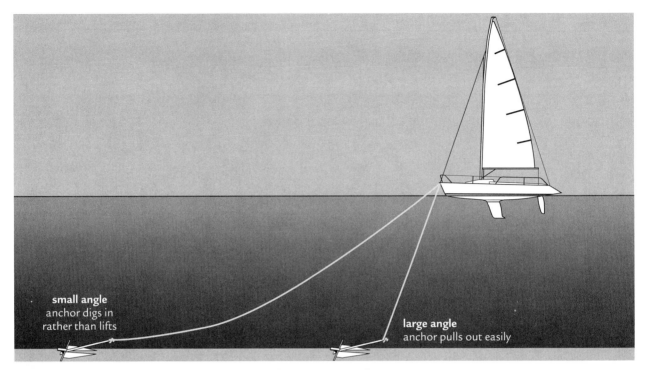

small angle
anchor digs in
rather than lifts

large angle
anchor pulls out easily

Figure 7-3. A smaller rode angle holds better than a larger angle.

HOW TO ANCHOR

- Make sure end of anchor rode is tied to a cleat on boat
- Head into the wind to stop the boat and allow the sails to luff
- Roll up or lower the jib
- When you are stopped, lower the anchor over the bow and let the boat drift backward
- Cleat the rode after sufficient scope is let out
- Check for dragging
- Lower or roll up your sails
- If you are too close to an anchored boat, raise your sails and move

opposed to throwing it overboard. Anchors have flukes that allow them to dig into the ground below; if the anchor line is tangled around these flukes, the anchor may not hold. Make sure the flukes are clear and the line can run freely.

When you head into the wind, release the mainsheet and the jibsheets. As the boat starts to drift backward, feed out your rode until you have let out five times as much line as the depth of the water. When you do this, your *scope* will be 5:1. For example, if the water is 20 feet deep, you should let out about 100 feet of line at first. In many cases, a scope of 5:1 is adequate for small boats when the bottom is good for holding, there isn't much wind, or you are anchoring for a short time. For peace of mind, increase your scope to 7:1 in a lot of wind and anytime you want to ensure you won't start *dragging*, or drifting backward.

As you let out more rode, the angle the rode makes with the bottom gets smaller; this in turn gives your anchor greater holding power. A smaller angle allows the line to pull the anchor against the bottom, which causes the flukes to dig in. With a larger angle, the rode will lift the anchor up, which can release the flukes.

Anchor lines and docklines are usually made of nylon because this type of line stretches and absorbs shock. A boat at anchor is constantly moving as current and wind direction change, however small those movements are. A speed boat rushing by can cause a wake; this is bad etiquette, but it also makes your boat bounce up and down. As the wake causes your bow to rise and fall, the anchor line needs to be able to stretch and go slack without breaking or dislodging the anchor.

When you feel you have eased out sufficient scope, snub the anchor line around a cleat. The momentum of the boat will jerk the anchor *home* (make it dig in), just as a fisherman sets the hook when a fish is caught. To check that your boat is secure and not dragging, place your hand on the anchor line forward of the bow. If you feel vibration, this usually means the anchor is dragging along the bottom.

Unless there is a lot of current or no wind at all, your boat will line up into the wind when the anchor is set. If you haven't done this already, roll up or lower your jib, then lower your main as soon as possible to avoid wear and tear on the sails.

Small sailboats, because they are so light and often have short keels or just centerboards, tend to move around more than cruising boats when anchored. From time to time, glance at points on shore and the other boats around you to see if the angle and distance have dramatically changed, bearing in mind that you may just be swinging. If you find you are uncomfortably close to another boat that was there before you, heed this rule: the boat that anchors last, moves first!

When you are ready to leave, reverse the process. Raise your main, but don't trim it in. Ask a crew member on the bow to *overhaul* the anchor line—pull it onto the boat. As he or she does this, the boat moves towards the anchor; when your bow is directly above the anchor, it usually comes up quite easily. If it seems to be stuck, take the anchor line back to a jib winch and crank it up. You may find a lot of mud or grass on the anchor as it emerges from the water. Before you bring it aboard, bounce it up and down in the water to dislodge the gunk, to avoid bringing mud aboard. When you are free and the anchor is aboard and stowed, unroll your jib, trim your main, and get underway.

If your boat has a motor, you can power toward the anchor as a crew member brings the line aboard. If you encounter resistance while you are under power, you can use the motor to move around and pull the rode from different directions until it releases. When you start sailing on cruising boats, you will learn about electric winches called *windlasses*, which help you bring up anchors on larger boats. Regardless of the size of your boat, the winches you use to help raise and trim your sails work pretty well on a stubborn anchor.

HOW TO DOCK UNDER SAIL

Docking under sail takes practice, but the techniques are easy to learn. If you take time to prepare before approaching the dock and think through each step, you will be the envy of all those type A people watching from ashore! We do a lot of women-only programs, some of which are held at pop-

"Successful docking maneuvers are the result of a combination of lots of practice, the right feeling for the size of the boat, the right timing, and an understanding of wind conditions and their effect on the docking procedure. One has to feel *how the boat is affected by the wind and* feel *how the actions taken against this take effect. Then the theory comes a lot easier."*
CLAUDIA LOGOTHETIS (35), DREIEICH, GERMANY

Figure 7-4A. On initial approach to dock under sail

Figure 7-4B. Turned into the wind with the mainsheet eased

Figure 7-4C. Turning alongside. Back mainsail if necessary to kill speed

Figure 7-4D. Drifting along dock

Figure 7-4E. Holding shroud and about to tie up

ular boat shows. It always amazes the onlookers when five or six Colgate 26s slide into their slips or alongside a dock without a voice raised or a snag in the procedures.

In Figure 7-4, Offshore instructor Beite Cook is approaching the dock single-handed (alone). To kill speed, Beite has rolled up his jib and his mainsail is luffing (A). He has brought the boat into the wind (B). He has released the mainsheet and he's using just the boat's momentum to slip in alongside the dock (C). If he were coming in too fast he would back the mainsail against the wind to reduce speed. The boat is drifting along the dock, close enough for him to step off while holding onto the shrouds (D). Beite is ready to secure the boat to the docklines he left in place when he departed (E). He also left fenders along the dock so he didn't have to rig any on the

Figure 7-5. Tie fenders to the boat before docking.

boat; however, you should always consider placing fenders alongside the boat's hull just in case.

Well in advance of your approach, get your fenders and docklines out. Attach the docklines to cleats in the bow and stern on the same side—starboard or port—when you know which side will be alongside the dock. Tie fenders to that side of the boat using a clove hitch and two half hitches, as described at the end of Chapter 5.

Gauge your approach and roll up your jib first, then sail into the marina under mainsail alone. When you feel you can drift alongside or into the dock bow-first with boat momentum only, lower your mainsail and steer without any sails. If you misjudged and can't quite make it, scull with your tiller—move it back and forth rapidly—to gain forward momentum.

In very light air you can sail into the dock with your main up as Beite did. The main can act as a brake and you can push the boom out against the wind to slow down if necessary. In heavy air, the boat will have a lot of forward momentum after the sails come down. Timing is everything. But with practice you will get to know how fast and far your boat will move as you approach with full sail, with just your main, and with no sails up at all.

Consider the safety of your crew and boat when you plan to dock. Warn your crew against using their feet or hands to fend off another boat or the dock. Don't ask a crew member to jump off the boat onto the dock until you are close enough for someone to step easily ashore. Quite often, someone is waiting on the dock to take your line, help bring the boat in close, and tie your dockline around a cleat or post for you. When you are ready to go ashore, pass your belongings to someone on the dock if you can—rather than carry them and run the risk of dropping a wallet, a phone, or your sunglasses overboard. Always check the way your boat is tied up to make sure the knots can be easily untied (but won't come undone on their own).

Wind Direction and Your Approach

Under sail, docking isn't much different from picking up a mooring or someone in the water. The boat has to be headed into the wind to stop. Although it may be blowing hard outside the marina, a relative calm usually exists when you get inside the breakwater and near the docks. The wind inside may still be strong, however. But over time you will get used to how your boat drifts in different wind strengths, so this will be less of a factor when docking under sail. Figure 7-6 shows how to approach in various wind directions: with the wind parallel to the dock (A); blowing from the dock to the water (B); and perpendicular to the dock (C).

If the wind direction is *parallel* to the dock (A), just shoot the boat into the wind and come to a stop parallel to and alongside the dock.

If the wind is blowing away from the dock and toward the water (B), shooting into the wind takes you straight into the dock, so approaching at an angle is better than head-on. If you are going too fast, remember that you can back your main to slow down. In scenario B, avoid coming in perfectly parallel to the dock. As you luff your sails to slow down, the wind will push the boat away from the dock. If the dock is long, you might be able to salvage your landing by throwing a line to someone ashore or asking a crew member to step carefully to the dock with a line before the boat slows down too much.

If the wind is blowing perpendicular to the dock and toward it from the water (C), docking is more difficult. If the wind is heavy, the best approach is without

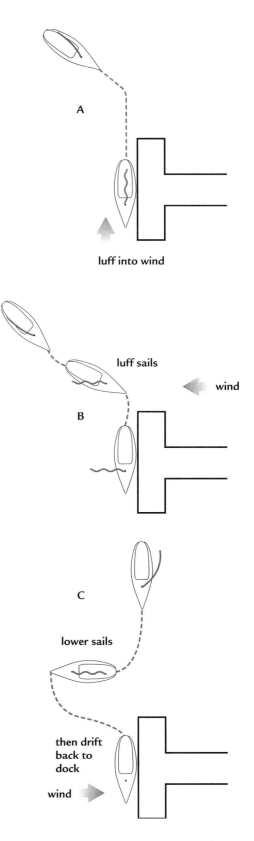

Figure 7-6. Docking a sailboat under sail alone

any sail up. If the wind is light, you might approach with only the jib up. Round up (point your bow) into the wind to windward of the dock and lower any sails that are still up. Then drift in. If you are on a boat like the Colgate 26, you should have enough momentum to keep sailing for a short while after the sails are lowered.

Tying and Tidying Up

When tying your boat to the dock, the bow and stern lines are only half the story. If you leave the boat with just those two lines attached, any movement could cause the boat to hit the dock. If the boat moves forward, the stern swings into the dock. If it moves aft, the bow hits the dock.

To solve this problem, *spring lines* are used. The *after spring line* runs from the bow of the boat aft to a cleat or piling on the dock and keeps the boat from moving forward. The *forward spring line* runs forward to the dock from the stern and keeps the boat from moving aft. All four lines—the bow, stern, and two spring lines—keep the boat parallel to the dock.

When approaching the dock, you tied fenders along the side of your boat that would rest next to the dock. You may have had one crew member with a free fender, ready to place it between the boat and dock if it looked like the two might hit. Now check those tied fenders to make sure they will stay in place where the hull touches the dock. Ideally, the place where the dock touches the fender should be just about at the fender's middle.

Most sailboat hulls are curved. If fenders are tied too high they can pop out of the space between the boat and dock. If placed too low, where the boat curves in toward the water, they can be ineffective. Depending on the length of the fender's line, you can tie it to the lifeline or base of a stanchion. Check all your knots. It's not uncommon to see a fender floating free in a marina because a knot came undone.

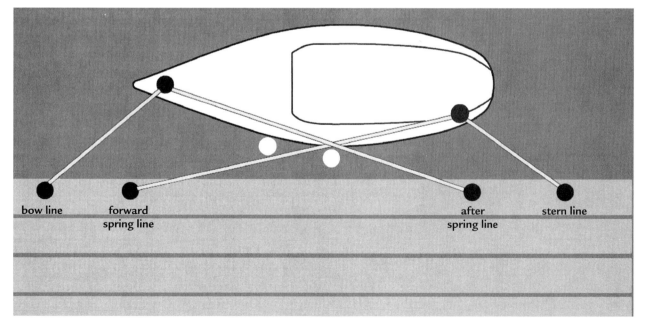

bow line   forward spring line   after spring line   stern line

Figure 7-7. Dock lines

right way to cleat   **wrong way to cleat**

Figure 7-8. The right and wrong way to cleat a dockline

If you are tied to a floating dock, you don't have to worry about tidal changes. But if the dock is fixed and you arrived at high or mid-tide, make sure you leave enough slack in the lines to keep the cleats on the boat from pulling out or enough slack to keep the docklines from breaking when the tide goes out. It doesn't matter if this means the boat is sitting several feet away from the dock. You can always pull the lines in to get aboard.

Adjust your lines from the boat, not from the dock; this way, any excess line stays aboard. If someone helped catch your docklines and cleated them for you, check how those lines are tied. Sailors are a helpful group, but not all sailors know how to properly tie a bowline, a cleat hitch, or other knots used for docking.

IF YOU GO AGROUND

It's not hard for a small sailboat like a Colgate 26 to go aground when sailing in channels that constantly need dredging. Tack a little too close to the edge of the channel, and you may bump. If you keep sailing in that direction, you can truly go *hard aground* (get stuck on the bottom). So what do you do if this happens? First, think! You want to get into deeper water as quickly as possible, which is usually the direction you just came from. The stronger the wind, the more urgent it becomes to get into deep water. Greater seas (waves) come with more wind, causing your boat to pound on the shoals. If you are in a rocky area, this can result in damage to your hull if the pounding continues. Depending on the wind direction, you may also find your boat being pushed farther and farther onto the rocks.

Sometimes you can get off a sandy shelf simply by trimming the sails in tight and getting all the crew to sit or stand on the leeward side of the boat. This heels the boat and gets the keel out of the sand. Keep the boat heeled over as it starts to move forward and have someone steer toward deep water before you let the boat go upright again.

Figure 7-9. Heeling the boat with crew to get off a shoal

If heeling the boat doesn't work, you can try shoving the bottom with a paddle; but most likely, you'll have to *kedge off*. To do this, drop an anchor attached to the bow out in deeper water. (You might be able to throw the anchor out or get someone in a passing boat to help you. As a last resort, you or a crew member can swim the anchor out—but only if that swimmer is very strong and won't be fighting currents.) Once you've set the anchor and you pull the line, the boat should pivot around toward the deeper water and eventually set the boat free. Don't try to kedge off from your stern or you may damage your rudder. If nothing works, wait until the tide rises. Then you can simply drift off.

TEST YOURSELF

Mooring Pickup

To test your knowledge of how to pick up a mooring answer the questions below.

1. What is the shooting point?
2. Describe the best approach to the shooting point.
3. In a strong wind, is the shooting point closer to or farther from the mooring?
4. Does the boat stop faster in heavy or light winds?

Anchoring

The questions below will test your knowledge of anchoring techniques.

1. What factors affect where you can anchor?
2. How do you prepare your crew and boat to anchor?
3. When and how do you lower the anchor into the water?
4. How do you know if your boat is dragging?
5. What is scope and how much should you have?
6. If you go aground, how do you get off?

Docking Under Sail

Test your docking technique by answering the questions below.

1. How do you prepare for docking?
2. What do spring lines do?
3. Where should fenders be placed?
4. Which knot is best for securing fenders?
5. Why should you adjust lines from the boat?

8 RIGHT-OF-WAY RULES AND NAVIGATION

Out on the water, there are no stop and yield signs. You need to know the *Navigation Rules* (officially called the COLREGs—International Regulations for Preventing Collisions at Sea) to avoid collisions or uncertainty when in the vicinity of other boats—and that pertains to all kinds of boats, not just sailboats, in inland and international waters.

Navigating along coasts and waterways is very different from driving. There may be no road signs or lines in the water to delineate where you can sail. But there are buoys and channel markers, sounds, lights, and a *chart* (map) to guide you away from hazards.

This chapter will teach you how to sail confidently in the vicinity of other boats, and then give you an overview of the basics of navigation. There are many fine books that delve deeply into navigation—by line of sight, by the stars, and by GPS (Global Positioning System). In this chapter you will learn how to read a chart, find out where you are, avoid hazards, plot a course, and measure distance. In Chapter 16, your navigating skills will develop further as you learn to adjust for currents, drift, and a lot more to make you a savvy cruising sailor.

HOW TO DETERMINE IF YOU ARE ON A COLLISION COURSE

Before you go sailing for the first time, be aware that it is the responsibility of the person steering the boat to avoid a collision. You must be constantly on the lookout for potential trouble. If your boat is heeling and the sails block your view to leeward, peek under the boom occasionally. You might also delegate one crew member to help keep an eye out, but remember that the ultimate responsibility is yours. No excuses! Even if you know you have the right-of-way, the other boat may not be well versed on the rules, or they may not react quickly enough to avoid trouble.

If another boat is heading your way, there is one sure way of determining whether or not the two of you are on a collision course. Take a *bearing*—the angle from a point on your boat to another boat or object. Sight across your compass and note the bearing of the other boat. You can also line up the other boat with a vertical point on your boat, such as a stanchion or shroud. If, in a short time, you take the bearing again in the same way and it hasn't changed, you are on a collision course.

Another way to judge whether you are on a collision course is to watch land in the distance behind the other boat. If land is disappearing behind the bow of that boat, that boat is *making land* on your boat and will cross ahead. If land is appearing in front of its bow, as if it were going backward against the land behind it, you are making land on the other boat and will cross ahead of it. If the land remains stationary, watch out! You are on a collision course.

Relative speeds of the two boats make no difference at all. You could be sailing at 5 knots and be on a collision course with a ship traveling at 25 knots. Always be aware of your surroundings, use your eyes and your binoculars, and be ready to react when in the vicinity of other boats, rocks and shallow waters, landmarks, and buoys.

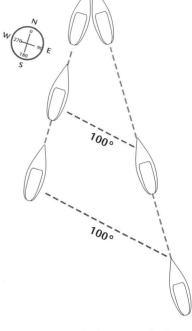

Figure 8-1. Take bearings to determine if you are on a collision course.

RULES OF THE ROAD

When Sailboat Meets Sailboat

There are only three basic possibilities, and three basic rules to follow, when your sailboat approaches another sailboat.

> Rule 1: When you are on the same tack as the other boat, the leeward boat has the right-of-way.
> Rule 2: When you are on opposite tacks, the starboard tack boat has the right-of-way.
> Rule 3: If you are overtaking the other boat, or it is overtaking you, the boat ahead (the overtaken boat) has the right-of-way.

In Figure 8-2, two boats are approaching each other and subject to the *same tack rule.* Sailors refer to the boat with right-of-way as the *stand-on vessel*—the boat that must *hold its course.* The leeward boat has right-of-way, and the windward boat has to keep clear, or *give way.* Which boat is the leeward boat? If you said the boat on the left, you were correct.

Figure 8-3 shows the *opposite tack rule.* The starboard tack boat is the stand-on vessel and has right-of-way. The port tack boat has to keep clear or give way. Which boat is on port tack? If you said the boat on the right, you are correct.

Figure 8-4 shows two boats involved in the *overtaking rule.* In this case the boat ahead is the stand-on vessel and has right-of-way. The overtaking boat has to keep clear or give way. Which boat is overtaking and what tack is that boat on? If you said the boat behind is overtaking and is on starboard

AVOID COLLISIONS

- Sight along the compass
- Line up the other boat with a stanchion or shroud
- Check if you're making land, staying the same, or losing land on the horizon
- If the angle or object on shore stays the same behind the other boat, you are on a collision course
- Difference in speed is not a factor

SAME TACK RULE

- Leeward boat is the stand-on vessel
- Leeward boat has the right-of-way
- Windward boat has to keep clear (give way)

OPPOSITE TACK RULE

- Starboard tack boat is the stand-on vessel
- Starboard tack boat has right-of-way
- Port tack boat has to keep clear (give way)

Figure 8-2. Same tack rule: boats are converging, leeward boat has right-of-way.

Figure 8-3. Opposite tack rule: boats converging, starboard tack boat has right-of-way.

Figure 8-4. Overtaking rule: boat behind is overtaking and has to give way.

tack, you are correct. Note that these boats are sailing downwind, with the wind pushing from behind, and they are on opposite tacks. In the *overtaking rule*, the difference in tacks is not relevant, unless you are racing. Over many years, a complete set of rules specifically for sailboat racing has been developed and administered by the International Sailing Federation (ISAF); but these are not relevant to recreational sailing.

When Two Boats Meet, Both Using Engines

New sailors often think a sailboat always has right-of-way over powerboats, even when the sailboat is running an engine or an outboard motor. This is not so. If a sailboat has an engine or outboard motor, it is classified as a powerboat

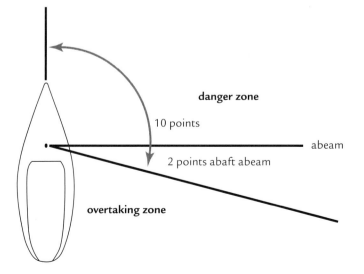

Figure 8-5. Powerboat rules: any boat in danger zone is the stand-on vessel.

WHO HAS THE RIGHT-OF-WAY?

- Stand-on vessel—has right-of-way, maintains course and speed
- Give-way vessel—does not have right-of-way, must alter course to avoid collision

when the engine is in use. Even if you have a daysailer with a tiny outboard motor, when the motor is running—whether your sails are up or not—you must abide by the *Navigation Rules* that apply specifically to motorboats.

Though there are many variables, the main thing to remember when boats under engine power are on a converging collision course is that the one in the other's *danger zone* has the right-of-way. The danger zone of a vessel under power is from dead ahead to two points (22.5°) abaft the starboard beam. Any boat approaching from that area is the *stand-on vessel* and has right-of-way. You are the *give-way vessel* and must keep clear.

The danger zone is described in points. That's why red and green side lights on boats are 10-point lights. A point is 11.25° and there are 32 points in a 360° circle, like a compass. Ten-point lights have a 112.5° arc, which enables you to see a red port side light at night when a boat is approaching your danger zone.

If you are the stand-on vessel you are obliged to hold your course and speed so you won't be misleading in your attempts to keep clear. What must be avoided at all costs is the kind of mix-up that occasionally happens to pedestrians going in opposite directions on a city street. You step to the left just as the person approaching steps to the right, so you both change direction and block each other again.

On a boat, this could bring about a serious collision. If your boat is the stand-on vessel you must maintain your course. But if, in the end, the other boat has not responded appropriately and it is obvious you will collide because of that, the rules (and common sense) say that you must do whatever is necessary to avoid a collision. If two boats are approaching each other from dead ahead, both should turn to starboard. If one is approaching the other from any point behind the danger zone, it is the overtaking boat and must keep clear of the boat ahead.

When Pure Sail Meets Power

The information above should be enough to keep you out of trouble when you are running your engine and meet another powerboat. But another set of rules applies when you are sailing and meet a powerboat.

You may assume a sailboat without an engine, or a sailboat not using its engine, always has right-of-way over a powerboat. Though this is usually true, there are a few exceptions: when the motorboat is anchored or disabled; and when the motorboat is being overtaken by the sailboat; when the motorboat is a commercial vessel over 65 feet long with limited maneuverability in a narrow channel. If you see a vessel with a round black shape hosited near the bow, it is anchored. One last point to remember: a rowboat or paddleboat has right of way over a sailboat!

NAVIGATION BASICS

How to Use a Compass

Your chief navigational aid—the compass—has certain idiosyncrasies you must understand to use it correctly. First, the compass does not point to the North Pole—*true north*—but to a magnetic mass called *magnetic north*. The difference

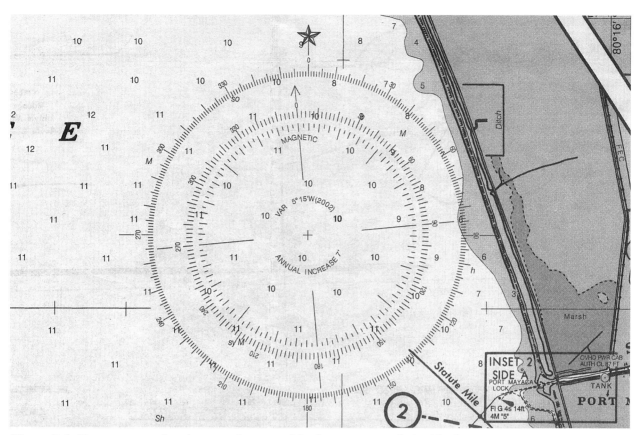

Figure 8-6. Compass rose showing two rings: outside shows true north, inside shows magnetic north.

between magnetic and true north is called *variation*. Variation changes with geographic location and is precalculated on the *compass roses* found on most charts.

The compass rose on a chart has two rings. North on the outer ring is true, while north on the inner ring is magnetic, which takes into account variation for the area you are sailing in. As long as you use the inner rose for plotting courses, you can forget about having to compute variation. Since your compass is magnetic, magnetic directions are all you care about, and these can be taken right off the chart.

However, compass readings can also be affected by metallic objects or electrical wiring on the boat. The resultant *deviation* usually requires that the compass be checked and adjusted when the boat or the compass is new. Although it's always there, deviation rarely amounts to more than one degree on a sailboat—and since you can't steer anywhere near that close, it is not often worth worrying about. Just be aware that deviation exists. You will learn more about variation and learn how to check your compass for deviation later, in the cruising section of this book (see Chapter 16).

Accuracy is a habit you should foster when navigating. You never know when you will be caught in a dense fog and need all the precision you can muster. You should be navigating all the time, even if you know where you are.

How to Calculate Distance

Vertical lines on a chart are called *meridians* or *lines of longitude*. On a globe, meridians converge at the North and South Poles, but they show as vertical, parallel lines when the features of a round globe are projected onto a two-dimensional coastal chart for navigation. This Mercator projection method causes some distortion, but it isn't significant except at very high latitudes.

Horizontal lines are called *parallels* or *degrees of latitude*. There are 60 minutes in a degree of latitude. Each minute of latitude (and longitude at the equator) equals 1 nautical mile.

To measure distance, use the latitude gradations along the sides of the chart. Each mile is divided into tenths for accuracy and ease in measuring distance. If

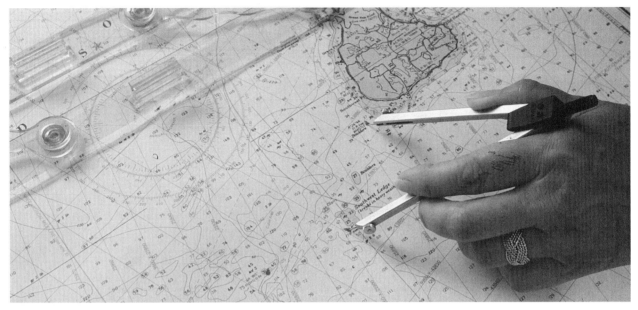

Figure 8-7. Finding distance using dividers

Figure 8-8. Measuring distance on the side of a chart

you want to know how far it is between two buoys, place one point of a set of dividers on one buoy and spread them so that the other point is on the other buoy. Then move them to the edge of the chart and read how many minutes fall within the points. If the distance is 7 minutes, that converts to 7 nautical miles.

If the distance you want to measure is greater than the spread of your dividers, choose a workable distance on the chart's edge and measure that distance in minutes of latitude. A good distance is 5 miles from tip to tip. Then point one tip on your starting point, with the other resting on a spot 5 miles down the course. Rotate the points of the dividers 180°—first one tip, then the other, as you *walk* the dividers toward your destination. Normally, the last measurement is something less than 5 miles, so you will have to bring the outer tip in until it rests on your destination. Then measure this last bit of distance on the edge of the chart and add it to the number of steps you had to make. Each 180° rotation is a *step*, in this case 5 miles.

On many charts, where only a rough estimation of distance is needed, you can use your hand. The spread between your thumb and little finger might be around 10 miles, allowing you to measure 70- to 80-mile distances quickly and within a few miles of accuracy.

Many boats have speedometers, called *knotmeters*, which tell you how fast your boat is going. A knot is 1 nautical mile in an hour. Boat speed is expressed in knots, not knots per hour.

How to Plot a Course

The line between your departure point and destination is called a *course line*. When you draw a course line on a chart, you want to know the magnetic direction of the line because it represents your boat moving on a compass course. The inner circle of the compass rose on the chart equates to your boat's compass, oriented to magnetic north. It would be great if you could simply move the compass rose right over your course line and read your course direction as if it were the boat's compass. But since the rose is printed on the chart, you can't do it that way. The next best thing is to move the course line to the compass rose.

To do this, use a *parallel ruler*. This nautical gadget allows you to move a line from one chart position to another while keeping that line exactly parallel to the original line so that its direction remains the same.

Lay the edge of your parallel ruler along the desired course. Press down on one leg and move the other out in the direction of the nearest compass rose. Then press that one down and move the first in parallel. Alternately press-spread, press-spread the parallel edges of the ruler until you center one

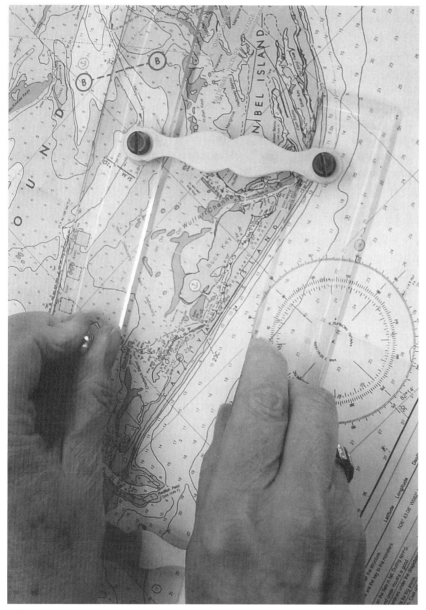

Figure 8-9. Using parallel rulers

MEASURING DISTANCE

Bear in mind:

- One minute of latitude is always one nautical mile
- One minute of longitude is a nautical mile at the equator but shrinks to nothing at the poles
- So when measuring distances from chart-edge gradations, use *only* the left or right edges, *never* the top or bottom edges

TIPS FOR USING PARALLEL RULERS

- Press firm against the chart: if rulers slip, they are no longer parallel to your course line
- Read the course off the inside (magnetic) rose, not the outer (true) rose
- Read the correct increment: smaller rose lines are at 2°; every degree is marked on larger roses
- Read the correct edge of the circle for a heading—i.e., not 270° (west) when you are actually traveling 90° (east)

Figure 8-10. Typical lighted buoy

edge directly over the cross in the center of the compass rose. Then read your course, in degrees, on the inner (magnetic) circle of the compass rose. Be sure to read the side of the compass rose pertinent to the direction you are sailing. For example, let's say you are traveling in an easterly direction somewhere between 45° and 135°. When you move your parallel ruler over the center of the compass rose, you will have two options. In this case, one side of the rose may read 104° and the other 284°. Obviously, you need to select the 104° course.

How to Read a Chart

Buoys are marked on a chart as small diamonds with a dot underneath to indicate their exact location. The color of the diamond, usually red or green, corresponds to the color of the buoy. The most common buoys are *nuns* and *cans*. Nuns are red, conical, and even numbered. Cans are green, cylindrical, and odd numbered. Next to the diamond on the chart is a notation. For example, that notation might be N "4" to indicate this buoy is a nun with the number 4 painted on it. Or it might read C "3" to indicate a can buoy marked with the number 3.

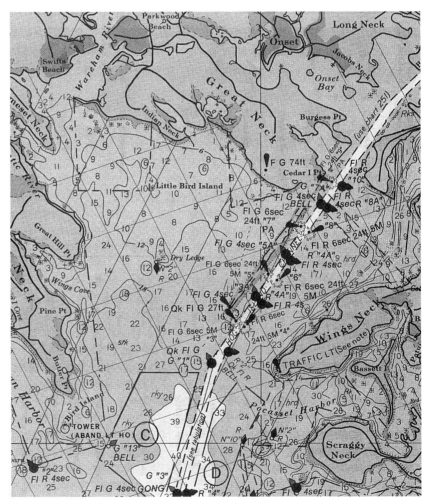

Figure 8-11. Detail of a chart

If the dot under the diamond is in the center of a small purplish circle, it means the buoy is lighted. The characteristics of the light are written alongside. "Fl R 3 sec" means a red light flashes every 3 seconds. "FG" marks a fixed green light that doesn't flash. A note on the chart like "60 FT 13 M" means that the light is 60 feet above the surface of the water and has a visibility of 13 miles. Study a chart and familiarize yourself with other abbreviations.

The colors on a chart are important. White areas are deep water, light blue is usually under 20 feet deep, and green is out of the water at low tide. Check how the depth is indicated. On most U.S. charts the depths are in feet at mean low water, but depths are sometimes measured in meters or fathoms. A meter is about 3 feet and a fathom is 6 feet. Also, note contour lines at certain constant depths, which give you an idea of how the bottom is laid out.

When trying to decide which side of the boat a red or green buoy should be on as you pass, remember the time-honored navigational aid for U.S. waters: *Red-Right-Returning*. This means that red buoys are kept to starboard when entering a harbor or when sailing from a larger body of water into a smaller one. If you are on the Intracoastal Waterway, the saying *Red Dirt, Green Sea* will help you remember which side to pass the markers. Red markers are on the mainland side of the channel—the dirt side—and the green markers are to seaward of the channel.

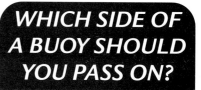

WHICH SIDE OF A BUOY SHOULD YOU PASS ON?

- ◆ Red-Right-Returning—keep red buoys on boat's starboard side when returning to port or sailing from larger body of water into smaller one
- ◆ Red Dirt, Green Sea—red markers on mainland side of channel (dirt), green markers to seaward side of channel when sailing on Intracoastal Waterway

Taking Bearings

Navigation on a sailboat is slightly complicated by the fact that you can't always steer the course you want. If your destination is dead upwind, you have to tack back and forth. On a powerboat you could plot all your courses the night before and run the preset courses with only current to worry about. But when sailing, you must keep track of your location as you sail along and continuously adjust your course to the desired destination.

One of the best ways to determine your position is to take bearings. To do this, pick two or three different lights or landmarks that you can identify visually, and make sure these are marked on your chart. Sight across your compass at each one in rapid succession and record the compass heading—your bearing—to each point in degrees. A portable hand bearing compass, which you can keep in your pocket, makes it easier to take bearings as you can hold it at eye level to take readings. The first bearing you should take is the one closest to your bow or stern, since its angle changes the least.

Figure 8-12. Using a hand bearing compass

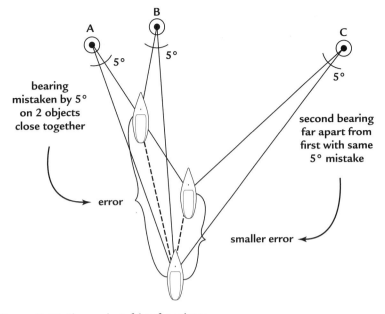

bearing mistaken by 5° on 2 objects close together

error

second bearing far apart from first with same 5° mistake

smaller error

Figure 8-13. Errors in taking bearings

Using your chart, locate the same compass bearing for each of the readings you just took on the nearest magnetic rose (inner circle). Place an outside edge of your parallel ruler on both this number on the rose and the cross in the very center of the rose. Walk the other outside edge of the ruler to the charted light or landmark you took the bearing on, then draw a line through that object and out into the water. You are located somewhere along this line. Now repeat the process using the second and third bearings you took. Three bearings will give you a small triangle—a *cocked hat*—when plotted, which is a bit more accurate than the cross you get from only two bearings. You are somewhere in the triangle. If the triangle is large, take your bearings again; one was probably inaccurate.

When you choose lights or landmarks, make sure there is a good distance between them. If you use only two bearings you will get greater accuracy if the two marks are 90° apart from your position. Figure 8-13 shows bearings taken with a 5° error in each. Note that using landmarks A and B produces a much larger aggregate error than using A and C, which are farther apart.

TEST YOURSELF

Right-of-Way Rules
Answer the questions below to test your understanding of right-of-way rules.

1. What is a bearing and when should you take it?
2. If two sailboats are on the same tack, which one is the give-way vessel and what should it do?
3. Explain the opposite tack rule.
4. Explain the overtaking rule.
5. When does a sailboat not have right-of-way over power?
6. Where is a powerboat's danger zone and when is it used?

Navigation
1. Explain variation and deviation.
2. What distance is represented by 2 minutes of latitude?
3. When using parallel rulers to plot a course, what four common mistakes should you avoid?
4. What does Red-Right-Returning mean?

9 *TRANSITION TO A CRUISING BOAT*

A lifetime of opportunities to see the world under sail tempts many a new sailor to learn more. Now that you have covered the basics, you are ready to learn about sailing a larger boat and pursuing the cruising lifestyle.

Sailors look at cruising in many ways. Is your goal to gain just enough knowledge to sail with friends who own cruising boats? Do you dream of chartering a yacht in the best cruising areas of the United States, Caribbean, and abroad? Perhaps you'll buy a boat you can comfortably live on with family or friends and cruise close to home on weekend escapes and week-long getaways. You may be preparing to cruise for extended periods of time—along the coast, down to the Bahamas and the Caribbean, then through the

"Fast Track to Cruising was a terrific beginning that opened a new world to us. We purchased our own boat in June 2002 in San Diego . . . Our future plans include sailing San Francisco Bay, then down the Pacific Coast to Cabo San Lucas and into the Sea of Cortez—all in the next three to five years. We would not have had these plans had we not taken the course . . . It has given us a dream— goals and plans for the future—that we never thought possible."

JOHN QUINN (51),

CARBONDALE, CO

Figure 9-1. The cruising lifestyle

Panama Canal and to the Pacific. Sounds exotic? It is! Think it's possible? Absolutely! The world is yours to see under sail. All you need is the skill and a little time.

CRUISING LINGO

All those new words you learned in the first part of this book are used on larger boats to describe the same parts and techniques. But because cruising boats have living quarters and other features not found on smaller boats, there are a few more terms to learn.

Cruising boats all have at least one cabin and creature comforts to make you feel at home. The general living quarters are called the *main saloon*, and in that area you sit on *settees* (bench-like couches with storage lockers underneath). On many cruising boats the stove in the adjacent *galley* (kitchen) is *gimballed* (mounted on a swinging mechanism) to allow level cooking when heeled underway. In port or on calm days, the stove can be locked in place. Most galleys now have refrigerators

with *holding plates* (also known as *cold plates*) that must be periodically recooled with refrigerant from a compressor; the compressor is powered by a belt of the main engine or off an AC- or DC-powered motor.

Nearby is the *nav station*, where the boat's electrical panels, a table for chart work, and electronic equipment are generally found. In individual cabins (and sometimes in the main saloon) are the *berths* you sleep on. Here you find drawers, *hanging lockers*, and *cubbies* for your clothes and sundries. When you need to use the facilities, you go to the *head* where the toilet, sink, and shower are located. Under the floor of the shower there is usually a sump pump to drain out water after it is used.

When leaving the cabin you are going *topside*, generally right into the *cockpit*. Often the cockpit is protected from the sun by an awning called a *bimini*, which is either permanently in place or on a frame that can be lowered. Sitting on the deck of a cruising boat gives you a much higher feeling off the water than sailing a small

Figure 9-2. Main saloon on a cruising boat

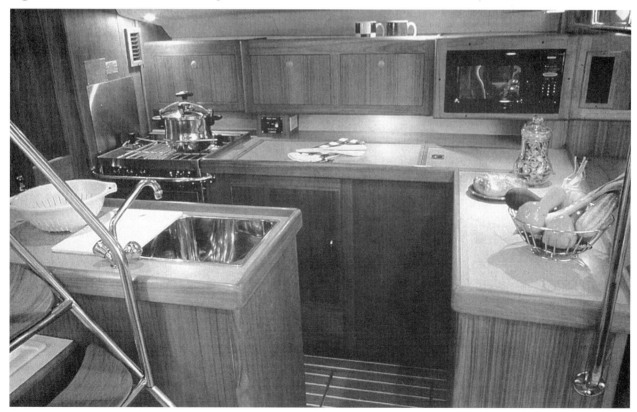

Figure 9-3. Galley on a cruising boat

Figure 9-4. Nav station

boat, because of the cabin space below. That distance from the top of the deck to the water results from higher *freeboard*.

To get to the cabin you go *below* (or *belowdecks*) through the *companionway* opening, down the companionway stairs, and onto the cabin *sole*—the floor of the cabin. The *floorboards* of the cabin sole can be raised in sections or have small openings in them through which to check the *bilge*, where water and other liquids like oil can collect. The *overhead* (ceiling) of the cabin might have a *headliner* (these are removable panels, sometimes made of fabric) that covers the electrical wires running through the boat.

Portholes (windows) in the sides of the cabin allow light in and can be opened for more air. If these windows cannot be opened, they are *portlights*. Hatches—hinged doors on the roof of the cabin—are opened

when in port or on light-air days to allow air to flow through the cabin. Portholes and hatches are fastened tight by *dogs* that look like wing nuts. Two other sources that allow you to bring air into the cabin are *dorades*—L-shaped funnels mounted on the deck—and a fabric *wind scoop*, which you can attach to a halyard and tie down over the companionway opening or a hatch to direct air belowdecks.

A couple of other terms you should know relate to safety and how the boat is built. *Chainplates* found on the sides of the hull are where shrouds are fastened. This area can be a source of leaks on older boats, and savvy sailors always check the chainplate areas before stowing dry foods on a cruise or making an offer on a potential purchase.

Many cruising boats have masts stepped right on deck, sitting in a mast step. On larger boats, however, you may find that the mast goes through the deck down to a mast step under the floorboards. The boom on any boat, regardless of size, is attached to the mast by a *gooseneck*. This fitting should be checked often for signs of fatigue or cracks, as it takes a lot of abuse, particularly when a flying jibe occurs.

If you cruise where the water and weather can be rough, you should rig *jacklines* the length of your deck when headed offshore. These are usually made of sturdy stranded wire and are shackled to padeyes near the bow and stern of the boat. When on deck in heavy weather, always wear a *harness* with a strong tether that hooks into the jacklines by a *snap shackle*.

In case someone should ever go overboard, you should mount on your boat's stern a *horseshoe life preserver* to toss to the swimmer as a flotation aid until you can get him or her back aboard. Alternatively, carry a *LifeSling*, which is packed in a bag for rapid emergency deployment; this piece of gear includes a long tether that helps you haul the swimmer back aboard (see Chapter 6). You also should carry an *EPIRB*—emergency position-indicating radio beacon—which will broadcast a distress signal rescuers can home in on if you ever get in serious trouble, and an inflatable *life raft* that can carry the full complement of your crew.

Figure 9-5. Wearing a harness in heavy weather

Figure 9-6. LifeSling shown coming out of the bag with tether attached

Figure 9-7. Horseshoe life preserver is mounted on stern rail

"I was apprehensive about learning the boat's mechanical systems, since I knew nothing about engines or water systems or batteries—and the 38-foot boat felt like the Queen Mary. *I found I really enjoyed learning about mechanics and I got over the boat-size thing."* BECKI QUINN (55), CARBONDALE, CO

LEARNING THE SYSTEMS ABOARD

The procedures for operating the devices that make your cruising boat a home—including your engine, electrical, water, and battery systems—may differ from boat to boat; but the theory is the same. In a cruising course or during a charter check-out you will be thoroughly briefed on how to operate everything safely and for optimal performance. New boats usually come with operating manuals that provide step-by-step maintenance procedures.

Diesel Engine

Most cruising boats are powered by diesel engines. Diesel engines require three components to run: fuel, air, and compression. If you have trouble starting an engine, 90 percent of the time it is because of fuel.

Fuel flows from the fuel tank to a primary filter with a water separator. Since water is heavier than diesel fuel, it sinks to the bottom of a cup and the

Figure 9-8. Diesel engine

water can be drained out. This filter also takes out impurities. Next, the fuel goes through a fuel lift pump, which operates mechanically but can be operated manually to push fuel through the system. Then it passes through a secondary filter, and on to the injector pump. This pump delivers diesel fuel at high pressure to the injectors, which spray atomized fuel into the cylinders where it mixes with air, is compressed, and ignites. The tolerances are very tight for the injector pump, so don't fool with it unless you are a qualified mechanic.

One of our instructors uses the memory jogger *SSBB* to help you understand how a diesel engine works. Though a bit graphic, this stands for Suck-Squeeze-Bang-Blow. This describes the four piston strokes shown in Figure 9-9: the inlet stroke *sucks* air into the cylinder (1); as the compression stroke *squeezes* and the air within becomes superheated, the injector sprays diesel fuel into the combustion chamber where it immediately ignites (2); the resultant explosion—the *bang*—forces the piston down for the operating stroke (3); and the exhaust stroke *blows* the spent gasses out of the system (4).

When you are troubleshooting a failure to start, there are several points to check. If you clean the fuel filters and bleed the air bubbles out of the fuel system but the engine still won't start, lack of air could be the problem. You may have to clean the air filter so air is able to mix with the fuel.

The last problem could be lack of compression, but there isn't much you can do about that without a total engine rebuild. This usually comes from the engine being run without oil or from overheating.

Before you go out sailing, there are a couple of engine checks that need to be done. First, check the oil level and color. The oil dipstick, like a car's dipstick, has marks that tell you whether you need to add a quart or two, which is not uncommon with diesel engines. For convenience, you want to have a couple spare cans aboard at all times. The oil should be jet black. If it looks like chocolate milk, most likely there is water in the oil, which will affect the efficiency of your engine. You should consider draining and replacing the old oil as soon as possible.

Next check the freshwater cooling level. Eyeball the level when you remove the cap and add water if needed. Be very careful not to put water in the oil receptacle or oil in the water reservoir. This may sound silly, but it is a common mistake made on cruising boats.

When you turn the key, a loud engine alarm should sound. This tells you oil pressure is low. The noise will stop when the oil pressure rises to the operative range. In cooler climates you may have to hold in a *preheat* button before you press the starter button.

After starting the engine and before putting it into gear, there are a few more checks to make. Always let the engine warm up in neutral for a few minutes and check to make sure water is coming out of the exhaust. Your boat will have gauges—usually in the cockpit near the starter switch—which read the oil pressure and water temperature. The engine manual will tell you what these levels should be. Oil pressure is usually 55 to 65 pounds and water temperature 120° F to 150° F. The ammeter should read on the plus (+) side, telling you the batteries are being charged.

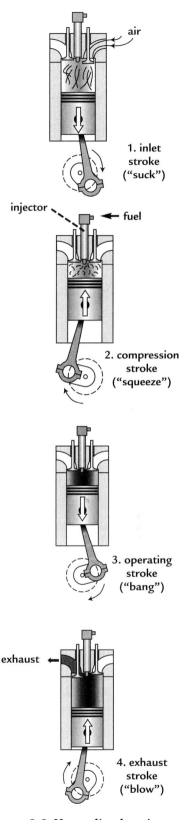

Figure 9-9. How a diesel engine works

IF ENGINE WON'T START

- Check that the battery switch is on
- Check fuel level
- Clean fuel filters
- Bleed air out of system
- Clean air filter
- If no compression, call the mechanic

The freshwater system in a diesel engine is cooled by seawater sucked through an intake, circulated through coils, and sent back out. If you don't see water spitting out of the exhaust, you should do some more checks before using the engine. The raw-water pump impeller may be burned out, or the intake through-hull valve (called a *seacock*) that passes seawater to the pump could be closed or plugged with seaweed. The pump impeller is made of rubber so the pump can't be damaged if sand is sucked in. Because of this, it needs to be replaced from time to time. A raw-water strainer between the seacock and the pump keeps seaweed and other matter from getting into the engine, and periodically it needs to be unclogged. If the cap on the strainer is not seated tightly, air can get into the line, which causes overheating.

When you no longer need your engine and want to shut it down, pull out the engine *kill switch* until the engine stops. The low pressure alarm will go on and stay on until you turn the key off.

In some parts of the world where you might charter a boat, the person who checks you out may not be proficient in English. Question anything that doesn't seem right. On a cruise in Croatia many years ago, we were told that we could turn the engine key to "off" while the engine was still running. We questioned this statement but listened to the guy checking us out, not our intuition—at least at first. By turning off the key, we soon found we lost all our gauges and alarms and decided to leave the key on. Later in the trip we lost oil pressure and had to get one of the boats in our flotilla to tow us in for repairs. Had we followed the check-out guy's advice, we wouldn't have known about the oil pressure loss until it was too late, causing severe engine damage and a spoiled cruise.

All of this may seem complicated and confusing at first, but don't dwell on it. Diesel engines are highly reliable. If you do the simple checks described, seldom will you run into problems. At some point, if you intend to spend extended time aboard, away from boatyards and mechanics, you should consider taking a diesel engine maintenance course. These fun and informative weekend programs are held periodically throughout the country by Mack Boring, the distributor for the popular Yanmar engine used on many cruising boats.

Electrical Systems

Batteries power electrical systems and are controlled by circuit-breaker panels. Many boats carry two separate batteries: a house battery for all the lights, pumps, and other electrical systems; and a second battery that exclusively powers the engine starter. When the engine is running, both batteries are charged.

Every sailboat has at least one master breaker switch that turns the battery power on or off. Some boats may have two; one for the engine battery and one for the house battery. There may also be one for shore power. The 110–120-volt shore power alternating current has to be adapted to 12- or 24-volt battery power by an onboard converter. When at a dock hookup, you will use a heavy-duty power cord that has a special fitting at one end for the dock receptacle. The other end usually plugs into a cockpit receptacle. Before leaving, be sure to turn your shore power off, disconnect the power

PRESAIL ENGINE CHECKS

- Oil level and color
- Water level
- Oil pressure
- Water temperature
- Water spitting through exhaust

cord from the dock, and stow it either aboard or ashore.

Some sailboats also have an inverter that changes the battery's direct current (DC) to AC current for use with shore-type appliances like blenders, toasters, hair dryers, and microwave ovens.

After you've turned your main power switch on, you can go to the circuit-breaker panel and turn on the lights, instruments, and other functions (they should all be labeled). There will be a breaker for bilge pumps, cabin lights, navigation lights, instruments, anchor windlass, radio, stove solenoid, stereo, fans, water pressure, water heater, and many others. Make sure you have flipped on the ones you plan to use while sailing.

Water Systems

Top off your water tanks before leaving for a cruise. The fill pipe is on deck and marked "water." Another fill pipe on deck is marked "fuel" so be sure not to confuse the two. Don't laugh, it has been done many times; the fill-pipe covers, which are flush on the deck, look exactly the same.

There should be a number of water tanks aboard, each with an ON-OFF valve. Open all of the valves so the water will fill all of the tanks. When full, the water will start to back out the fill pipe. Close all of the valves except the tank you want to use first (usually the forward-most tank). On many modern boats, there is often a deck-fill pipe for each individual tank. Make sure you don't miss any. Otherwise you'll have to open the inter-tank valve later on. Water use and conservation is further discussed in Chapter 17.

PROPER ENGINE USE

When operating an engine, shifting in or out of gear should always be done with the throttle at idle. Some boats have two levers: one to shift gears, one to throttle up and down. Other boats have a single lever, as shown in Figure 9-10, which when pushed forward first pops into gear and then throttles up as it is pushed farther ahead.

To warm up the engine, start in neutral position so you can increase revolutions without moving. When using a single lever control to keep the engine in neutral, pull the center hub of the handle out with the handle in the vertical position, then push it forward slowly until you reach the desired revolutions. When the engine sounds like it is running smoothly, pull the handle

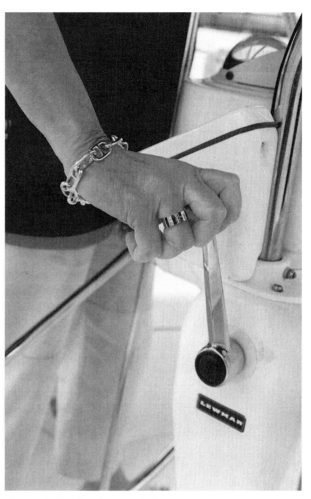

Figure 9-10. Engine throttle

slowly back to the vertical position where it will pop back in automatically and engage the gears. To accelerate and move ahead, push the handle forward from neutral (the vertical, center position). As you continue to push the handle, the boat continues to accelerate. To go into reverse pull the handle back to neutral, pause, and then continue to pull back slowly. The farther back you pull, the more the engine accelerates in reverse.

You can damage your transmission if you jam the lever forward fast, then pull it back into reverse without pausing when the handle is vertical. Consider the advice of instructor Michael Domican, who cautions his students: "Slow is pro!" Put the handle forward just enough to hear a "clunk" into forward gear before revving it up. When you pull back, pause with the handle in neutral, count to five, then continue back just enough to hear the engine "clunk" into reverse before going for speed.

Some handles, like the one shown, have a button in the middle that is in the *out* position when the engine is engaged. To rev the engine in neutral, press the button in and simultaneously push the handle forward slowly. When you pull the handle back to vertical, the button pops out automatically, allowing the handle to engage in forward or reverse.

Through new technology and materials, modern cruising boats are lighter than older ones. Newer engines generate more horsepower with less weight and volume to push. This means your boat will accelerate faster under power and stop faster when you put it in reverse. The only way to *feel* how your boat reacts under power, in forward and reverse and at different speeds, is to practice.

You want to be in control: know how long it takes to stop, how well the boat tracks in reverse, how it pulls when you gun it in reverse, what sort of turning radius you have, and how much the wind will affect you as you maneuver in tight quarters.

MANEUVERING UNDER POWER

Driving your boat under power in a perfect circle is a good exercise for understanding how it handles. Normally, the wind will cause the circle to be egg-shaped. But by advancing the throttle as you turn upwind and throttling back as you turn downwind, you can learn to control the shape of the circle. Watch your wake to see how your circle evolves.

Make a tight full circle in forward gear to port and then to starboard. The boat will turn in a smaller radius to port than to starboard, because of the direction of rotation of the propeller. A propeller that rotates clockwise in forward gear is called a *right-hand* prop. Clockwise rotation *walks* the stern to starboard in forward gear and to port in reverse gear. Most cruising boats have only one engine with a right-hand prop so, for descriptive purposes, all the exercises in this section are for boats with a right-hand prop. If your boat has a left-hand prop, it will act opposite to the

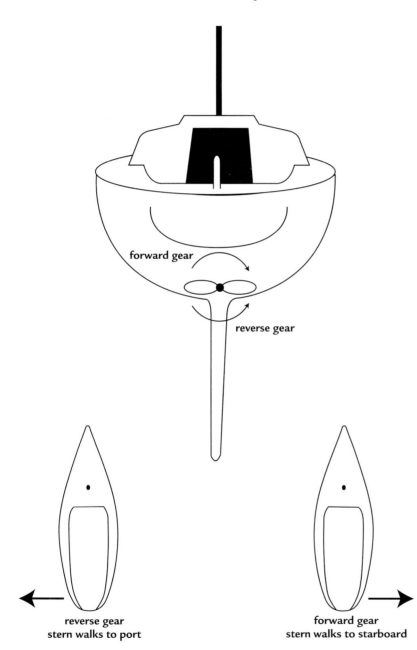

forward gear

reverse gear

reverse gear
stern walks to port

forward gear
stern walks to starboard

Figure 9-11. Prop walk with a right-hand propeller

examples in this section. To find out if your boat has a right- or left-hand prop, go into forward gear while tied to a dock with bow, stern, and spring lines. If your stern pulls the boat to starboard, you have a right-hand prop. If it pulls to port, you have a left-hand prop.

Naval architects, engine manufacturers, propeller engineers, and other experts differ on why prop walk occurs. Regardless of the true reason, think of the blades as having greater bite at the bottom of the rotation than at the top, so in forward gear with a right-hand prop the stern walks to starboard and in reverse it walks to port. Imagine the propeller blades resting on the bottom like a wheel. As the wheel turns counter-clockwise—facing forward—it rolls to the left. As it turns clockwise, it rolls to the right.

Next, practice making a tight, full circle going backward in reverse, first to port and then to starboard. Note how much tighter the turn is to port than to starboard.

By using the knowledge you now have of the difference in forward and reverse when turning to starboard and port, you can use forward and reverse gears to make the smallest possible circle in each direction. This comes in handy if you are powering into a small harbor to look for an open slip, find nothing, and need to do a 180° turn to exit the harbor.

This maneuver—the *back and fill*—is demonstrated in Figure 9-12. Put the helm over to starboard to initiate the turn with the engine in neutral (2). Reverse the engine with short bursts of power, leaving the helm hard over (3). You should be able to turn the boat completely around in little more than its boat length. If the boat starts going backward you may need a few spurts in forward to complete the turn. With the helm hard to starboard, prop wash counteracts the tendency for the bow to go to port in forward.

Next try a turn to port (Figure 9-13). Put the engine in *idle reverse*—very slow speed in reverse—and initiate the turn by putting the wheel to port as you coast to a stop (2). Then give the engine short bursts in forward gear alternating with slow reverse (3). This will kick the stern to starboard without creating much forward motion.

When you learn how your boat reacts in reverse, you can use it to your advantage to stop along docks. If your boat has a right-hand wheel, approach at an angle, port side to the dock. When you give it a slight burst in reverse to stop the forward movement, the stern kicks in to port and you end up parallel to the dock at the same time the boat stops.

Next try making your circle in reverse gear. This helps you understand how the bow follows the stern

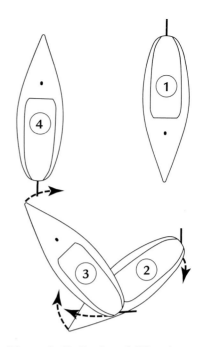

Figure 9-12. Back and fill: using prop walk to assist a tight turn to starboard

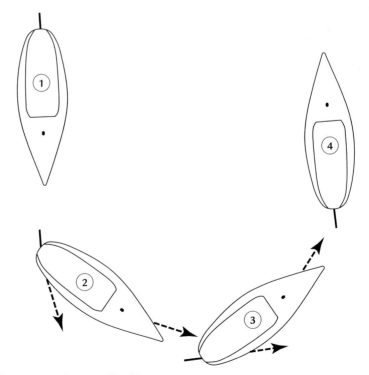

Figure 9-13. Prop walk effect on a tight turn to port

STARBOARD TURN UNDER POWER (WITH RIGHT-HAND PROPELLER)

1. Approach in neutral to decrease speed.
2. Turn the wheel hard to starboard.
3. Apply reverse bursts to lose forward momentum and use prop walk to pull the stern to port.
4. When boat loses all momentum, apply forward gear in short spurts with wheel hard over to complete the turn.
5. Tendency for the bow to turn to port in forward is offset by prop wash against the rudder.

and how wind affects it. Don't power in reverse into heavy seas because water can flow over the exhaust loop and get into the engine.

When cruising under power, engine fuel consumption is greatly dependent upon engine *rpm*—revolutions per minute. For good fuel economy and to reduce engine wear, cruise at no higher than 75 to 80 percent of maximum rpm. To determine that level, when you put the engine in forward gear after warming it up, give it maximum throttle for a moment. If it registers a top rpm of 3,000, you should cruise at about 2,400 rpm. On a cruising boat, the greater the rpm you use, the more fuel you consume with only a modest amount of increased speed.

However, you can get increased speed by *motorsailing*—using the engine in conjunction with the sails. In moderate winds this can be more effective than the sails or engine alone. When you are sailing close-hauled it is particularly useful to combine just your mainsail and the engine, because you can sail so close to the wind. Avoid motorsailing in heavy winds. The heel angle may be bad for the engine under load and the intake for the seawater cooling system may be out of the water if you are heeled over.

When you are motorsailing in international waters and inland U.S. waters on a boat over 39 feet long, you are supposed to display an inverted black cone; however, we have seen very few of these.

PORT TURN UNDER POWER

1. Approach the turn with engine idling in reverse.
2. Turn the wheel hard to port.
3. Maintain idle reverse to stop all forward way and maintain speed level.
4. Watch the bow against the shoreline to see when the boat stops turning or loses forward momentum.
5. With rudder still hard over, apply forward bursts and return engine to neutral after each burst until turn is completed.

TEST YOURSELF

Cruising Lingo

Describe the following on a cruising boat:

 1. Cabin sole
 2. Chainplates
 3. Companionway
 4. Mast step
 5. Gooseneck
 6. Jacklines
 7. Topsides
 8. Freeboard
 9. What is the purpose of a life ring and a LifeSling?
10. What does an EPIRB do?

Engines and Onboard Systems

Answer the questions below to test your knowledge of proper engine use and onboard systems.

 1. What is powered by the house battery?
 2. Which of these does a diesel not need to run: fuel, water, air, compression?
 3. With a right-hand prop in reverse, does the stern go to port or starboard?
 4. What percentage of maximum rpm should you use when under power?
 5. How much throttle should you use when shifting gears?

10 *GETTING UNDERWAY*

Regardless of the type of cruising boat you sail, you need to take time to prepare before getting underway. That preparation should include checking weather forecasts for any changes that might occur. The day may start out calm, but a summer squall could pop up later. You also need to prepare your boat to go sailing, keeping the safety and comfort of everyone aboard in mind. Think of the mess that can occur if loose items start to fly and hatches are open at the wrong time!

BEFORE YOU LEAVE

While you are still at the dock, on a mooring, or at anchor, make a last-minute check in all the cabins below. If you are planning to sail and it is blowing fairly hard, all loose items have to be stashed away or tied down before the boat heels. A bottle that isn't properly stowed could fly to leeward and make a mess—or worse, it could hurt someone.

Make it a habit to check the bilge before starting the engine. Not only will this keep moisture and damage out of the boat, but it helps you spot leaks early, before they develop into major ones. If you see water in the bilge, manually or electrically pump it out. Larger cruising boats have electric bilge pumps. While the engine is warming up, turn on the pump and listen for water sucking out. Check the exit hole in the hull by looking down from the deck to make sure water is leaving the boat.

Pump the bilge while the boat is level, under power or at rest. If you don't think about pumping the bilge until after the boat starts heeling, most of the water will have left the *sump* (the deep part of the bilge) and you will never get the bilge dry. A more serious outcome is the chance you may drown your batteries if you set sail with a lot of water in the bilge. Most batteries are positioned low in the boat because they are so heavy.

Close hatches and portholes and dog them tight. When the boat heels, portholes on the windward side will be close to horizontal. If they are left open, someone walking on deck could step right through the porthole—which happened to Steve on a race when he accidentally stepped through one, right up to his thigh. Luckily he was only bruised.

Close any open seacocks that could let water in when the boat heels. Remember, seacocks are valves that open and close the fittings that go through the hull for the head (toilet), sinks, and engine intake. A loop in the line leading to the head will keep seawater from getting into the toilet, even if the rubber valve designed to keep water out fails. Without a loop, the valves are not failsafe. The only seacocks that should remain open are ones that lead to the engine like the seawater intake. When you are living aboard your vessel in port, the seacocks are usually left open at all times. But, if you're leaving your boat for any extended period of time, close all seacocks in case the hose leading from one of them springs a leak or pops off. If this happens, the boat can fill with water and eventually sink. It is also a good idea to close the valves leading from the fuel tanks to avoid a fire if the fuel line starts to leak. So before getting underway, it may be necessary to open the seawater intake valve for the engine, the engine exhaust valve, and the fuel line valves. Also check the various belts on the engine; they should not be able to slip under load.

Make sure you have enough fuel. If you run out of diesel, air gets in the system and you have to *bleed* fresh fuel through the whole system before you can start the engine again. This can take a few minutes to an hour—depending on how often you've done it before. Your engine manual describes how to bleed the system. Some engines have an automatic bleed system that saves a lot of work when you run out of fuel. Next, advance the throttle, make sure the gearshift is in neutral, start the engine, and do your instrument checks (oil pressure, ammeter, and water temperature).

LEAVE THE DOCK IN STYLE

Leave a dock in a controlled and orderly fashion. To do this, think ahead: assign jobs to your crew members and plan your exit. Many situations will come up requiring different methods for getting underway from a dock, depending on which direction the wind is blowing and the space you have to maneuver.

Several different situations are outlined below. Regardless of which method you choose, the last two docklines you bring onboard should have been doubled back to the boat. Have a crew member loop the dockline around a cleat or piling on the dock and temporarily cleat it back on the boat, so when you are ready to get underway your crew can simply pull the line off the dock cleat or piling as you motor away. This allows all crew members to be on the boat before it pulls away from the dock, eliminating potentially dangerous leaps from the dock to the departing boat.

◆ Situation 1: If the wind is blowing from the dock, anywhere from about 45° to your bow to 45° to your stern, you can just drift out and get underway. Double the bow and stern lines back to the boat with the short end of the line cleated on top of the long end. Ask a

---

BEFORE GOING SAILING

◆ Secure everything below
◆ Tie down items on deck
◆ Pump bilge
◆ Dog hatches and portholes
◆ Close head and sink seacocks
◆ Open engine saltwater intake and exhaust valves
◆ Open fuel valves
◆ Check fuel level
◆ Check oil pressure and water temperature after starting engine

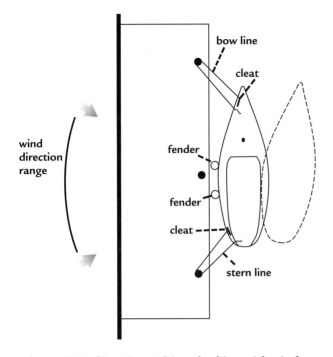

Figure 10-1. Situation 1: Disembarking with wind blowing from dock

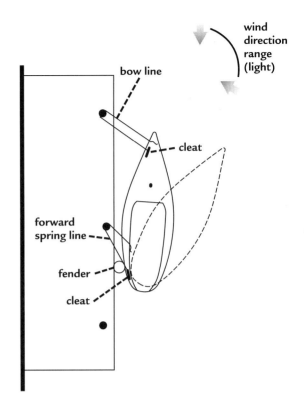

Figure 10-2. Situation 2: Disembarking with wind from anywhere between the bow to an angle blowing toward the stern

crew member to release the bow line and pull its slack back to the boat. When the bow has blown sufficiently away from the dock, retrieve the stern line in the same manner. Put the engine in forward and drive off.

◆ Situation 2: When the wind is light and in a range from dead-on your bow to blowing at an angle toward your stern and the dock, you should leave the dock by *springing* the bow out. Double the bow and spring lines as shown here. Remove all other docklines and ask a crew member to place one or two fenders near the stern. If the wind is shifty, apply a small amount of reverse to keep the stern against the dock. Release the bow line and use reverse to back the boat against the spring line. This will draw the stern toward the dock and force the bow away from the dock. When the bow is sufficiently off the dock, shift into forward and drive off slowly to allow time for the spring line to be retrieved. Since your propeller is forward of the rudder and prop wash in reverse flows away from it, turning the rudder will have no effect on the boat while springing the bow out. But prop walk does become important as you pull away from the

dock. When the boat shifts into forward, the stern *walks* to starboard. If your port side is toward the dock as in Figure 10-2, prop walk makes life easy for you because the stern walks away from the dock. If the starboard side is tied to the dock and you execute the same maneuver, prop walk works against you. In this case, simply spring the bow a little farther out than otherwise necessary and turn the wheel slightly toward the dock as you engage forward. Prop wash is deflected to starboard by the rudder and mitigates the effect of prop walk.

◆ Situation 3: If your boat is tied to the dock with the stern into the wind, turn the rudder toward the dock and put the engine in forward with just an after spring line attached. This will force the bow in and the stern out. Again, fenders should be placed toward the bow. When the stern has moved sufficiently away from the dock, power away in reverse as the spring line is brought aboard. In reverse, the propeller pulls the stern to windward and

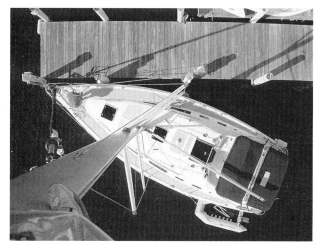

Figure 10-3. Situation 3: Disembarking with wind blowing toward stern

Figure 10-5. Removing a dockline from under other docklines

the bow just follows. The boat is under complete control. No surprises.

♦ Situation 4: When you are in tight quarters you may need to pivot the boat around the corner of a dock. Double the forward spring line back to the boat on a corner piling and put the boat in reverse against it. Make sure fenders are carefully placed to avoid any damage to your hull against the corner of the dock. As you ease the spring line, the boat should pivot more than 90° around the dock. When the bow is pointed in the desired direction, shift the engine to neutral, retrieve the spring line, and power off.

Figure 10-4. Situation 4: Pivoting around the dock in tight quarters on a forward spring line

Docklines often have spliced loops at one end to make it easier to grab a piling when docking. If you are the first boat in, you may find your loop under one or more docklines from other boats when you get ready to leave the next day. If this is the case, you don't have to take the other lines off to get yours off. Just pull your loop up inside the other loops, over the top of the piling, and back down through those loops.

After you cast off the lines, make sure none are dangling over the side of the boat where they can tangle in the propeller and render your engine useless. Remember how important that engine is to you when you get in a tight spot. Keep the jibsheets in the cockpit rather than on the deck so they can't be kicked overboard accidentally. Coil and stow your docklines. Take off any hanging fenders and stow them away too. Nothing looks more landlubberly than fenders dangling over the side, bouncing on waves.

SETTING SAIL

After leaving the dock, take some time to tidy up and think through the next steps. Assign crew members jobs in preparation for raising the sails. Figure out where the wind is coming from and how strong it will be when you get out into open water. Make sure all your lines are free of kinks and are led through the proper fittings. Get the jib ready to be unfurled.

When you are heading out into open water or on a windy day, it may be prudent to take off and stow the mainsail cover and attach the halyard to the head of the mainsail before leaving the dock. This minimizes

SAFETY TIP WHEN RAISING MAINSAIL

Keep the bow about 10° off the wind so the mainsail luffs slightly to the side. This keeps reef lines away from the person steering and the boom away from crew working on the halyard winch.

the amount of time you or your crewmates need to stand on the top of the cabin in rough conditions. This also allows you to raise the main quickly if your engine dies suddenly. If so, your salvation lies with the anchor or your sails. Have them ready to use immediately. If your engine does die and space is tight, anchoring is probably safest. But if you have room to maneuver, go ahead and put your sails up.

Don't remove the sail ties until you are headed into the wind and ready to raise the mainsail. Be sure you closed any hatches you could fall through while working on deck before you left the dock. When you are clear of the dock and other boats, check once more to make sure you don't have any fenders or lines dangling over the side.

When you are in an open area with room to maneuver, head into the wind to raise your sails. Slow the engine down to about 800 rpm and try to keep the boat in one place and headed right into the wind. If the boat starts to fall off, use forward gear to gently bring the bow back into the wind.

First, raise the mainsail, which acts like a weathervane to keep the boat headed into the wind. Just like you did on a smaller boat, look up before hauling on the halyard to make sure it isn't caught around a spreader. As you raise the sail, check often to make sure the leech of the main and the battens don't foul in the shrouds on the way up.

Everything that keeps the boom from swinging freely needs to be loose to allow the sail to go up easily. That includes the mainsheet, cunningham, boom vang, and reefing lines along the leech. Ask a crew member to control the mainsheet and ease it out as the sail goes up. When the leech starts getting tight, the mainsheet should be released completely so the sail won't fill with wind before it is all the way up. Tighten the cunningham after the sail is up to get the stretch out of the lower part of the sail along the luff.

Most boats have a *topping lift* that holds the boom up when no sails are set. When reefing or furling the mainsail, the topping lift keeps the boom from falling; but when the mainsail is raised, the topping lift should go slack. If it doesn't, you may have to ease it to allow the sail to be trimmed properly.

Unlike the mainsail on smaller boats, the mainsail on a cruising boat is larger and more powerful; you'll want to use proper technique for hauling the halyard up, which we cover later in this chapter (see the section on Safe and Efficient Winch Use).

When the main is all the way up, fall off on the desired tack and—before you stop your engine—look around. If there are no obstacles to leeward, such as reefs or moored boats, cut the engine and enjoy the peace and tranquility of sailing. If there are potentially dangerous objects to leeward, keep the engine running until you are well clear. It is also good practice to run the engine at least 15 minutes at the beginning of a day's cruise to evaporate any

IF YOU ENCOUNTER RESISTANCE WHEN RAISING SAILS

- ◆ Look up and around
- ◆ Free the halyard if it's caught around a spreader or twisted on another halyard
- ◆ Loosen the mainsheet, boom vang, cunningham, and reef lines
- ◆ Check for twists in the sail as it goes up
- ◆ Ease the topping lift if it's holding the boom up
- ◆ Continue to loosen reefing lines as the sail is raised

Figure 10-6. A genoa is a jib that overlaps the mainsail.

condensation that develops—and even longer if your batteries need charging.

On a cruising boat the jib is often called a *genoa*, and the sheets attached to it are called jib—or genoa sheets. The genoa is a large jib, so large its clew extends past the mast to overlap the mainsail as opposed to fitting between the mast and the forestay—as it does on many small boats.

On most cruising boats, the genoa is furled (rolled up) around the headstay. On this type of roller-furled jib, you set it by pulling on the jibsheets, and you *douse* it when you are done sailing by pulling on the furling line—rather than hauling it up and down on a halyard. When the headstay and furling gear are installed, the halyard tension is set for the desired luff tension and does not need to be adjusted each time you go sailing.

To unfurl the genoa underway, sail on a reach and let the wind help you pull it out. Uncleat the line that turns the roller-furling drum and let it out slowly while another crew member pulls on the jibsheet. If you just let the furling line go, as soon as the wind starts to fill the sail it will unroll extremely fast; this can cause the line on the drum to spin into a tangled mess that may

be hard to sort out when you try to roll the jib back up again. By easing it slowly, with one turn around a winch or cleat so it can't get away, it will roll back up evenly on the drum.

Figure 10-7. Proper way to put wraps around a winch

Figure 10-8. Proper way to use self-tailing winch

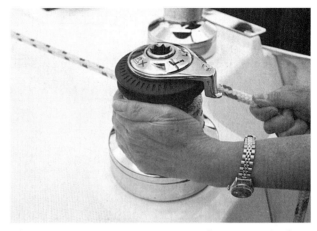

Figure 10-9. Proper way to ease a sheet on a winch

Make sure there is a stop knot in the end of each genoa sheet (see page 22). To trim the genoa, put two wraps around the sheet winch and add more wraps as you pull the sheet in. Use one hand so you can let it slide through your fingers if there's too much strain. Remember to wind the line around the winch clockwise as you look down on the winch from above.

Your cruising boat will probably have *self-tailing winches*, which make it easy for one person to trim a sail. When you've run out of steam and can't pull the sheet manually any more, jam it around the top of the winch and crank the winch handle. On a self-tailing winch, the line from the drum must go over the stainless steel guide before you jam it into the cleat.

Watch the sail as you trim, not the winch. Use both hands and center your shoulders right above the winch. As you winch in the jib, look up at the luff and the direction of the wind to make sure you don't bring the genoa in too far for the direction you're heading. Too many sailors concentrate on the winch and pull the clew right into the block, or so far that the spreader ends up poking into the leech of the sail.

To ease the genoa sheet when adjusting to a slight change in wind or course, place one hand over the coils on the drum with your thumb touching your index finger, not sticking out where it can get caught in a loop.

Ease the end of the line with the other hand. Your hand on the coils acts like a brake to control speed and flow as the genoa is eased. If you just uncleat the sheet and let it loosen on its own, the coils will first stick on the drum, then suddenly jerk out and catch you by surprise. At best, the sheet will probably go out too far and you have to laboriously crank it back in. At worst, your hand holding the free end could suffer rope burns and be pulled into the coils around the winch.

SAFE AND EFFICIENT WINCH USE

On a cruising boat, you will use winches both to trim your sails and to ultimately tighten your main halyard (and your jib halyard, if you don't have roller furling). All halyards are usually led back to the cockpit through *rope clutches*, which act as a brake to hold a line in place when you set a sail or make other adjustments. If this is the case on your boat, close the lever of the rope clutch as you prepare to raise the halyard; then pull the halyard toward you through the clutch, hand over hand, until you can't raise the sail manually any farther. Up to this point you should not have any of the halyard wrapped around a winch.

When you raise the sails you will probably need to use a winch to get the last bit up, and it is only at that point that you put turns around the winch, not before. Wrap one or two turns of the halyard around a winch using one hand. Remember to let the halyard slide through your fingers as you circle the winch. Do not make a loop around the winch with two hands or you might catch your fingers between the winch and the line.

As you pull directly from the winch, another crew member can help by *bouncing* the halyard. Note how

Figure 10-10. Halyards and other lines from mast led through rope clutches on deck

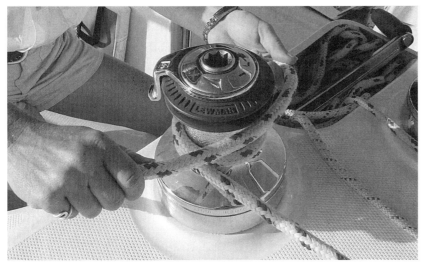

Figure 10-11. Improper way to add wraps to a winch

THE RIGHT WAY TO PULL ON A LINE

- Grab the line in your right hand with your fist over the top, thumb and forefinger toward you and pull to your right side (like swimming).
- Then grab the line with your left hand, fist over the top, and pull to your left side.
- Alternate as above, until line is trimmed in (or winch is needed).
- Instead of pulling it to you, this method uses your whole arm with broader, more efficient motion.

the crew in Figure 10-12 are using their body weight, with arms extended, to pull out and down on the halyard. A crew member should be on the winch to simultaneously take in the slack.

When the bouncer slows down, you need more wraps than two or three on the winch to create friction and keep the line from slipping around the drum if you do not have rope clutches. Pull the halyard coming off the winch toward you about a foot, then wrap that part quickly around the winch and pull again until you need more help. Then, and only then, should you insert the winch handle. If the winch handle is inserted while you can still pull manually on the halyard, you have to go around the whole handle when you need an extra turn of line on the winch, which is very awkward. Until the sail is all the way up, keep tension on the free end of the line to keep it from slipping. As someone cranks on the winch, another crew will have to *tail* the free end coming off the winch. *Tailing* means to pull on the line to keep it taut so it can't slip back.

Figure 10-12. Bouncing the halyard

AVOID WINCH OVERRIDES

- Start with two or three wraps and pull manually
- Add more wraps as tension occurs
- Make sure someone tails and keeps tension on the sheet
- Use one hand when adding wraps
- Add additional wraps before inserting the winch handle
- Remove the winch handle when the sail is trimmed in

Figure 10-13. Releasing a winch override with a rolling hitch

Most halyard winches have double gears: high when turning the handle in one direction, low when turning the other direction. When you can no longer turn in the high direction, reverse to low. Or you can ratchet back and forth, pulling toward you in high gear and pushing away in low.

If you have too many wraps on the winch you may get an *override*. The part of the halyard going onto the winch has crossed over and pinched the part leading off the winch. If this happens, you won't be able to continue pulling on the halyard and must get all the turns off the winch and start again; but this requires relieving the tension on the override. Using a spare line, tie a rolling hitch to the line leading to the winch with the override, as shown in Figure 10-13. The rolling hitch won't slip under pressure, so crank it tight on another winch to relieve the original line and then untangle the override.

TIDYING UP ON DECK

All lines, and particularly halyards, should be neatly coiled. When the sail is up as far as it will go, cleat the halyard, coil it, and then put the winch handle away. Never leave the handle in the winch, as it can get lost and is expensive to replace.

All the excess halyard now lying in your cockpit or on deck needs to be coiled and cleated in such a way that it can be easily uncoiled if you suddenly need to lower the main. Make your coils clockwise to minimize kinking. Always coil from the *fast end*—the end that is attached to something—toward the free end of the line to work any kinks out. How many times have you coiled up a garden hose only to find it trying to go the other way with interminable kinks? The hints in the sidebar help you avoid that same situation with lines on a boat.

"A clean deck is a happy deck!"
WILLIAM LEE (30), BOSTON, MA

KNOTS TO KNOW

A rolling hitch can slide in one direction but will stay in place when tension is applied in the opposite direction. Some common uses are: to relieve tension on another line that may have an override in it; to secure a halyard to a stanchion or rail; to tie a line to an anchor rode of a stuck anchor so you can use a cockpit winch to help bring it up; and when lashing a dinghy on deck.

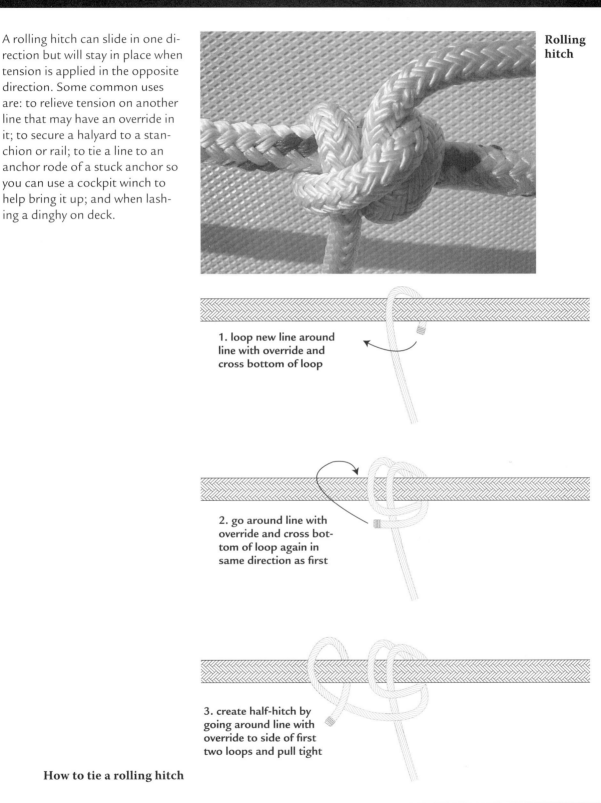

Rolling hitch

1. loop new line around line with override and cross bottom of loop

2. go around line with override and cross bottom of loop again in same direction as first

3. create half-hitch by going around line with override to side of first two loops and pull tight

How to tie a rolling hitch

TO TIDY UP A HALYARD

1. Tighten the halyard and make one turn around the base of the cleat before criss-crossing it. The last loop should be a *half-hitch*, which keeps the line from uncleating accidentally.

2. Coil the line, starting from the end fastened to the cleat.
3. Reach through the coil to the cleat and pull the bottom section of the half-hitch through the center and over the top of the coiled line.
4. Loop that section of the half-hitch over the top of the cleat to neatly hang the halyard.

If a sudden squall hits, you need to be able to release halyards quickly, without any tangles. To do this, take the hanging coil off the cleat and flake out the halyard on the deck. The bitter end of each halyard should be secured with a stop knot so you can just let the halyard go, get on to the next emergency, and know that the halyard won't be lost up inside the mast. The jibsheets should also be coiled and laid down in the cockpit with the coils running off the top. If coils run off the bottom and you have to do a quick tack to avoid a collision, the sheet can knot up and jam in the sheet block when it is thrown off the winch.

If you didn't have time to coil and stow your docklines before getting the sails up, this should be done now. Since the docklines are no longer attached to anything, it doesn't matter which end of the line you coil first, unless there is a spliced loop in one end. If so, start with that end and bring the coils to it. It doesn't matter which hand you hold the coils in; but make your loops clockwise to avoid kinking as shown in the sidebar. Braided line has a tendency to make figure-eights with each loop. That's okay; the loops don't have to be perfect ovals.

HOW TO COIL A DOCKLINE

1. Stretch one arm out the same distance for each coil and collect loops in your other hand.

2. Finish the coil off by wrapping the end of the line around the middle of the coils a few times and pass a loop through the top part of the coiled line.

3. Pass the same loop over the top of the coils on either side and pull tight on the end of the line.
4. If you are hanging the line, run the bitter end through loop (instead of passing the loop over the top of the coils), leaving enough line to hang the coil.

TEST YOURSELF

Getting Underway and Setting Sail

To test your knowledge of how to get underway and set sail, answer the questions below.

1. Why should you close your portholes or hatches before leaving?
2. Why should you pump the bilge before leaving?
3. When do you have to bleed fresh fuel through a diesel engine?
4. Why and when do you double docklines back to the boat?
5. Describe springing the bow out.
6. When you set sail, which sail should you raise first? Why?
7. When you unfurl the genoa, what do you do with the furling line?
8. As you winch in a genoa sheet, what should you watch?
9. Why should you coil lines after use?
10. What does bouncing a halyard mean?
11. Describe how a rolling hitch can be used.

11 BASIC MANEUVERS UNDER SAIL

When you sail a cruising boat, you use the same two basic maneuvers you use on a smaller boat: tacking and jibing. Since it is a longer process to tack a cruising boat, cruising sailors tend to stay on one tack for a longer period of time and only tack when necessary.

WHEN AND WHERE TO TACK

Plan your tacks with your destination and surroundings in mind. If you tack indiscriminately, you may discover a stand-on vessel or an obstruction such as a moored boat right in your path—and you'll have to tack back again.

Assuming you are close-hauled and sailing 45° off the wind, you will head approximately 90° from your current course when you tack. If you pick a landmark directly abeam to windward from the high side of the boat, you can get a good idea of your heading on the next tack. In the absence of a landmark, use your compass as described below. Make sure there is no danger in that direction and look aft to windward for boats that could have right-of-way over you after you tack.

One of the most common errors when tacking a cruising boat is to turn the boat too far. On a small boat, the jib is trimmed in immediately after a tack—so you can tell almost instantly whether the boat has turned too far or not by observing whether the jib is luffing or stalled. On a cruising boat, however, it may take quite a while to winch the genoa in all the way, and during that time the sail is luffing. Unlike a small boat, this makes it hard to determine if you are sailing too high or too low.

If you fall off to fill the genoa before it is all the way in, you will have turned the boat well past 90°. This makes it hard on your crew, as the genoa is now full of air. To avoid this problem, note your compass heading on the original tack. Then add or subtract 90° depending on which way you plan to turn the boat. Most compasses have 90° *lubberlines* that make this exercise

Figure 11-1. Sailing on a long tack

90° lubberline

If 148° is your course, steer 238° as if that was the boat's heading.

Figure 11-2. Steering a compass course by the 90° lubberline

easy, or you can use a screw on the compass rim.

Test that you are as close to the wind as possible on the original tack before you take your reading. Another caveat is that the wind may shift as you turn. The compass course is only a temporary crutch. As soon as the jib is trimmed in, sail by the jib—not the compass—until you settle down.

If you are steering a compass course and are more comfortable sitting to windward or leeward of the wheel, you can steer your course by watching the 90° lubberline. It takes a little practice, but works the same as the forward lubberline—as long as you remember it is 90° from your actual compass course. In Figure 11-2, the boat is being steered about 148°. In this case, keep the course close to 238° on the 90° lubberline as shown.

HOW TO TACK A CRUISING BOAT

Because of its large overlapping genoa and greater displacement, tacking a cruising boat is a slightly different process than tacking a Colgate 26. As the cruising boat's bow turns into the wind to tack, the genoa sheet has to be released as soon as a good luff appears on the luff of the sail. If the sheet is not released early enough, the sail will *back*—fill with wind on the other side—and force the genoa into the spreader and swing the bow hard over. Though there is usually no danger involved, it is bad for the sail to rub against the tip of the spreader under pressure; this also puts excessive strain on the spreaders. Even worse, when the sheet is finally released, it takes off with a vengeance and could catch a crew member as it flies out.

As the sail starts to luff, ease the genoa sheet a few feet and then throw the turns off the winch by lifting straight up and flicking the turns off at the same time. A common mistake is to release the genoa sheet at the moment the person steering calls, "Hard alee!" This is typically too early to release the sheet. Remember, the luff in the sail should control your release, and the person handling the genoa sheet must watch the sail carefully. The opposite could also happen: if the command to tack is made late, that person must release the sheet before the sail backs.

When a genoa backs, the boat can seldom return to the original tack without the sheet being released—because the sail is pushing the bow across. If you are on the genoa sheet and you aren't positive of the intentions of the person steering, but the boat turns into the wind, you can't go wrong to release the sheet when the sail starts to back. Realize, however, that a backed jib is under tremendous load and the sheet will zing out fast when released—creating a more dangerous situation than a normal tack.

Always be able to release the sheet easily and quickly when necessary. With self-tailing winches, just free the line from the jam cleat on the top and flick it off. If your boat doesn't have self-tailing winches, the sheet will be held by a separate cleat. In this case, don't use half hitches because they are slower to take off. Take one turn around the cleat base, crisscross the cleat in the normal fashion once, and then take one last jamming turn around the base of the cleat to keep the line from uncleating. As the genoa comes across during a tack on a cruising boat, the flailing sheet may catch on a winch, the edge of a hatch, or other "stuff" on the deck. If you take up on the new sheet fast enough, this may not happen. But if your boat has a tendency to do this, station a crew member well forward of the mast to help get the sail and sheets across the foredeck by pulling the sail forward along its foot and passing it overhead. Caution: don't position anyone near the mast where the genoa's clew can hit them as the sail comes across.

As you learned earlier, the most efficient way to crank a winch is to stand with your shoulders over the winch and your feet spread for balance. You should be able to turn the handle continuously in one direction until you can no longer turn the winch. Then change the direction of your rotation to use the lower gear. Always watch the sail as it comes in. If it touches the spreader or the clew hits the sheet block, you have gone too far.

Normally, the faster you trim the better. It is much easier to trim the sheet in all the way before the genoa fills with wind, but this practice may not be very efficient. After a tack, a boat moves slowly and needs to pick up speed. Full sails, versus flat sails, will help the boat accelerate quickly. Leave a little belly in the jib at first, or ease the jibsheet slightly to help the boat get going. Then crank in the last few inches as the boat accelerates. If the sail fills prematurely, ask the person steering to head up and luff the sail; this will make it easier for you to crank in the jib.

Again, always be sure to remove the winch handle from the top of the winch when you are finished trimming, then stow it in an accessible place, such as a cubby in the cockpit, so it can't be lost overboard.

HOW TO JIBE A CRUISING BOAT

Jibing is a fairly simple procedure. Although the mainsail is pretty much ignored when tacking, it must be carefully controlled during the jibe. On the Colgate 26 you were concerned with the boom swinging over and hitting someone. On a cruising boat, where the forces are so much greater, the mainsheet is just as much a threat. If somebody gets tangled in the mainsheet as the boom swings across the boat, they can get hurt quite badly.

For this reason, you should overhaul the mainsheet in a jibe—trim it as the boat turns. As soon as the boom crosses the centerline of the boat (the imaginary line running from the bow to the middle of the stern of the boat) let the mainsheet out fast.

Boats that stay in hot climates usually have a bimini top for shade, which also keeps the boom and mainsheet away from crew in the cockpit during a jibe. Even so, you should trim in the mainsheet to keep the boom from flying from one side to the other, which also puts extra stress on the gooseneck.

TACKING A CRUISING BOAT

To avoid backing the genoa in a tack, release the leeward genoa sheet as soon as the luff of the sail goes soft.

Figure 11-3. A blanketed jib twists around the forestay when eased too far in a jibe.

Accidental jibes are dangerous for unsuspecting crew members. If you are running dead downwind in rough seas on a cruising boat for a long period of time, you should rig a *preventer*—a line running from the end of the main boom forward to a cleat near the bow that stops the boom from traveling across the centerline. Make the line to the bow long enough so it will stretch rather than break if you get off course and the wind fills the other side of the main. That stretch gives you time to get back on course.

Boom preventers are often used in conditions of low visibility when it's harder to see wind changes and on long downwind passages. But these are too complicated to set up for a short run. On short runs, it is up to the person steering to keep the boat from sailing by the lee. The crew should always be aware that at any time during a run the boom could come swinging across.

If your boat has a rope and block boom vang

arrangement you can unsnap the whole boom vang from its connection at the base of the mast and snap it to the rail as far forward as possible, then pull it tight for a combination vang-preventer. However, many boats have solid vang systems like the tubular one shown in the photograph, which are not easily detached for this purpose. If you have a preventer on to keep the boom from coming across, or the boom vang is led to the rail for the same reason, you must release it before jibing.

To execute a jibe, ask a crew member to start pulling in the mainsheet on the command, "Prepare to jibe!" When you see the main approach the center of the boat, say "Jibe ho!" and turn the boat. Slightly delay the jibe, because there is no way a crew member can trim in the main as fast as you can turn the boat—except in very light air conditions.

In very heavy air you may have to sail the boat

slightly by the lee to relieve the force on the sail and allow the crew to bring in the main. Never use a winch handle when bringing in the mainsheet. Simply haul it in, hand-over-hand with one or two turns around the winch so the sheet can't fly out uncontrolled when you start to ease after the jibe. For more control in heavy air, center the traveler car and tighten the blocks at each end, so the car can't slide across the boat and hit someone in the way.

The genoa takes very little effort when jibing. Just ease out the old sheet and pull in the new one. Avoid easing the old sheet too far or the sail will fly out beyond the bow of the boat. If this happens, the whole sail will have to be pulled across the headstay when you try to pull it in on the new side. The accompanying friction and the flogging of the jib can make pulling it across very difficult. The new sheet should be trimmed as the old one is eased, keeping the clew of the sail from going too far forward of the mast as the boat jibes.

When sailing downwind, winging the genoa on a cruising boat with a spinnaker pole (if you have one) can be very effective. The genoa is easily blanketed by the mainsail, so getting it to windward—opposite of the main—greatly increases the sail area projected to the wind.

To sail wing and wing on a run with a spinnaker pole, rig the pole to rest on the headstay with the windward genoa sheet through it. Ease the leeward sheet and pull the clew to the pole with the windward sheet. When it reaches the pole, keep trimming and the pole will pull the genoa out to windward. Trim the sail as if the leech of the genoa is now the luff. Too far back and it collapses, so ease it forward, and vice versa.

To go back to normal sailing, ease the pole forward to the head-stay, trip the windward jibsheet out of the pole's jaw, trim the leeward sheet, and then stow the pole away.

If your boat doesn't have a spinnaker pole, you can pull the genoa to the side opposite the main just using your windward genoa sheet. But you have to be on a dead run to keep the genoa full.

CONTROL YOUR JIBES

1. Make sure the preventer (or boom vang led to rail) is released.
2. Overhaul the mainsheet before the jibe begins.
3. Bring the main to the center of the boat as the boat turns.
4. Let the mainsheet out quickly as the boom crosses the centerline of the boat.

"This past fall when I was sailing back from Tuscany, Italy, to Toulon, France, with 40 knots of wind behind us, we were doing a wing and wing with a spinnaker pole on a genoa. My boat was surfing down waves at 15 knots!"

WILLIAM LEE (30), BOSTON, MA

DOUSING SAILS AT DAY'S END

As you head back to your home port or into a new harbor to spend the night, start planning well ahead of time. Decide when you are going to get your sails down and, once again, assign tasks to your crew. It is fine to take in the genoa and continue sailing under main alone while you sort out where you want to dock or anchor. But before you lower both sails completely, turn on your engine and keep it idling until you need it to stay in position or maintain direction.

In moderate conditions you are probably sailing with both your main and genoa. If so, the genoa is furled up or taken down first. To furl the sail, simply pull on the furling line. Remember, this is the line that leads from the

Figure 11-4. A furled genoa with dark UV cloth protection along leech

Figure 11-5. Taking down the main

drum at the base of the jib aft to a winch near the cockpit. The furling line rotates the whole head foil as it rolls up the jib.

To furl the genoa you must let it luff completely. Free the sheet and head up to reduce speed and heel angle, but don't flog the sail against the shrouds. This will increase friction and make it more difficult to furl the sail.

If the genoa furling line is hard to pull, do not put it on a winch and start cranking. First check that the genoa halyard is really tight. Turning a foil that is curved takes a lot more force than turning a straight one, and this may be the case with your headsail. The luff of the jib needs to be stretched tight or the furling mechanism won't work well. If this is the case, take the time to tighten the halyard with the sail luffing. Assuming you planned your takedown well in advance, checking the genoa headstay for excess sag at that time would have been prudent.

If your halyard is tight and there is still resistance, check the upper furling fitting to see if another hal-

yard got wound up in it. If that furling fitting turns freely and seems clear, but it is still hard to pull the furling line, head downwind and blanket the jib behind the main to reduce pressure on the jib. Only after you've exhausted other options should you attempt to use the winch to furl the genoa. If the jib won't furl at all, something must be broken and the headsail should be lowered to the deck.

When the sail is rolled up, it's still exposed to sunlight and subject to ultraviolet deterioration. Sailmakers therefore add a panel of UV-resistant material along the leech. This panel ends up on the outside of the roll and protects the rest of the furled sail. After the sail is completely rolled up, add a few extra turns to wrap the jibsheets around the outside of the sail. This locks the furl in place and keeps the wind from catching an end of the sail and unfurling it.

When lowering a main with slides attached to the luff, the slides remain on the mast, piling one on top of the other at the boom as the sail comes down. Flake

Figure 11-6. Tying the mainsail on the boom

the sail along the boom by positioning a crew member at both ends. Starting at the clew, make continuous folds onto the top of the boom, following up by folding the leech in the same manner as you go. Then, using sail ties made out of nylon or rope, tie the flaked sail securely to the top of the boom. An easy knot for this purpose is half a bow. Instead of two loops each with a tail, make only one loop with one tail. To untie it, just pull down on that tail. Some sailors like to use elastic cord with a loop toggle for securing the mainsail.

An alternative method is to make a pocket—like a hammock—along the foot of the sail by grabbing the leech four to five feet from the clew and folding the rest of the sail into the pocket formed by this portion of the sail. Then roll it up on top of the boom and secure it with sail ties. The sail is furled and looks neater if you have no sail cover, or if you are just making a stop and plan to go sailing again shortly.

After the sail is tied on top of the boom, the sail cover goes on. Tie the wide end of the cover around the mast, pull the other end to the end of the boom and tie it tightly. Then fasten the grommet snaps, or shock cord threaded through hooks and eyes along the edges of the sail cover under the boom. Start at the gooseneck and work aft.

Like the genoa, the mainsail is also highly susceptible to the sun's ultraviolet rays. The best solution is to protect the sail with a cover made out of Sunbrella cloth. Removing the sails completely to store them out of the sun isn't practical on cruising boats.

However, you can now find cruising boats with mainsails that furl in-

Figure 11-7. A halyard secured to the rail

side the mast. In this case, the mainsails do not have battens (for obvious reasons) so the leech is cut concave, which makes for a less efficient sail. Furling mains and jibs, electric winches, and other features on new cruising boats make cruising so much easier—and the shape of the sails is less important.

Always remove the halyard from the head of the mainsail when you are finished sailing. You can secure the halyard shackle to a ring on the mast; but in windy or rolling conditions, the halyard will clang against the mast and keep you—and everyone else in the harbor—awake. Better to attach it to a spot on the *toerail* (the vertical lip or rim along the outer edge of the deck, usually where the deck meets the hull) or the bottom of a stanchion, then tighten and cleat the other end. You can also snap the shackle to any handy loop positioned away from the mast.

Last, after coiling all the lines and tidying up, lock the steering wheel with the rudder amidship. There is usually a brake on the side of the steering pedestal that keeps the wheel from spinning when sailing is done for the day.

TEST YOURSELF

Tacking, Jibing, and Dousing Sails
Answer the questions below to test your knowledge of tacking and jibing a cruising boat and dousing your sails.

1. Before you tack, how can you estimate your course on the next close-hauled tack?
2. What's the best way to cleat a jibsheet?
3. Describe backing a jib and how it occurs inadvertently.
4. If the genoa is full but not trimmed in yet, what can the helmsman do to help the crew trimming the sail?
5. What is the main concern when jibing the genoa?
6. What is the main concern when jibing the mainsail and how is it alleviated?
7. When you are finished sailing, which sail do you douse first?
8. Describe how you put away the sails after sailing.

SETTLING DOWN FOR THE NIGHT

12 DOCKING AND MOORING A CRUISING BOAT

After a great day on the water, you're ready to return to the dock. Your sails are down, your engine is running, and you've assigned jobs to your crew to make your landing successful.

Your objective in docking a cruising boat is to put it alongside the dock so lines can be secured without risk to crew members or the boat. Approach very slowly: reverse gear on a cruising sailboat is not very effective.

APPROACHING A DOCK

When docking a boat under power, three factors come into play: wind, current, and boat speed. Given the choice, always approach the dock into the wind so you can control the boat better with higher engine rpms. This gives you better steerage because the propeller is pushing more water past the rudder. To slow down, throttle back and the wind will help brake the boat.

Be aware of current direction and strength in the dock area and allow for it as you approach. Observe the speed and direction of floating objects (like seaweed) in the water. Look at the pilings. If there's a strong current, you'll see what looks like turbulence (a wake) on one side. That side is the down-current direction.

Preparation when docking is always important. If you are in charge, make your plan of action early and discuss it with each crew member. Assign specific tasks. Make sure fenders and docklines are rigged well in advance of your arrival.

Place fenders over the side, tied to the lifelines or stanchions with a clove hitch backed up by two half hitches, or—at a minimum—a round turn with two half hitches. (Too often, fenders tied only by clove hitches end up floating behind the boat!) Rig a bow line, stern line, and two spring lines early on the docking side of the boat. One end should be cleated or around a winch, with the line led through a chock and back over the lifelines in

Figure 12-1. Preparing fenders and docklines before docking

Figure 12-2. A fender secured to the lifeline with a round turn and two half hitches

preparation for tossing the free end ashore. Put a decent-sized loop on the free end so you can ask someone on the dock to just drop it over a piling or cleat. Then you can adjust the line length from the boat without having to rely on that person ashore, who may not understand how you want your docklines adjusted.

Just as you did when leaving a dock, you must figure out your approach and actual landing relative to the wind strength and direction. Current is not a factor unless it is very strong, which is unusual in a protected marina. However, you might experience strong current if you are docking on a river or inlet. The scenarios below outline several different situations.

♦ Situation 1: The wind is parallel to the dock, which has little effect on your approach. If the dock is on your port side and you have a right-hand prop, approach the dock at an angle between 15° to 45° (see A in Figure 12-3). As the bow nears the dock, go into reverse to walk the stern to port. If the dock is on your starboard side, your approach should be more parallel to the dock because your stern will walk away from the dock in reverse. In either case, ask your crew to put the bow and forward spring lines ashore first. When they are tied or cleated, back the boat against the spring line until the stern and after spring line are secured. Rarely will you get into trouble by coming in with too little speed. Sure, you need some boat speed to be able to maneuver; but it is unlikely you can hurt much if you are not moving. Re-

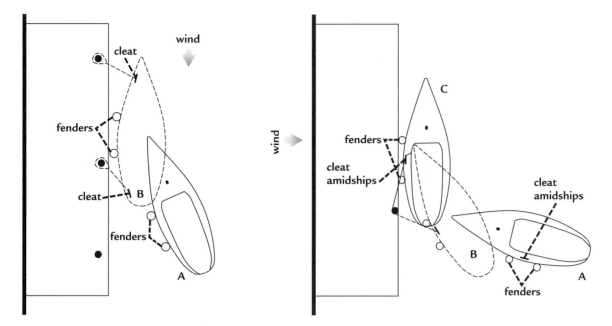

Figure 12-3. Situation 1: Approaching with wind parallel to the dock

Figure 12-4. Situation 2: Approaching with wind perpendicular to the dock

member: *Slow is pro!* A heavy cruising boat cannot stop quickly. Approach a dock or slip too fast and your boat's momentum will forge ahead, possibly causing damage to your boat or nearby boats. The slowest possible approach is always preferable.

- Situation 2: The wind is perpendicular to the dock; this has the greatest effect on your approach. If the wind is blowing from the dock, approach with your bow heading almost directly into the wind (see A in Figure 12-4) then turn parallel to the float at the last possible minute. To slow down, you have to put the engine in reverse; but this gives you far less directional control because reverse on a sailboat is notoriously ineffective. So make sure someone is prepared to get a spring line leading aft ashore first to stop your forward motion (B). With a right-hand prop, the stern will walk to port when you put the engine in reverse to stop the boat. If your port side is to the dock, this will pull you closer, so allow for prop walk in your approach. After you have stopped alongside, put your engine in forward idle to pull against the spring line until all lines are secure (C).

- Situation 3: The wind is blowing you sideways onto the dock. In this scenario, you should make your approach as if you are going to land on

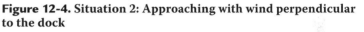

INSTRUCTOR TIP

"Glance sideways to judge your speed during docking, anchoring, and mooring maneuvers where 'slow is pro.'"

MICHAEL DOMICAN, CRUISING INSTRUCTOR,
BRITISH VIRGIN ISLANDS

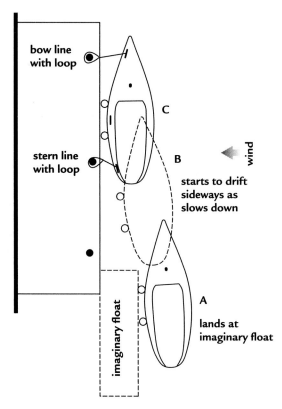

Figure 12-5. Situation 3: Approaching with wind blowing boat toward the dock

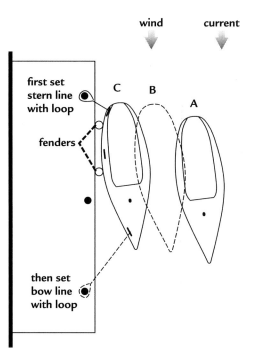

Figure 12-6. Situation 4: Approaching in reverse with wind and current combined

an imaginary float between you and the actual dock (see A in Figure 12-5). As you approach, target your landing at the imaginary upwind float. As you slow down you'll drift sideways (B) into the actual dock (C). When you are at a dead stop you should be resting gently alongside the dock, just where you want to be.

♦ Situation 4: The wind and current are coming from the same direction, pushing your boat forward. When used properly, current helps you get in and out of tight docking situations. Normally, you approach a dock in an up-current direction, which enables you to power a knot or two through the water and still remain in the same place over the bottom. If you turn the bow a few degrees across the current, the boat will crab sideways and can be fit into an extremely tight spot between other boats. But this won't work when strong wind combines with current. The wind will tend to blow your bow to one side or the other, forcing the boat across the current. A solution in this case is to back against the current and the

wind. Put the engine in reverse to pull your stern into the wind and current, and the rest of the boat will line up downwind like a weather vane. Then steer so your stern is at a slight angle to the current. The boat will then crab sideways directly into the docking space or slip.

In many cases you can secure the boat by leading a spring line from a winch through a chock or a block amidships, then aft along the dock. The chock must be at the center of lateral resistance of the hull, keel, and rudder. To find that point, attach a line to the toe rail or a block near the middle of the boat and pull the boat sideways. If the bow comes in more than the stern, move the block aft until pulling on the line brings the boat in sidewise and parallel to the dock.

Set this pivotal line up as one of your spring lines. As you approach the dock, get that line ashore first and ask the person helping you to drop it over a cleat or piling aft, near the stern of the boat. A crew member should stand ready at the winch to ease this line, to avoid crunching the topsides against the dock if the boat is moving too fast. However, this line describes an arc when secured; any forward motion of the boat brings the whole boat alongside the float parallel to it, because of the location of the lead.

Figure 12-7. Using a spring line to pull a boat in

The last line to secure, which is optional, is the *breast line*—a single line from the middle of the boat to an opposite pier or piling. This line is tied to keep the topsides away from the dock. If you plan to leave the boat unattended for a while, breast the boat a good distance from the float in case of bad weather. To do this, ease all the lines substantially and take up on the breast line. Then temporarily pivot the bow or stern into the dock so you can get off and finish tightening all the lines to keep the boat parallel to the dock. If you are tying up to a non-floating dock, remember to allow enough slack to accommodate the rise and fall of the tide.

PICKING UP A MOORING

Dock space in the United States and around the world is in great demand. Quite often you will have to anchor or pick up a mooring for the night. In some areas you will find permanent moorings set out for cruising boats to use. This preserves the ecology and protects reefs where constant anchoring has taken its toll. When you are out cruising, you may call ahead to a local yacht club or marina and they will tell you to pick up a specific guest mooring. You may even have a designated mooring in your home harbor. So how do you pick up a mooring?

Approach the mooring buoy slowly from the downwind side so you are heading directly into the wind as you motor toward it. The crew member on the bow should be giving you directions by pointing at the mooring—using

---

DOCKING CHECKLIST

- ◆ Get fenders ready
- ◆ Get bow, stern, and spring lines ready
- ◆ Check and prepare for wind and current
- ◆ Approach slowly
- ◆ Secure lines ashore
- ◆ Adjust lines on the boat

Figure 12-8. Using hand signals when picking up a mooring

hand signals. Verbal instructions are often hard to hear, and yelling just draws attention as you enter a harbor.

After the mooring line or the pickup buoy (a small buoy that is easily grabbed from the deck of a boat) has been retrieved, make sure you hold the boat in position until the line is secured to the cleat. To do this, put the engine in neutral. If you see your crewmate struggling to pull enough mooring line aboard to tie it down, power the boat gently forward for a short time to gain some slack in the line.

If the mooring line has a loop in the end, your crewmate should place it over the bow cleat. The light line that attaches the pickup buoy to the heavy mooring line is then cleated on top of the loop, to ensure the loop doesn't slip off the cleat. This can happen if the mooring line is stiff and the loop is large and the bow of the boat pitches down off a wave, creating slack in the line.

In some cases the mooring has no line attached and you are expected to use your own; so it's a good idea to make a pass first and check if you need to set up your own line from the boat. If this is the case, cleat a dockline on the port bow cleat, pass it through the port bow chock, then through the mooring ring, back through the starboard bow chock, and to the starboard cleat. When it is time to leave, all you need to do is release one end.

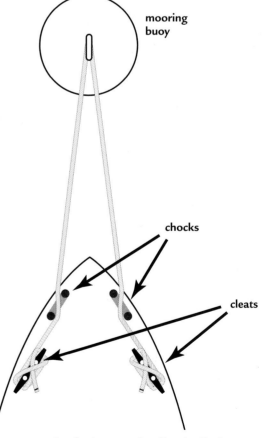

Figure 12-9. The proper way to cleat a mooring line to the bow

This system is very susceptible to chafe, so be sure to use an oversized line and use only for a short time in moderate conditions. One or two safety lines tied directly to the ring is better for overnight and heavier wind conditions.

MED-MOOR DOCKING

As dock space becomes tighter and tighter, maneuvering among docked and moored boats is becoming more of a challenge. The Mediterranean style of mooring stern-to a dock, which is commonly called *Med-moor*, allows more yachts to tie up in an area and is becoming common in the States. But this kind of docking takes coordination: become proficient at mooring stern-to and you will be revered by your peers.

When we cruised in Greece, we ended most days by dropping our anchor about five boat lengths from the dock and backing down to the quay. First, select the spot where you want to end up. If you are in port early enough in the day, you may find a sufficiently wide-open space between two boats—wide enough to accommodate the beam of your boat without touching the others. But this is rare abroad, where you look for any space you can find between two boats—no matter how narrow—and make it larger by pushing the others aside. In many Med-moor situations, might makes right.

> ### MOORING CHECKLIST
>
> - Approach slowly
> - Head toward the buoy from downwind
> - Use hand signals for forward, neutral, reverse
> - Secure the mooring line loop on a cleat

Figure 12-10. Med-moor docking in Rhodes, Greece

Figure 12-11. Backing in to a dock in Greece

It is far easier for a larger boat to push two smaller boats aside than the other way around.

Be careful if you see small boats all huddled together rather than intermingled with larger boats. The water in that area may be too shallow for your boat.

Once you have decided where you want to be, maneuver your boat into position so you are lined up to your landing spot and parallel to the others. Drop the anchor about five boat lengths out, or whatever distance seems appropriate for the size of the harbor. Water depth is not the determining factor; what's more important is that your anchor holds well enough to keep your stern from hitting the quay. In many harbors your anchor will hold quite well with short scope because it catches some of the other anchors and ground tackle if it drags. Also, latecomers often lay their anchor chain over yours, which increases your holding power. When the anchor is down, the key is coordination between the person on the bow, who is easing out the anchor chain, and the person who is backing the boat into the space.

Steering in reverse takes practice. Some sailors like to stand in front of the wheel facing the stern to steer, just as if they were going forward and turning the wheel in the direction they want the stern to go. Though this is a common and fairly popular method, it is a bad habit because your back is to the bow and you can't see what sort of trouble the rest of the boat is getting into. Keep in mind that when you are in reverse, a sailboat's bow makes large swings when the stern moves only a little.

A better position is to stand sideways, perpendicular to the wheel. When you pull the top of the wheel toward you, the stern comes toward you. When you push the top of the wheel away from you, the stern goes away from you. You can turn your head over one shoulder to look forward and the other to look aft (see Figure 12-11).

While backing in, a couple other crewmates with *roving fenders*—fenders that are not secured in place but ready to be placed where needed—are very helpful. At first, the crew on the bow should ease a lot of scope so the boat can maneuver moving backward. If the bow starts falling off in one direction or the other, the bow crew should stop easing until strain on the anchor straightens the boat out again. Ideally, the anchor should be secured early, requiring quite a bit of power in reverse to get the stern near the quay bulkhead.

Figure 12-12. Stern lines run through rings on a seawall and back to the boat.

Lines from either side of the stern are then led to rings or cleats on the quay and doubled back to the boat. As the engine is reversed, take in the slack on one side and then the other. When you are ready to leave you can just throw off the short end of the line and pull it through the ring or around the cleat, with less chance of getting a tangle or snags. Finally, put a stern plank to shore to get on and off the boat. Tie it securely to the boat and allow enough overlap on the quay so it can't drop in the water in the event of a big surge.

HOW TO BACK IN FROM A PRESET MOORING

In some parts of the world, such as the southern coast of France, you pick up a preset mooring and back in. The approach is the same as the Med-moor, except you are not dropping an anchor. Instead you have to power backward toward the quay until you can reach the mooring and its messenger line. Since each boat has a mooring and does not need to drop an anchor, this system is obviously less chaotic than the Med-moor, both on arrival and departure.

If your boat pulls hard to port when you reverse, line it up at an angle as shown in position A in Figure 12-13. By the time you reach position B, the boat has some momentum in reverse and you are lined up with the slip and can reduce power. With steady, low rpms the boat will back in a straight line. Problems can occur if you *jockey* the boat—race the motor in forward, reverse, forward, and reverse again. With each jolt of power, the stern kicks out or in—so take it slow.

Position a crew member on the bow with a boat hook to snare the bow line attached to the mooring, or to pass your own line through an eye in the mooring buoy. Then bring the line back to the boat so you can ease back as you wish. There will also be a messenger line that leads from the mooring to the quay. As the bow crew is picking up the mooring, another crew member in the stern should pick up the messenger line and help guide the boat backward.

You might find there is no mooring buoy, just a messenger from the bow mooring line to shore. When you are almost docked, have someone snag the messenger line with a boat hook and follow it to the mooring line, then secure it to your bow. The messenger line can

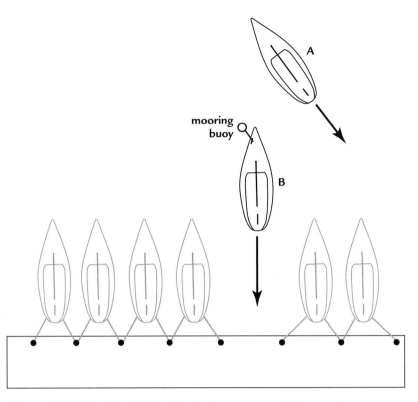

Figure 12-13. Backing in to a dock when prop walks to port

be messy with seaweed and growth. You may want to let the line run over the boat hook out over the side of the boat, rather than bring it aboard, until you get it to the bow.

Whether you Med-moor or pick up a preset mooring to back in, always have plenty of fenders on both sides of the boat and reposition these for maximum protection after you are tied up and settled down. Since the position of your boat relative to those alongside depends on the length of your plank to shore, there isn't much you can do about your spreaders' proximity to another sailboat's spreaders. However, you'll be pretty tight against the other hulls and won't move much and in all the cruising we've done overseas, we've never had issues with spreaders touching. This is far more common when sailboats *raft up* (tie up alongside each other) from a mooring or an open anchorage.

SHUTTING DOWN

Whether you are docking, anchoring, or picking up a mooring, you always follow the same procedure when shutting down your engine. Put the engine in neutral at idle speed and pull the engine cut-off lever out hard. Hold it out until the engine quits and the engine alarms go on, then be sure to push it back in and turn off the key to stop the alarms. If you push the cut-off lever in before the engine alarms go on, the engine might start again. Though loud, be thankful that your alarms are working. Switching off the key cuts off the alarms. If you forget to push the cut-off lever back in, the next time you turn the key to start the engine, the alarms will sound and the engine will crank over but won't start until the lever is in.

Some sailors like to charge their batteries before shutting down for the night, but the noise of a running engine and the smell of exhaust can disturb an otherwise beautiful sunset; so you may want to charge batteries while you are out powering or motorsailing. On long passages, you should run your engine an hour or so each day to keep your refrigeration cool and house batteries up.

TEST YOURSELF

Returning to the Dock
Test your knowledge of docking by answering the questions below.

1. What is the proper approach when the wind is parallel to the dock?
2. What is the proper approach when the wind is perpendicular to the dock?
3. What do spring lines do after securing the boat?
4. How is a midship spring line used during docking?
5. Do you adjust dock lines from the boat or the dock?
6. What does a breast line do?
7. Should you approach a mooring down-current or up-current?
8. Which direction should you face when steering in reverse?
9. Describe the steps you should take when doing a Med-moor.
10. How do you shut down the engine?

13 *ANCHORING YOUR CRUISING BOAT*

Spending the night at anchor can be one of the most peaceful aspects of cruising. A full moon casts a long streak of light across the water, illuminating the masts in the harbor. The quiet lapping of water against your hull lulls you to sleep. Life is good—if you anchored correctly.

Anchoring problems often occur in the middle of the night when you are half-asleep. Poor anchoring procedures and not knowing the characteristics and capability of your anchor and ground tackle can trigger such problems. In this chapter, you'll learn how to avoid these problems so you can enjoy tranquil evenings on the hook.

ANCHORS AND THEIR HOLDING POWER

Five variables affect how well an anchor will hold:

- Type of anchor
- Weight of anchor
- Type and weight of anchor rode, chain and/or rope
- Angle anchor line makes with the bottom
- Type of bottom you are anchoring in

In general, the best bottom for anchoring is hard sand. And the heavier the anchor, the better the holding power. But different types of anchors work best in different conditions.

A *Danforth* anchor holds well in a muddy, rocky bottom, but it holds poorly when the bottom is grassy or covered with seaweed. A *plow* anchor is better at grabbing on a grassy bottom. A *fisherman's* anchor has to be heavy to be effective and is awkward to handle. The *Bruce* anchor and the *spade* anchor, though not as popular in the States as in Europe, are probably the most effective all-around anchors.

Figure 13-1. At anchor in Maine

WHICH ANCHOR SHOULD YOU USE?

- Danforth for muddy, rocky bottom
- Plow in grassy or seaweed-covered bottom
- Fisherman is heavy and awkward to handle, but is an excellent anchor for rocky bottoms
- Bruce and spade anchors are the most effective all-around types

As you learned in Chapter 7, the smaller the angle the anchor line makes with the bottom, the better the holding. If the line is almost vertical, the anchor will lift rather than dig in. If the line is almost horizontal, the anchor will dig in hard. To reduce the angle, let out more scope. While a scope of 5:1 is enough for temporary anchoring, such as when you take a lunch stop, a minimum of 7:1 scope is recommended when you settle in for the night.

New factors come into play when you anchor on a cruising boat. Because the boat has higher topsides, you must consider the distance from the anchor chock to the water when anchoring in tidal waters.

For example, suppose your boat's freeboard measures 4 feet and you are anchoring in an area known for 6-foot tides. At high tide, the water depth will be

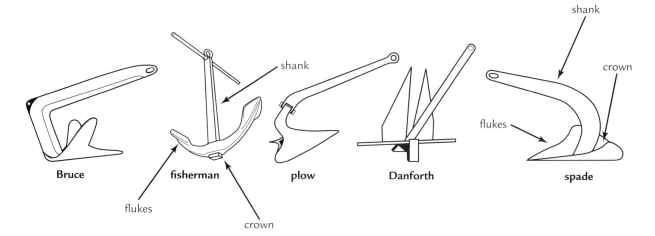

Figure 13-2. Anchors and their parts

TIDE AND FREEBOARD AFFECT SCOPE

- ◆ Determine the water depth
- ◆ Check the tide tables for depth at high tide
- ◆ Add depth at high tide and the boat's freeboard to determine scope

14 feet (8 at low tide). Add your 4 feet of topsides and you will need to let out scope based on 18 feet of depth. A 7:1 scope for low tide without accounting for topsides is 56 feet, less than half of the necessary 126 feet! When the current starts to flow fast you will probably drag with such a short scope.

Most cruising boats have a *depth sounder,* which is very useful to determine water depth when you anchor. But it doesn't tell you how to measure your anchor rode to get the right length. Until you are well aware of how much line the calculated scope represents, you can use colored plastic markers, tape, even nail polish to mark your rode at 20-foot intervals.

Many sailors determine how much line to let out by flaking the anchor line from the anchor well up and down the deck —about one-fourth of the length of the boat (this will give you a flake of 10 feet on a forty-footer)— until you have about 100 feet of line out. When that 100 feet is over the side, eyeball the angle of the line to judge adequate scope as you let more out. Figures 13-3 and 13-4 give you an idea of what inadequate and adequate scope look like. Remember that refraction makes the angle look less acute than it really is.

Another way to increase holding power by reducing the angle the anchor rode makes with the bottom is to drop a weight—a *sentinel*—along the anchor rode. To do this, use a *messenger*—a lighter line attached to the sentinel with a snatch block at one end—and attach the messenger and sentinel onto the anchor line. Lower them about 20 feet. The line from the bow to the weight becomes more vertical than before, while the line between the anchor and the weight lies nearly flat.

If the sentinel rests on the bottom, it reduces your boat's swinging radius and keeps the anchor line from wrapping around the keel. Adding a rode—or length of chain between the anchor and line—also increases holding power, because the chain must be lifted before the anchor is affected.

The pin of the shackle that connects the anchor rode to the anchor can work loose over time or in rough conditions, resulting in the loss of your anchor. Use seizing wire to keep the pin from turning—and always check the shackle before you use the anchor.

Figure 13-3. Inadequate scope

Figure 13-4. Adequate scope

WHERE TO ANCHOR

When you are at anchor, the boat moves as wind, current, and other boats come and go. But if set right, the anchor will remain stationary while your boat pivots (swings) on a radius from the anchor. Boats of the same type swing about the same way. A deep-keeled sailboat lines up more with the current while a shallow-draft powerboat with a high superstructure lines up more with the wind. As you sail near a harbor you might see sailboats pointing in one direction and powerboats in another. In a crowded anchorage try to drop your anchor slightly aft of another boat with similar characteristics, so when you swing—as long as you both have comparable scope—you won't touch.

If you pick a spot behind another boat, drop your anchor slightly aft and to one side of its stern to allow room to get your anchor up easily when you want to leave should you find that boat dead ahead the next morning. If you find your anchor directly under another boat, power up very close to that boat, take in all the slack in the anchor line, and reverse your engine. Since the anchor line is almost vertical, scope is minimal and the anchor easily drags out.

ANCHORING CHECKLIST

- Make sure scope is at least 7:1 when tide is high and freeboard is added
- Use the right anchor for the bottom conditions
- Anchor line angle off the bow should not look steep
- Consider dropping a sentinel on your anchor line or adding chain for extra holding power
- Use seizing wire to keep the pin in the anchor shackle from backing out

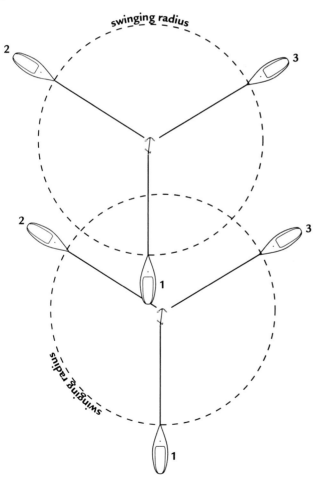

Figure 13-5. Drop anchor slightly aft and to one side of neighboring boats to allow for swing.

A 360° anchor light is required unless you are anchoring in a *special anchorage* area designated by the Coast Guard and stated on charts. Check your chart and, if a light is required, turn it on or place a portable one on your bow about six feet above the bow fitting.

In very protected waters with only a light breeze on a hot summer's night, consider anchoring from the stern. With your stern headed into the wind, the light breeze can come down the companionway and any aft-opening hatches to cool off your sleeping area. The best way to accomplish this is to anchor the normal way from the bow. Then snap a snatch block over the anchor line with a line through a turning block on the stern and back to a jibsheet winch. Pull on this line to bring the anchor line to the stern outside all the standing rigging and lifelines.

The last thing you want in the dark during a squall is to try to detach an anchor line from the stern and reattach it to the bow, so don't uncleat the line on the bow. After the boat has been turned around with the stern toward the wind, cleat it again at the stern. If an unexpected squall comes through in the middle of the night, all you have to do is uncleat the stern, ease the snatch block line, and the bow will swing back into the wind.

SETTING YOUR ANCHOR

As you approach the anchorage, have your anchor ready on deck. If the anchor line is stowed in the *forepeak*—a locker under the deck at the bow—have enough line out on deck so the anchor will reach the bottom without having to pull more line out. If you are towing a dinghy, snub it in close to your stern or alongside the hull so the painter can't get under the boat and the propeller. Keep the dinghy on the side opposite your exhaust, so sooty water doesn't spit into the dinghy as you maneuver under power.

You should have carefully stowed the anchor line before setting out, to avoid tangles in an area that's hard to reach when you next need the line. Make sure the bitter end is tied off—either to a cleat or ring in the forepeak or on deck—before the anchor is put over the side. Don't throw the anchor. After the boat has come to a complete stop, lower it into the water gently until some of the weight is reduced by water pressure; then let go.

After the anchor is down, be patient. Let the wind blow the boat downwind and settle back on its own. Gunning the engine in reverse not only makes it difficult and dangerous for the crew in the bow letting out line: the anchor can also start to drag before enough

line has been paid out. Ease out line as the boat drifts backward. When all the line you wanted is out, snub it around a cleat to allow the momentum of the boat to set the anchor.

Sometimes wind tends to blow the bow way off to leeward—so far that the stern ends upwind of the bow. In this case, power forward downwind to set the anchor, but be careful not to run over the anchor line and wrap it in your prop. When enough scope is out, put the engine in neutral. As the anchor sets, the bow will turn toward the anchor upwind. Now, either leave the engine in neutral and let the wind blow your stern around or use the engine in reverse.

As you drop back, the crew member in the bow should apply gradually increasing pressure on the anchor line by looping it around a cleat. When everyone feels the anchor is set, secure the line, and then reverse the engine to test it. The method used to tell if you are dragging on a small boat (mentioned in Chapter 7) is the same as that used on a cruising boat. Grasp the line beyond the bow and if you feel vibration, the anchor is not set. If it becomes obvious that you are ending up too close to another boat that was there first, raise your anchor and try again.

Take compass bearings on nearby landmarks or lights as a safety check before you relax or go for a swim. When you take bearings again later on, this might help you determine whether or not your anchor has dragged.

However, there are three caveats to this method that show how taking bearings can have limited value. If the landmark is nearby, normal swinging at anchor will radically change the bearing; you may think you are dragging when you are not. If the landmark is far away, you have to drag a long distance before the bearing changes. If visibility deteriorates between the time you anchor and the next check, you might not be able to see the landmark. Sometimes it's better to check your relative position to other boats or moorings in the harbor, if there are any.

If the bottom is rocky, before putting the anchor over the side you may wish to attach a *tripline*—a light line attached to the anchor's *crown* (where the arms are joined to the shank). This allows you to pull the anchor out backward if it becomes snagged. Attach a small buoy to the tripline. The buoy will float directly above the submerged anchor, giving you a mark to head for in order to get the boat right over the anchor before raising it.

WHEN TWO ANCHORS ARE BETTER

Limited room and current changes might be good reasons to consider setting a second anchor. If you are in a small or crowded anchorage, you may want to set out two anchors at 45° angles off the bow to reduce the distance your boat can swing. Although using two anchors does not add much holding power, if one anchor gets loose the second will probably keep you from dragging.

If you are anchored with a single Danforth anchor and the current changes, the anchor could flip over. If the bottom is grassy or a stone becomes wedged between the shank and a fluke, the anchor might not dig in again. With two anchors out at approximately 45° off both sides of the bow, the greatest angle either one can rotate on the bottom is 90°—even if the wind swings 180°. When set, each anchor will rotate rather than pull out.

Figure 13-6. Prepping anchors

However, you don't get double the holding power with two anchors. To compare holding power, take the square of the weight of the anchor, or of the two anchors combined. For example, a 12-pound anchor's holding power is 144. An 8-pound anchor, squared, is 64. Two 8-pound anchors give you a holding power of 128, which is lower than that of a single 12-pound anchor. So the reason for using two anchors versus one heavier one is based on how much swing you can tolerate at anchor.

The best way to set two anchors across the wind is relatively simple. First, measure out the rode you will need for both anchors and leave them flaked on the starboard and port sides of your deck near the bow. The bitter ends should be securely cleated and the anchors ready to be lowered over the bow. Under power, choose where you want to drop your first anchor (see A in Figure 13-7). With the wind on your beam, start

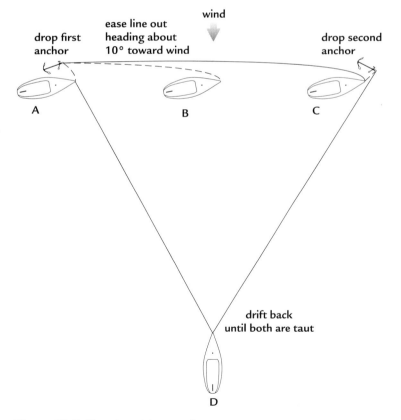

Figure 13-7. How to set two anchors

THREE WAYS TO SET TWO ANCHORS

1. Drop the first anchor; power across wind while paying out anchor line on the windward side of boat, until the end of the line is reached; drop second anchor with same amount of anchor rode and drift back.
2. Drop the first anchor and drift back to set it; keep the rode tight as you power to a position abeam of the first anchor and drop the second anchor.
3. After the first anchor is set, take the second anchor out in dinghy with the bitter end attached to bow of boat; have a crew member pay the line out from the cruising boat until the drop point is reached.

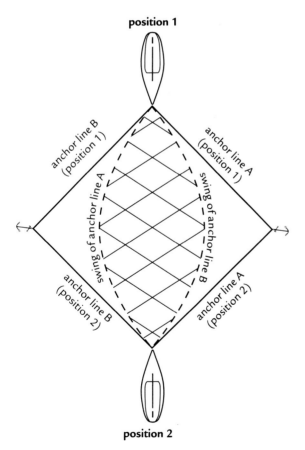

Figure 13-8. Total swing area (crosshatched) with two anchors

paying out the first anchor (B) while powering at about 10° closer to the wind. Since the wind is roughly abeam, it will push you to leeward as you power across it, so you need to steer slightly higher. When the end of the first anchor line is reached (C), put your engine in neutral, drop the second anchor and pay out its line. The boat will drift back and end up solidly anchored by the two anchors, able to absorb all sorts of wind and current changes without excessive swinging (D).

A second way to double anchor is to drop the first, then drift back and set it as if it were the only anchor. Then keep the line tight as you power to a position abeam equally upwind of that anchor, drop the second, and fall back.

A third way to set two anchors is to get the first one down as you normally would. Then, take a second anchor attached to the bow of your cruising boat out in a dinghy and drop it when you reach the right distance and angle from your boat. Unless you are trying to do this alone, leave the bulk of the anchor line on the cruising boat. It is far easier for the person in the dinghy to carry just the anchor while another crew member feeds the anchor line out from the bow of the sailboat.

ANCHORING IN DEEP WATER

When anchoring in areas where the water is very deep, like the Society Islands of Tahiti, a combination of chain and nylon line works quite well. An anchor rode combining 60 feet of chain and 300 feet of nylon line seems to be a good answer for anchoring in 70 to 90 feet of water every night. The chain increases holding power and resists the abrasion of coral heads, and the rope reduces the weight of the whole arrangement.

Your boat should have a *windlass*, a piece of equipment that will make it easier on you and your crew when you start sailing cruising boats over 30 feet in deep-water anchorage areas (especially when you are using chain). The windlass is an electric winch mounted in the anchor locker under the deck in the bow as is the case in Figure 13-9. Most newer boats house the windlass under the deck, not on it, to reduce clutter and for safety reasons (lines can catch around it, toes can get bruised). A foot button on deck near the windlass allows you to activate the windlass as you *weigh anchor*—bring the anchor up. The windlass has a brake, which is used to release the chain when you lower the anchor, so make sure the brake is tight before you get ready to raise the anchor. After the rope section of the rode comes up and chain reaches the windlass, pause to switch from the rope drum to the chain drum if necessary.

With the 60/300 combination described above, you'll be using all chain when you anchor in shallow water. As the wind increases and you add scope, you gain the cushioning advantages of stretchy line. You should also have a smaller anchor aboard with all-line rode; this is good for lunch stops in a protected area where a mud or sand bottom won't snare or chafe the line.

There are other places, such as Turkey and parts of the Caribbean, where the bottom goes out from the shore at a shallow gradient for a few hundred feet and then drops off steeply to a depth of 100 to 150 feet. In an area like this, anchor in the shallower water and then take a line from your stern ashore to a tree or rock. In some places rings are even provided for this purpose (see Figure 13-10). Floating lines are much easier to use for this and are less likely to get wrapped around the prop. If the anchor drags at all, it will drag into shallower water and increase the holding power. Without a

Figure 13-9. Button under crew's right foot activates the windlass

Figure 13-10. Tie the stern to a tree, rock, or ring when depth drops sharply

line ashore, the anchor can drag toward the deep water; in the middle of the night, you might find you are drifting around in deep water with the anchor dangling off the bow.

One other way to increase holding power is to *back an anchor*—put two anchors in line with a short piece of chain connecting them. This arrangement is rarely used; but if you expect a storm and don't have two long anchor rodes, you can tie two short rodes together into a long one and back the anchors. This arrangement holds far better than two anchors on two short rodes. Even if one pulls out, the other remains set.

SPECIAL CIRCUMSTANCES

On one of our flotilla cruises in Tahiti, our six boats anchored close together near some reefs. In the middle of the night, we woke up to find we were bumping against the bow of a companion boat. In driving rain with near-zero visibility, our impulse was to immediately get the anchor up and move to another spot, but this would not have been prudent.

First, since the wind direction had completely reversed, we started the engine and took up enough scope to stop bumping, but held off getting underway until we plotted a safe course. We couldn't head in the direction we had previously been pointing, or we would end up on a reef. So we plotted a course that would take us back to a safe area of the harbor, figuring out how many minutes we would need to power in that direction to get there. (You will learn about time and distance in Chapter 16.) When you are disoriented, sleepy, and have a problem to face, try not to do anything rash. Take the time to plot a safe course, decide on how many minutes to run that course, turn on your running lights, and trust your compass—the best friend you have in this sort of situation.

On another flotilla cruise—this time in the British Virgin Islands- -we headed into the harbor on Jost Van Dyke in the late afternoon. The anchorage was already crowded and the wind was blowing onshore. We rounded the sterns of the anchored boats and headed out between them to drop our hook. It was clear that we would be unable to drop the anchor and drift backward without hitting one of the boats on either side, because we couldn't track in a straight line until we had enough scope out for the anchor to bite. We therefore used a system that is rarely called for; but under special circumstances, it really works.

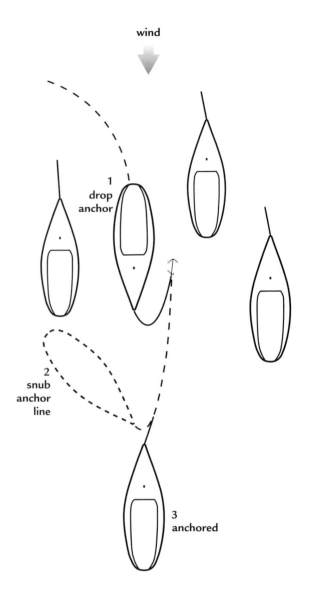

Figure 13-11. Anchoring in tight quarters

We went upwind of the fleet, then powered straight downwind through the fleet and dropped the anchor over our bow between two of the anchored boats. When there was enough scope out to position us behind the other anchored boats, but not too close to shore, we snubbed the anchor line. The anchor grabbed and spun us around 180°—right in the spot we wanted to be for the night. There was a lot of yelling and pointing from the other boats as we executed this plan, and a sudden hush in the harbor when we spun around.

The crucial part of this maneuver is to put the engine in neutral as you drop the anchor and pay out the

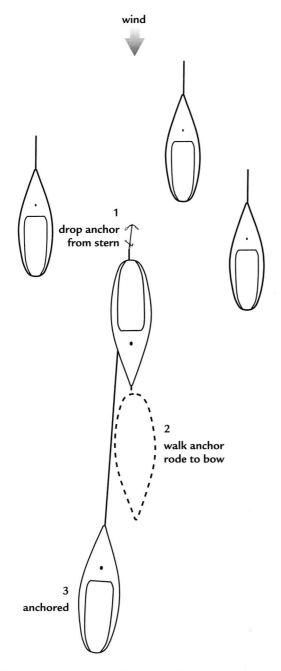

wind

1
drop anchor
from stern

2
walk anchor
rode to bow

3
anchored

Figure 13-12. Anchor by stern, then cleat the anchor rode to the bow

line fast, so it can't get caught around the prop. The bitter end must be cleated, and the anchor line must be flaked on deck so it can stream out quickly without snagging. You must be powering at a good clip when you drop the anchor, so you will continue in a straight line when you put the engine in neutral.

If you are concerned about dropping the anchor from your bow because you might foul your prop, take your anchor and anchor line to the stern. Power slowly downwind and drop the anchor where you want to place it. You will have complete control, able to power between other closely anchored boats. Since you don't have to put your engine in neutral, you can power more slowly, which makes it easier and safer to pay out scope. When you reach your desired location, snub and cleat as before. When securely anchored, take the end of the anchor line up to the bow—outside all stanchions and shrouds—cleat it, then release the line at the stern. Though this method takes more effort and preparation, it is surer and safer in a crowded anchorage.

HOW TO GET GOING AGAIN

To raise the anchor, start the engine and motor toward it. If you are steering, you won't be able to see where the anchor line is; ask a crew member to stand on the bow and point toward the direction of the line, as someone else gathers it in. Voice communication may be lost in the noise of the engine, so hand signals are important. The signals used are: point to port or starboard to indicate direction to turn bow toward anchor; raise a fist in air to tell the person steering to go into neutral and come to a stop; push palm back toward cockpit for reverse gear; point or pulse hand forward for forward gear.

If you are gathering the rode (line or chain) aboard the bow, retrieve the anchor rode by hand or with a windlass until it is vertical. Signal the person on the helm to put the engine in neutral so you can secure the rode around a cleat. At this point, the forward momentum of the boat will break the anchor out. As the anchor comes up from a vertical position, the engine should be in neutral and the boat should be at a complete stop. If the boat is still moving forward, the anchor can bang against the bow and put dings in your hull.

Figure 13-13. Use hand signals when raising the anchor

If the anchor doesn't break free with the boat's forward momentum, cleat the line and signal the person steering to put the engine in forward gear. You can then attempt to break the anchor out as the boat throttles over it. If at first you don't succeed, try different angles.

If you are anchored in swells, when the bow goes down in a trough, take up slack in the anchor line and snub it. As the bow rises on the next wave, the boat's buoyancy may break the anchor free. The slack may have to be taken in on a series of waves before the line is vertical enough for this maneuver to work. If the anchor still won't budge and you don't have a windlass, lead the anchor line back to a jibsheet winch and try to winch it up.

Failing this, don your mask and flippers to look for a solution—unless the water is just too cold for swimming. If, after close inspection, you find the anchor line is snagged on a rock, debris, or a coral head, ease out 60 feet and power with the helm hard over, pointing your bow away from the anchor. The boat will circle around the snag with a constant outward pull on the line (keep-

ing the line from wrapping around the keel). To reverse the direction of rotation, reverse the engine until the boat and anchor are in line, turn the wheel to put the bow to the other side of the anchor, then power forward with the wheel hard over. For counterclockwise circling, put the helm hard to starboard in forward gear. For clockwise circling, put the helm hard to port.

This maneuver should clear the line, if you can see which way it is wrapped. If you can't see, circle in both directions. If you can't feel any give or loosening in one direction after two or three circles, go four to six circles in the opposite direction. The nice thing about this method is that you are putting great outward pressure on the line with the boat almost parallel to it, pulling every degree of the circle rather than just a few angles.

If your anchor has caught on the anchor line of another boat, a simple and safe procedure is pictured in Figure 13-15. Cleat about 10 feet of spare line to the bow, bring your anchor up within reach (2), and pass the free end of that spare line under the other anchor's line and cleat it too (3). Lower your anchor to unsnag the

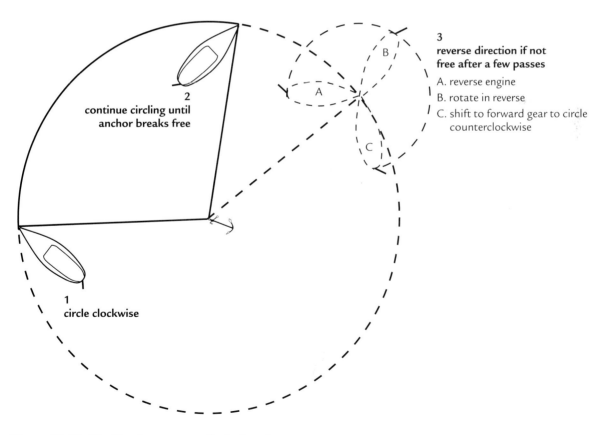

Figure 13-14. Circling to unwrap a fouled anchor

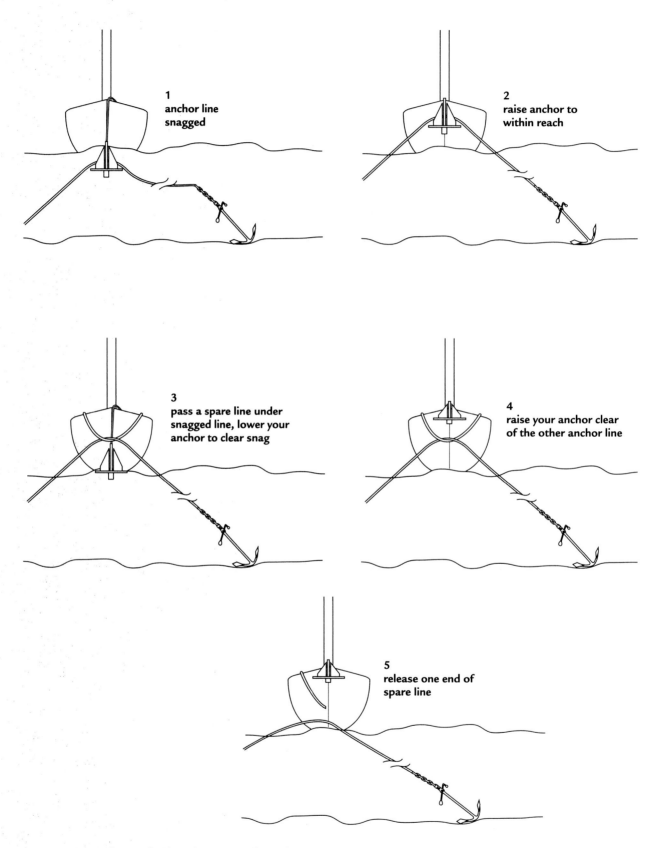

Figure 13-15. What to do if you've snagged another boat's anchor

other anchor's line, then bring your anchor all the way up (4). Uncleat one end of your spare line, and let the other anchor line drop (5).

During the night, as wind and current change, the boat might do 360° turns. If you have two anchors set, both lines could end up wrapped around each other; when you try to pull them apart on deck, the wrap tightens as you move down the lines. Instead, work on one line. As you pull it in make big loops on the other line and then drop those loops down the tight line (see Figure 13-16). This makes it easy to get the second anchor line up, after the first one is raised.

The same vagaries of wind and tide in the middle of the night may wrap your single anchor line around your keel. When you attempt to leave the next morning, you find the boat is anchored by the keel—not your bow. To solve this, turn your engine on but keep it in neutral; then tie a fender or floating

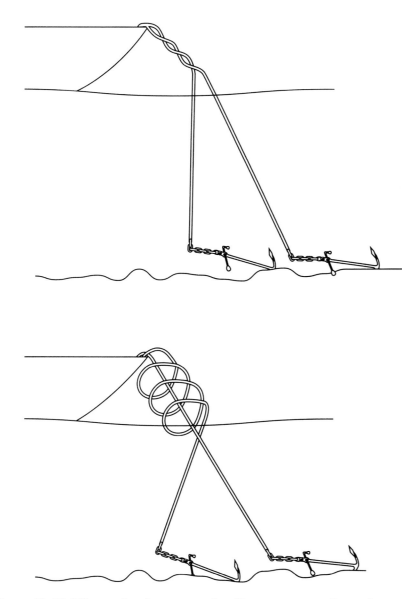

Figure 13-16. What to do when two anchor lines are wrapped together

Figure 13-17. Weighing the anchor without a windlass

cushion to the end of the anchor line and drop the whole thing over the side. Send someone in the water to loosen the wraps around the keel so the anchor line can drop off the keel. As you drift free, pick up the crew in the water and then pick up the fender and line under power. Be sure the anchor line is well secured to the fender or cushion. If you use a bowline, back it up with a couple of half hitches: bowlines can, and do, untie by themselves when floating around in water. Of course, don't put the engine in gear until the swimmer is back aboard the boat.

Some sailors raise their mainsail before raising their anchor. If you have a dead engine, this is necessary. Otherwise, don't do it. Why? Imagine that your mainsail is up and your anchor is not coming off the bottom as you power forward. You snub the anchor when the line is vertical and then power forward to break the anchor out. The anchor, however, sticks; but with the sail up, the boat pivots across the wind or even downwind. The mainsail is now full and you may be heading at an anchored boat nearby when the anchor suddenly releases. In this moment of truth, you realize it is better to get the anchor up and stowed under power first, with no sails set, and then motor to open water to raise the mainsail!

If you are sailing on a medium- to large-size cruising boat and don't have a windlass (or it breaks), it may take two of you to get the anchor up. While one crew member overhauls the rope or chain by hand, the other takes up the slack and keeps the rode tight around a cleat.

When the anchor eventually breaks the surface, clean the mud off before bringing it aboard. Then make sure it is well lashed down on deck before setting sail.

TEST YOURSELF

Anchoring
How well versed are you in anchoring technique? To test your knowledge, answer the questions below.

1. How do you unhook your anchor if you discover it is snagged on another boat's anchor?
2. What is a special anchorage; how do you find one; what are the rules?
3. Which has better holding power: a single 10-pound anchor or two 6-pound anchors?
4. How much scope is considered acceptable?
5. Describe two methods of setting two anchors.
6. How can you tell if your anchor is dragging?
7. Why shouldn't you raise your main before you get your anchor up?

TECHNIQUES FOR SUCCESSFUL CRUISING

14 SAIL TRIM FOR CRUISING

N ow it's time to take a closer look at the set of your sails and how to maximize your cruising boat's performance. The principles you covered in the learn-to-sail section on the points of sail (Chapter 3), how wind powers your sails, and how to read the wind (Chapter 4) apply to cruising boats too. A quick review of those chapters is a good refresher here. The skills you learned for a smaller boat can be transferred easily to a larger boat. Two main differences affect how you handle a larger boat: larger and more powerful sails—particularly genoas—and a heavier hull that's not as responsive to course changes.

HOW TO STEER COMFORTABLY

Even the largest racing boats have telltales on their sails to read and adjust for wind flow. On cruising boats, telltales on your jib are a terrific aid when steering to windward or on a reach. Most sailors use brightly colored strips (about eight inches long) that you can buy in marine stores.

Telltales should be attached (usually taped) with equal lengths on both sides of the sail. Attach these strips along the luff of your genoa or jib at three levels; make sure you can see the lower telltales when you are steering. For a 30- to 40-foot cruising boat, appropriate levels are one-quarter, one-half, and three-quarters of the way up the luff, 8 to 12 inches back from the headstay.

Reading telltales on a cruising boat is the same as reading them on a small boat. If the windward telltales flutter, you are sailing too high or the sail is eased too far. If the leeward telltales flutter, you are sailing too low or the sail is trimmed too flat. If the upper windward telltales flutter before the lower windward telltales flutter, then your jib lead is too far aft. If the lower windward telltales flutter before the upper telltales flutter, the jib lead is too far forward. It's as simple as that.

Luff tension is also important. When sailing close-hauled in moderate conditions you want a tight luff on both the main and genoa, with your sails flat and the draft forward. To achieve this on the main, tighten the luff with the downhaul and cunningham. To tighten the luff on a roller-furled genoa, you must tighten the halyard. Notice how flat the sails are on the racing boat *Condor*, shown in Figure 14-1, as she smokes to windward. The telltales in the window on the genoa are streaming aft perfectly.

Figure 14-1. The telltales on *Condor*'s genoa window are streaming aft.

Figure 14-2. Feeling comfortable and sailing "in the groove"

On a reach or run, a loose mainsail luff and full sails with the draft well aft are desired. In this case you should ease the main's downhaul and cunningham.

Sometimes the transition from tiller to wheel takes a little practice before you settle down and feel like you are "in the groove." It is easy to *oversteer*—turn the wheel too far and too quickly. Cruising boats are so much heavier than daysailers, and they are slower to react to changes in direction. So when you correct by steering back the other way, you may go too far again. If you look back at your wake, you begin to see a series of curves—not a straight line.

Another tip for getting the feel of steering a bigger boat is to hold the wheel lightly. Let it move naturally and correct gently as the bow goes off, as it might if you hit a wave. Place a marker on the center of your wheel to tell you when the rudder is directly in line with the keel. When you change course, this will help you get back on track when you settle down on a new tack. Practice moving the wheel to starboard or port a lot, and then try moving it a little in both directions (when no other boats are around, of course). See how far the boat turns and whether or not it keeps turning when you change direction again.

When you are cruising you want to look good. Speed may not be that important, but good seamanship is. So always try to keep a tight luff upwind, particularly on your jib. Scallops along the forestay or large wrinkles working aft from the luff not only look bad: they also disrupt airflow over the jib and reduce your sail's efficiency. To correct this, you may have to tighten the halyard. With a roller-furling sail, however, this is not a quick and easy adjustment. Happily, most sails cut for new cruising boats look pretty good when set properly.

WHEN WIND VELOCITY CHANGES

Take the time now to review the apparent wind diagram (Figure 4-24 on page 61). Note what happens to the apparent wind if the true wind suddenly dies. Boat speed remains constant while the wind velocity lowers to 6 knots, causing apparent wind to go forward. One way to remember this is to imagine the wind dying completely—as if someone had switched off a giant fan. In the absence of any wind, the only breeze you feel is that produced by the forward motion of the boat, coming from dead ahead and flowing toward you. So any reduction in true wind velocity must bring the apparent wind forward.

This happens quite often on light-air days, particularly to large cruising boats that have a great deal of momentum. The sails start luffing and it seems as if you are sailing too high or too close to the wind. The boat may actually be traveling through a light spot, a *hole* in the wind. To make your next move, you must decide if you are in a valid

---

INSTRUCTOR TIP

"Use the jibstay like a rifle sight. Line up on an object in the distance and hold it steady in your 'sights.'"

CLIFF BARE,
CRUISING INSTRUCTOR,
ST. PETERSBURG, FL

wind shift (a header) or just a hole. Head off 10° and if the sails are still luffing badly, you are probably in a hole. If it is a header, then head off to fill the sails. If you are in a hole and you head off, you will kill what little speed you have. In this case, you should shoot through the light spot with whatever momentum you have and pick up the breeze on the other side.

There are other cases where wind speed remains constant but boat speed varies. If the boat starts surfing down the face of a wave, the apparent wind goes forward. Sometimes, when a boat is sailing downwind with a *spinnaker*, the apparent wind goes so far forward it flattens the spinnaker back against the mast and rigging! When a sailboat slows down suddenly for

WHEN SAILS LUFF ON A LIGHT-AIR DAY

- ◆ Look for puffs ahead
- ◆ If you are in a header, head off to fill sails
- ◆ If you are in a hole, shoot through it

WHAT'S A SPINNAKER?

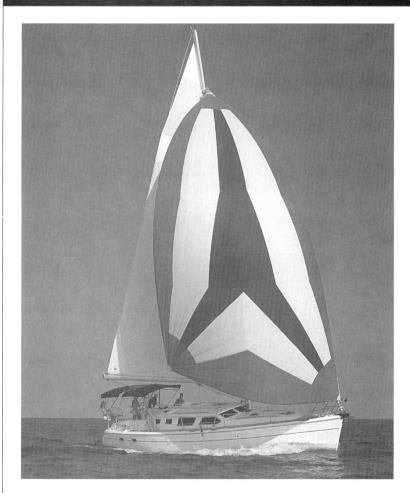

Spinnakers are large, usually colorful, balloon-shaped sails that are used on all sized boats for greater speed downwind. They may be symmetrical or asymmetrical, but require a pole to hold the tack out and expose the full sail to the wind. Many cruising boats carry a *gennaker* for broad reaching as in the photo. The gennaker, a light deep-draft sail made of nylon, does not need a pole. Instead, a *pendant*, which places the whole sail higher off the deck, is sewn to the tack and attached to a shackle at the bow.

CAUSE AND EFFECT OF APPARENT WIND CHANGES

- ◆ Wind dies, feels like a header
- ◆ Wind increases, feels like a lift
- ◆ Boat speed dies, feels like a lift
- ◆ Boat speed increases, feels like a header
- ◆ Boat turns to leeward, feels like a header
- ◆ Boat turns to windward, feels like a lift

some reason, the apparent wind comes aft and its velocity increases. As the wind velocity doubles, the pressure on the sails and rigging quadruples.

When a boat runs hard aground at high speed, it can be dismasted. This is because the rig and sails have a tendency to keep on going—even though the hull has stopped. But another important reason is that the apparent wind pressure on the sails has increased suddenly. So always remember that whenever there is a change in boat speed or direction, or wind velocity or its direction, there must also be a change in the apparent wind. Be alert, and either change course or ask a crew member to trim or ease the sails.

WHY SAIL SHAPE IS IMPORTANT

Poor sail shape and trim can increase heeling, which is undesirable for a number of reasons. When a boat heels, the bow digs in and the center of effort of the sails falls outboard rather than directly over the hull's center of lateral resistance (as discussed in Chapter 5). This causes strong weather helm, and the boat has a tendency to round up into the wind when you take your hands off the wheel. You also feel great pressure on the helm as you try to keep the boat sailing straight. This occurs because the rudder is at an angle, creating drag and slowing the boat down.

In Figure 14-3, the boat on the left is making more leeway—which causes it to slow down. When a boat is heeled over, the sails do not expose as much area to the wind; and with less *lateral plane*, the keel is less effective in preventing leeway, so the boat slips sideways more. This is not an efficient way to sail. When the rail buries in the water, various fittings—such as the toe rail, stanchions, turnbuckles, and sheets—create turbulence and increase drag, causing the boat to slow down even more.

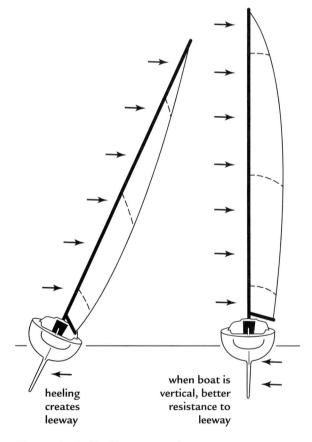

heeling creates leeway

when boat is vertical, better resistance to leeway

Figure 14-3. Heeling creates leeway

Figure 14-4. "On your ear"—sailing with the rail in the water

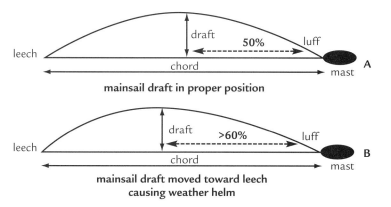

Figure 14-5. Draft position is expressed as a percentage of the chord length aft of the luff.

For many sailors, it is decidedly less comfortable to be "on your ear" all the time, particularly if you are trying to relax or cook up a meal.

Although you can reduce heeling by reefing (discussed in Chapter 6), there may be other reasons why you are heeling too much. Before you reef, some very simple things can be done to improve sail shape. These adjustments can reduce weather helm and heeling and improve boat speed and comfort. First, ease the traveler to leeward. This spills air out of the lower part of the mainsail. If this isn't enough, ease the mainsheet to allow the top of the sail to spill air.

Most cruising sailors don't replace sails as often as competitive sailors do. Well-used sails may not look tired, but they tend to lose shape before you realize they are no longer efficient. When Dacron sails get old, the draft moves aft toward the leech as the material stretches. This is also common in new Dacron sails as wind strength freshens.

Draft position—the location of the maximum depth of the sail at any given cross section—is usually expressed as a percentage of the *chord* length aft of the luff (see A in Figure 14-5). The normal position of the draft in a mainsail is 50 to 55 percent aft from the luff, and 30 to 35 percent aft for a jib.

When the draft moves farther aft toward the leech, as in B in the diagram, battens tend to cock to windward, and the resulting shape forces airflow to exit to windward on the weather side and separate into turbulence on the lee side. This shape stalls airflow and creates strong weather helm and a great deal of heeling. To counteract movement of draft aft in a sail, stretch the luff of the sail tight by increasing halyard or cunningham tension.

MAINSAIL CONTROL AND SHAPE

Too much mainsheet tension on a light-air day when sailing to windward will give your mainsail a tight leech; this also causes the draft to move aft. A tight leech disrupts airflow, so be careful not to trim the mainsheet too hard. Instead, move the traveler car to windward to bring the boom to the centerline of the boat. This results in less downward pull.

When mains and jibs have been used a few seasons, the leeches stretch and start to flutter. To cure this, tighten the *leech cord* (the line running inside

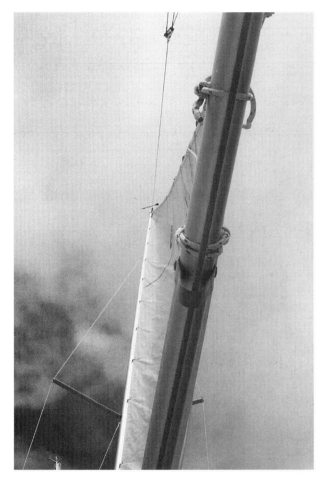

Figure 14-6. An over-trimmed sail (note how battens are cocked to windward)

Figure 14-7. Proper trim

the leech from clew to head) to stop the flutter. This also tightens and cups the leech, however.

On very light days, the weight of the boom can cause the battens to cock to windward and disrupt airflow over the sail even more. To solve this problem, tighten the topping lift to minimize the weight of the boom pulling on the leech of the sail.

In almost any wind condition, you can check if your mainsail is trimmed nicely when sailing to windward by sighting up the mainsail from beneath the boom. The second batten from the head should be parallel to the boom. In Figure 14-6, the sail is over trimmed and the tightened leech and battens are cocked to windward. In Figure 14-7, the mainsheet tension is reduced and the battens start to line up with the boom.

An absence of leech tension, which usually occurs when reaching, is almost as detrimental as too much

—except in heavy winds. The boom is out over the water, the wind force on the sail causes the boom to lift, and the upper part of the sail can actually be luffing even though the bottom part is full of air. This is called *twist* and is usually undesirable, except in a few situations.

Wind on the surface of water is slowed down by friction, which causes the wind at the top of the mast to be of greater velocity than at deck level. This means the top part of the sail is in a continual puff relative to its bottom area. Remember, apparent wind comes aft in a puff. So to keep apparent wind at the same angle to the luff over the full length of the sail, a slight twist at the head may be necessary.

Another exception to the harmful effect of twist occurs in very heavy air. Weight at the top of a mast can cause undesirable heeling, and the upper part of your sail can greatly affect how much your boat will heel. If

Figure 14-8. Racing boats broaching in more than 40 knots of wind

LIGHT-AIR
MAINSAIL TRIM

- Slide the traveler to windward
- Bring the boom to the center of the boat
- Sight up the sail from under the boom
- If battens cock to windward, ease mainsheet until second batten from the top lines up with the boom

MAINSAIL TWIST UPWIND

- Reduces heeling in very heavy air—ease mainsheet out, keep the traveler car in the center of boat
- Detrimental in moderate air—drop the traveler to leeward, tighten the mainsheet and boom vang

TO STOP ROLLING ON A RUN

- Tighten boom vang
- Trim main boom
- Harden up to a reach

you want to reduce heeling, simply reduce the effectiveness of the upper part of the sail by inducing twist. In this case, also ease the mainsheet. As the mainsheet is eased, the battens fall off to leeward and reduce the driving force of the sail.

Under moderate conditions, you want to reduce twist. To do this effectively, drop the traveler car to leeward and tension the mainsheet. This works until the boom passes the end of the traveler. Then the next step is to apply tension to the boom vang. The boom vang reduces twist in the mainsail. When tightened on a reach or run, it pulls the boom down and keeps the leech from falling off to leeward. The net result is that the same angle of attack of the apparent wind to the chord is maintained along the full height of the sail, making the sail a much more effective airfoil.

If you used the boom vang as a preventer, don't forget to remove it when you jibe—particularly in heavy winds. When the wind fills the other side of the mainsail, it tries to force the boom across. If the boom vang is working against this force, something has to give. The boom vang or boom may break; but if neither happens, the boat may *broach* out of control. During a broach, the boat lays over on its side, bringing the keel to a near-horizontal plane. The rudder is out of the water and can't be used to help steer the boat back up into the wind. Until the sails are released, the keel is useless as a counterbalance. Though this is more likely to happen on a racing boat carrying a lot of sail in heavy air, a broach is definitely something you want to avoid.

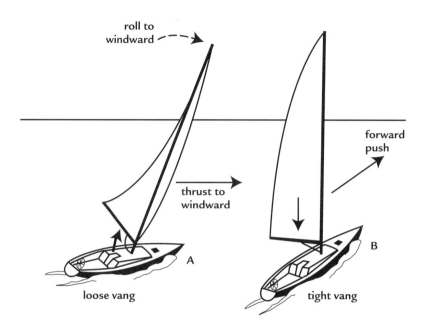

roll to
windward

forward
push

thrust to
windward

A

B

loose vang

tight vang

Figure 14-9. As mast rolls to windward, apparent wind goes forward

Compare the two boats in Figure 14-9. Note how much better the mainsail on boat B looks. By tightening up on the boom vang, the leech tightens and sail shape improves. On a run, lack of vang tension can enhance rolling. Though it is uncomfortable to roll wildly from side to side, this does not necessarily slow down the boat. Rolling is caused in part when the top part of the sail falls off to leeward because the boom is raised up in the air. The head of the mainsail may actually line up with the wind direction and pick up attached airflow, resulting in a drive to windward. Then a domino effect occurs, as the boat rolls from side to side. As the mast rolls to windward the apparent wind goes forward and airflow becomes attached farther down the sail, which adds to windward drive (as shown in A). Each roll makes the situation worse. To cure this, pull down hard on the boom vang to reduce twist at the top of the sail. This causes drive in a more forward direction (B). If rolling persists, trim the boom in a little and harden up to more of a reach.

PROPER GENOA TRIM

Draft in your jib or genoa should be farther forward than draft in your mainsail. A stretched out, baggy jib with the draft well aft will make your boat feel extremely sluggish. You will heel badly and sail slowly because a baggy leech creates drag. The slower a boat sails, the less effective the underwater surfaces are at reducing leeway. This whole scenario is inefficient.

Use strong halyard tension to keep the draft in a forward position. Slide your jib fairleads aft and use less jibsheet tension if the leech is cupped in too tight or the wind is heavy. If you see a lot of *backwind* in the mainsail (the front part of the sail seems to be luffing), the jib's draft is too far aft. This forces the wind to collide with rather than flow past the main as it comes off the genoa. A little backwind is fine; but when the sail burbles to windward

PROPER JIB LEADS

- Tighten halyard to move the draft forward
- If there is too much twist, move leads forward
- If the leech is too cupped, move leads aft

in moderate winds, the shape of the jib and not the mainsail needs work.

As described earlier, twist in the mainsail occurs when the top part of the sail falls off to leeward because of inadequate leech tension. The same problem exists with a jib. But it is the fore-and-aft placement of the jib lead—the block the jibsheet runs through—that determines the amount of twist in a jib.

If the lead is too far aft, the jibsheet pulls along the foot, downward tension on the leech is insufficient, and the top part of the sail tends to luff first. It is helpful to remember that the opening or slot between the jib leech and the body of the mainsail should remain parallel. If you induce twist in the mainsail in heavy weather—to reduce drive in the upper part of the main and thereby reduce heeling—you must also do the same to the jib.

Conversely, in light air, any fullness should be down low in the jib. You can accomplish this by easing the jibsheet, which has the same effect as easing the outhaul on the main along the boom. Easing the jibsheet increases draft by shortening the distance between the tack and the clew; this gives you greater drive in light airs and lumpy seas.

However, there is one detrimental side effect to easing the jibsheet: it frees the leech. As the clew goes out, the angle of the jibsheet is lowered. To regain the proper leech tension using less jibsheet tension, you must move the jib lead forward. Do the same as you fall off on a reach and ease the jib.

CONTROL IN HEAVY AIR

On cruising boats you should always reduce sail area when the wind velocity causes your boat to be overpowered. At this point, you are heeling so much that your speed has decreased and everyone on board is pretty uncomfortable.

You want to reduce sail equally between the main and jib to keep the boat balanced. So reef the main first. If the wind continues to increase and you are still overpowered, change to a smaller jib or roll the jib up partway. If the wind gets heavier, reef the main some more. If you are still not comfortable, roll up the jib or take it down.

When you reduce your genoa's sail area enough to keep the boat well balanced, gusts of wind can't blow the

Figure 14-10. Sailing in heavy weather under genoa alone

STEPS FOR SHORTENING SAIL

- Keep the boat balanced
- Take a reef in the main
- Change to a smaller jib or roll the jib in partway
- Take another reef in the main
- Roll up the jib or take it down
- The jib alone is OK on a reach or run, but not to windward

REEFING THE MAINSAIL

1. Ease the mainsheet
2. Lower the halyard
3. Hook luff grommet on the hook at the gooseneck
4. Tighten the halyard
5. Winch the leech reef line in tight
6. Secure safety line through the leech grommet and around the boom
7. Trim the mainsheet
8. Get comfortable and then tidy up loose sail along foot

bow off to leeward. On some boats, this may mean rigging a smaller jib in place of a cruising genoa—which isn't much fun when the going gets tough. If your boat has roller furling, simply roll the jib up partway. Make sure the furling line is in good condition, because there will be heavy strain on it as you pull in the sail. If you plan to do a lot of cruising on your own boat, an excellent heavy weather sail is a *fore staysail*, which is attached to the middle of the foredeck. Use it instead of the genoa when the wind gets over 30 knots.

On a reach or run, you can take the main down completely and sail with a small or partially rolled-up jib. If you roll the jib up halfway, the middle of the sail becomes very full because there is more sail area to roll up in the middle versus the top and bottom as it is furled. The clew is also affected, and it rises higher in the air as the jib is rolled up. This is fine when reaching in heavy air because there is less chance to scoop water; but doing this also raises the center of effort, which increases heeling. To compensate for these changes, adjust the jibsheet leads aft for the new angle made by the jibsheets when furled.

If you are beating to windward and douse the main completely, you could lose your mast. The mainsail absorbs a lot of shock when the boat pounds through a wave. If your boat hits a wave, the mast can whip forward and then aft. The mainsail, even when reefed, acts as a cushion to reduce that motion.

When you are caught by a surprise squall, the order changes. The genoa on a cruising boat often has much more sail area than the main, so that sail should be lowered or quickly rolled up first. A cruising boat has better stability than a small centerboarder, so there is no need to worry about dipping the main boom if the boat heels excessively. The boat should sail well under main alone. If you are still overpowered, reef the mainsail. Instructions for jiffy reefing, which were covered in Chapter 6, are reviewed below.

Jiffy Reefing

Someday, somewhere you will surely experience a sudden change in weather and you'll need to react quickly and competently. If you practice reefing in light and heavy air when you're out daysailing, cruising in rough weather will just be another day on the water.

INSTRUCTOR TIP

"When reefing the main, take care of the front of the sail completely before working on the leech. Get it down as quickly as possible and worry about tidying up the excess cloth later."
TYLER PIERCE, NORTHERN REGIONAL MANAGER AND INSTRUCTOR-TRAINER

Figure 14-11. Reef the main in bad weather.

Figure 14-12. Heavy weather sailing is a state of mind!

Enjoying the thrill of sailing in heavy weather not only involves your skill: it also takes the right mindset. A good friend of ours was very apprehensive about crossing the Gulf Stream—where the stream of the current running against the wind can kick up large seas—with her husband and son on their first cruise. The following question helped her to deal with her apprehension: "Ask yourself, is it life threatening or merely 'impressive'?" In nearly every situation, the latter is the answer.

Make sure your main halyard is extremely tight after reefing. A tremendous amount of pull on the head of the sail is transmitted along the leech because of mainsheet tension. When the head is near the top of the mast, the halyard pull angle is almost opposite the leech pull angle (see A in Figure 14-13). But when the sail is reefed, most of the leech pull is against the upper slides (B). That's why on a cruising boat, slugs (which go *in* a groove in the track) or slides (which go *over* the track) near the head of a mainsail are usually sewn on

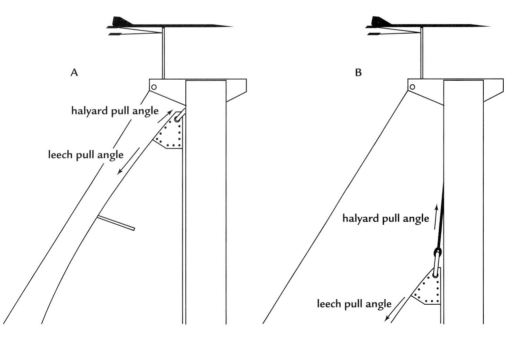

Figure 14-13. Halyard must be tight after reefing

with special care. Very tight halyard tension eases the strain on those slides to prevent them from ripping off—particularly on a beat, which produces the most mainsheet pull on the leech of the sail.

Heaving-To—Taking a Break in Heavy Air

Heaving-to is a versatile maneuver and can be used while sailing a small or large sailboat. You may be motivated by the desire to enjoy a peaceful lunch underway without anchoring; or you may wish to alleviate the pounding of sailing through heavy seas. While racing Olympic-class Solings (27-foot keelboats), we would heave-to for lunch between races as we were far out in deep water, unable to anchor. On one of our flotilla cruises in Belize and another in Greece the fleet had to heave-to for several hours in open water while a strong squall went through, as it was too dangerous to head into the harbor in rolling seas and poor visibility.

Simply put, the process of heaving-to puts the jib and main on opposing tacks, and the result is that the boat stays virtually in one place on a modest angle of heel. Back the jib to windward, forcing the bow to leeward. Then trim the mainsail to the point when the weather helm caused by the main balances the leeward push of the jib. Lash or secure the helm (your tiller or wheel) in a position that keeps neither the main nor the jib from overcoming the other. The boat will sit quietly in one spot, drifting slowly to leeward with no one steering.

TEST YOURSELF

Sail Trim on a Cruising Boat
1. What two factors make sails luff because of an apparent wind shift?
2. Explain draft in a mainsail.
3. Describe twist in a sail.
4. When is twist desirable?
5. How do you stop a boat from rolling on a run?
6. In what order do you shorten sail when caught in a sudden squall?
7. List the steps for reefing a mainsail.
8. What should you do with the genoa in heavy air?
9. Describe how to heave-to.

15 SAFETY AND HEALTH TIPS FOR CRUISING

Cruising is one of the safest lifestyles you can choose, providing pure bliss 90 percent of the time. But, as we saw in the last chapter on sail trim, when wind and seas build up, you and your boat experience a new set of stresses. These stresses can be easily overcome by careful planning and experience. Here's a good example of why it is so important to build strong knowledge and good boat-handling skills before jumping into cruising.

While honeymooning on a 43-foot yacht chartered from The Moorings in the British Virgin Islands, Tyler Pierce and his wife, Erika, met two other couples who were spending their honeymoons cruising too. In a remarkable coincidence, they were all starting out on the same day.

With a tropical depression coming through the islands, the base manager announced at the morning briefing that Tyler was not only from Offshore Sailing School, he was also a good sailor and the others should follow him to The Bight at Norman Island, a well-protected anchorage. Though not exactly what he wanted to hear on his honeymoon, Tyler later helped one of the other boats anchor in The Bight.

During a great week of sailing after the depression blew past, the Pierces ran into the couple they helped several times; but they never saw the other boat. Apparently, the husband on the third boat did not prudently raise his mainsail in the protected harbor. Instead, he waited until they were in rough conditions outside the breakwater, then sent his wife up on deck. He yelled at her because they were having problems with the sail. She yelled, "Take me back!" and left the island the following day. The honeymoon was, quite literally, over.

Tyler points out there are two morals to this story. First, nothing good ever comes of yelling at crew members on a boat. Second, nothing ruins a week in paradise quicker than getting in over your head. "You should work

Figure 15-1. Tyler and Erika Pierce shortly after their honeymoon

to master the key skills through study and practice so you can apply them in any condition you might encounter," he says.

Couples and families who plan to cruise together should strive for a strong, equal skill level. The best scenario is when everyone aboard can sail on par with each other and support one another when difficult conditions occur. Some women in the on-water portion of the Fast Track to Cruising course don't want to be the first to steer. But Mike Huffer, a branch manager, makes it clear at the outset that he expects husbands and wives who plan to cruise together to participate equally. "When choosing the 'skipper' the first day, I always choose a female," he says. "This eliminates apprehension and puts everyone aboard on an equal basis."

When conditions tend toward the other 10 percent of the time when sailing is not sheer bliss, tensions rise. As cruising instructor Barbara Stetson says, "The boat gets a foot shorter every day." When visibility decreases, navigation becomes harder. The boat can suffer problems and breakdowns. You might have a short in the electrical system, ripped sails, a broken boom, or a leak developing. But you are out there and have to cope with whatever Mother Nature dishes out.

"In less than two years I went from novice to taking friends cruising in the British Virgin Islands on 46-foot Moorings [boats] and 47-foot cats. I just purchased my own Beneteau 423 and plan to sail the islands. This is turning into an exciting retirement. I convinced my wife and kids to take Learn to Sail just to go with me and they are now very enthusiastic. Sailing has become a major interest during retirement and filled some of the holes left from leaving a corporate job. I'm a scientist and this fills an interest and need for technology learning, as well as meeting new people." **LARRY HANSEN (58), BONITA SPRINGS, FL**

Sometimes all it takes is motoring to a snug harbor to wait out a squall. Other times you may need to head farther offshore until the wind subsides—because there are obstructions near shore you are unable to see. Here are some safety and health tips to make your onboard life comfortable.

"I have gained enough confidence to expand my experience on my own boat, including crossing Lake Michigan for the first time, sailing at night, and taking a one-week cruise."

JOAN BYL (41), GRAND RAPIDS, MI

HOW TO AVOID BEING SEASICK

Some sailors are prone to seasickness—but they overcome it because the cruising lifestyle is too good to miss. If we haven't been sailing for a while, we often feel a few hours of queasiness on the first day out. But we soon get our sea legs and experience no further discomfort during the cruise. If you hear sailors boast they never get seasick, they no doubt haven't been in extreme conditions—like going through the Gulf Stream with the wind against the current. Happily, most of your cruising will probably be in comfortable conditions, with minimal sea and wind extremes.

If you do get into bad weather, make sure you have at least two people on deck at all times. When the going gets rough, the tough may not get tougher. Even on boats with experienced crew, half of the crew may be seasick and essentially helpless. With an inexperienced crew, there may be only one or two out of six crew members who are not sick (this is difficult for healthy crew members, especially if a storm is prolonged). Not only do you need an adequate number of crew; you also need a nucleus of crew members you can depend on in any sort of blow.

How do you know if you're about to succumb to seasickness? You might start to yawn a lot and feel sleepy. You might be experiencing indigestion and burping. If you or some of your shipmates are showing telltale signs or getting queasy, stay on deck where you can see the horizon and breathe fresh air. Talk to each other. Sing songs. Sip ginger ale, Coke, or Pepsi and chew on

Figure 15-2. Feeling queasy

"We were afraid of being seasick and that we would never learn to handle such a big boat. Our instructor kept us so busy with humor and confidence there was no time to get sick. After two days, the boat was like driving my pick-up truck."

TIM GAPEN (56), WISCONSIN RAPIDS, WI

"I was concerned about getting seasick since I have experienced it before on powerboats while going on scuba diving trips. I had no problems with seasickness on the sailboat."

ROD FARMER (51), HAWTHORN WOODS, IL

saltines or water biscuits. We asked a doctor why Coke or Pepsi helps and were told these beverages contain phosphoric acid, an ingredient in drugs used to control vomiting.

Take turns on the helm. Let the queasy crew member steer first, then rotate every 20 minutes or so. It helps to do something active that requires looking out at the horizon. Steering gives you the feeling and anticipation of what the next movement of the boat will be, which keeps your mind off what just happened. Keep busy on deck—as opposed to just sitting around and thinking about the prospect of getting seasick.

TIPS FOR AVOIDING SEASICKNESS

- Stay on deck and keep busy
- Take turns steering
- Sing songs or breathe deeply
- Look out at the horizon, not down
- Sip ginger ale, Coke, or Pepsi
- Chew saltines or water biscuits
- Don't sit downwind of engine exhaust fumes
- If you go below, stay in the aft half of boat
- Avoid greasy foods and alcohol the night before
- Carry wristbands and other remedies
- If all else fails, lean over the lee side and tickle your throat

Figure 15-3. Keeping busy on deck in heavy air

Stay in fresh air, but don't sit near the engine exhaust if you are motorsailing. If you feel like going below for a nap, lie on your back rather than your stomach—as this seems to keep your "innards" from bouncing around. If you have a choice of berths, stay out of the forward cabin and choose a berth in the center of the boat where there is less pitching motion. If you feel really terrible, ask a crew member to hold on to your belt for support or use a safety harness, tickle your throat over the lee side of the boat, and get rid of it. You will be amazed at how much better you feel.

Among the causes of seasickness, what you eat is high on the list. If you drink too much alcohol the night before sailing, you will be more prone to getting sick. If you eat greasy, hard-to-digest foods, you also increase your chances of getting sick.

There are seasick cures: some are good; some not so good. Seasoned cruising sailors recommend a number of prescription and over-the-counter drugs, some of which are not available in the United States. You can find out more about these drugs in magazines like *Cruising World* and on websites provided by cruising doctors. We particularly like Dr. Alayne Main's www.mainsailing.com/medical.htm, which includes a self-assessment page and the medical kit she and her husband used on a circumnavigation.

Ginger root has been a traditional cure for centuries and may be effective for some people in mild sea conditions. But when we offered ginger root pills to a number of Offshore Sailing School graduates on our Tahiti cruise—and then took them ourselves—we all swore, "Never again!" The passage from Bora Bora to Raiatea was a beat in reasonably brisk winds and steep seas. Burping ginger just made everyone feel worse.

An efficient, drug-free remedy for some sailors is a form of acupressure. Several manufacturers produce a bracelet with a button sewn in. When worn on both wrists with the button positioned at a point that is three fingers from the bend of your wrist between your two tendons, the wristbands reduce queasiness. Motion Ease is an emollient oil that, when dabbed behind the ears, seems to work well in combination with the wristbands.

While we're on the subject of acupressure, you may not think that hiccups are much of a problem; but for some people they can be life-threatening and can land you in a hospital. While cruising, it would be near impossible to get to a hospital, so remember this simple cure just in case you encounter a crewmate who needs help. The acupressure point for hiccups is exactly where the wedding ring is worn, but the treatment must be done on both hands. Press both fingers hard with your thumb and forefinger on the top and bottom of each ring finger until the hiccups stop. We have used this often—even on perfect strangers in restaurants—and it works!

OTHER HEALTH CONDITIONS YOU MIGHT ENCOUNTER

Hypothermia can sneak up on you. On one of our flotilla cruises in the Pacific Northwest a club member insisted on jumping in the water. He didn't last five minutes. When we fished him out he was shivering, weak, and slightly confused. If you encounter someone who seems to be suffering from hypothermia, warm the person slowly. Take off all wet clothing and wrap him or her with dry blankets. Warm liquids also help, but don't administer any alcohol.

Constipation can become an issue on long cruises where you're aboard all the time. Consider carrying a Fleet's enema in your medical kit, along with over-the-counter remedies to keep you regular. Unfamiliar sleeping habits caused by watch systems can throw off normal body functions in some sailors. Rough weather makes using the head so uncomfortable you might forego it for a while. Drink lots of liquids and give it a try every day, particularly the first few days—no matter how rough the conditions.

Sunburn is exacerbated on a boat because of the glare from the water. While cool breezes cover up the sun's intensity, you may be getting a lot more than you bargained for aboard. So cover up the first few days, use a sun lotion with a good sunscreen, and wear a hat and attach it to yourself with a lanyard that has clips at both ends to keep it on. Wear sunglasses to avoid damage to your eyes, again with a strap to keep them on. If possible, choose unbreakable frames with polarizing lenses, which will help you see reefs and contours better when sailing toward the sun.

It is a good idea to have a medical book aboard. Cruising is a great deal like mountaineering in that you have to be self-sufficient. There are no clinics you can run to if someone gets hurt. A good practical book with a lot of crossover to sailing is *Medicine for Mountaineering & Other Wilderness Activities*, edited by Dr. James A.

Wilkerson. This is the bible for travelers who are more than 24 hours away from medical aid.

EQUIPMENT FAILURES CAN CAUSE ACCIDENTS

On a cruising boat, equipment starts to break when forces become great. Anticipate what can break to minimize your chances of being hurt. Before sailing each day and fairly often if on a long cruise, make a tour of the deck of your boat (like a pilot does before taking to the air). Check for chafe on all lines, missing cotter pins, stressed or bent fittings, loose lifelines, and hairline cracks in turnbuckles, shroud fittings, and other areas of stress.

If you are cruising close to home and near marinas, getting replacement parts or help in fixing most problems is fairly easy. Regardless, your boat should carry various spares and tools: spare shackles, tools for tightening or adjusting fittings, duct tape for temporary repairs and covering areas that can chafe or rip sails and lines or harm crew.

Charter companies do a thorough check for the next party when a boat is returned after a cruise. When you start cruising on your own boat, you will occasionally also have to send someone up the mast to make sure all the rigging and fittings aloft are in good shape. Turning blocks are one of the most common areas that fail under strain. Your genoa sheet usually leads aft through a block and then forward to a winch. If the shackle holding the block lets go or breaks, the rig can become a big slingshot with the block as the missile. To avoid getting hit, don't stand forward or in the bight of a turning block. Even if the sheet only pops out of the block, it can trip you up if you are in the bight.

Another weak point is the main boom gooseneck, where tremendous strain occurs in heavy weather when sailing close-hauled. If the gooseneck separates from the boom, it will fly to leeward. Avoid walking forward or aft along the leeward side of the boat in heavy winds.

Throughout this book you'll find advice on how to avoid situations that could put you and your crew in harm's way. The more you sail the more you not only learn to naturally avoid trouble but how to quickly handle adverse situations when they occur.

If you are cruising for extended periods offshore, you should also have proper size wood plugs next to each seacock in case that fitting falls out or is knocked out, leaving a hole.

Dismastings are rare, but long-distance sailors also carry wire cutters, hacksaws and blades, a hammer, and large center punch to remove pins (commonly called drift pins). These are all necessary to cut away rigging if the mast goes over the side and you can't get it completely back aboard. In these very rare situations, safety for the crew is your first concern, but try to salvage as much as you can of the mast, boom, and rigging, and lash it down along one side of the deck if possible. If your sails were up they may be ripped but sometimes you can wrap them with the rigging too. Don't try to sort out the mess until you are in calm waters with calm nerves.

TIPS FOR GOING UP A MAST

Every year, accidents occur when sailors climb the mast or get hoisted up to retrieve a lost halyard or do a routine check of the rigging. The agile sailor who climbs the mast hand over hand and holds on while executing a task often forgets that hands can and do cramp up and involuntarily lose their grip. The only safe way to go up the mast is in a *bosun's chair*. And in rolling conditions, even using a chair can be dangerous if the procedure is not done properly.

If you use a rope halyard, tie it to the chair with a bowline, bypassing the snapshackle. You may have to use a snapshackle if you are going up on a wire halyard. In this case, tie a safety line through the chair rings and the eye of the shackle. For good measure, tape the snapshackle closed so the pin can't open if it catches on something as you go up.

Bring the free end of the main halyard back to a winch with at least three wraps around the drum. While one crew member hauls you up by grinding the winch, another should tail, keeping full tension in the end of the halyard coming off the winch. It is always easier on the crew doing the hoisting if the lightest crew member volunteers to go up the mast. If you are the one in the chair, your job is to help your crew hoist you up by pulling yourself up on the mast or a shroud. Be ever mindful of not losing your grip; if you do, you'll start swinging around the rig like a paddle-ball. It's not a good idea for crew to bounce the halyard when hoisting crew aloft. When the person going up the mast is fully hoisted, cleat the halyard securely or tie it to itself. Do not trust just the self-tailing winch jam or a rope clutch.

Unless it is absolutely necessary, don't go up in rough seas when the mast describes a big arc and it's

Figure 15-4. Crew in a bosun's chair, with safety downhaul attached

tough to hold on. Regardless, always have a downhaul line attached to the bottom of the chair with a crew member feeding out slack in the line as you rise. This keeps you from swinging if you lose your grip on the mast. As an added safety measure, snap a snatch block to the eye of the chair where the halyard is attached, then snap that block over any other halyard that runs all the way up the mast. That halyard, kept tight, acts like a track to keep you close to the mast as you go up. If there is a rope clutch you can use on the hoisting halyard, make sure it was closed for the hoist. Don't choose a halyard that you'll have to disconnect midway up. If no

other halyard is available, you can snap the block over the one that is taking you up; but this is not as desirable.

Remember the old axiom: One hand for the boat and one for yourself! Hold on. If possible, accomplish the task with one hand so you can save yourself with the other if something gives. And one last piece of advice: pack and tie all the tools you need into the bosun's chair *before* you start to go up.

To lower the crew in the bosun's chair when he or she signals they are finished: the crew managing the winch should sit down next to the winch and ease the halyard slowly and steadily, using one hand on the drum as a brake; the crew in the chair should remember to hold on on the way down.

WHAT TO DO IF SOMEONE GOES OVERBOARD

You have already learned what to do if a crew member goes overboard in Chapter 6. Take a few minutes now to review the three most-used ways to pick someone up who goes over the side: the Quick Stop Recovery Method, LifeSling Method, and Quick Turn Recovery Method. The techniques used on a large cruising boat are the same as those used on a small boat. But on a cruising boat, it takes more brute force to bring someone aboard because of the extra freeboard.

A study was done by the U.S. Naval Academy a few years ago to determine the cause of drowning from loss of a crew member over the side. It was determined that the chances of recovery are highest if the crew on board don't lose sight of the person overboard. Previous to the study, the standard sailing procedure was to have one crew member spot the person in the water while the rest of the crew prepared the boat to sail on a reciprocal course (180° from your original heading) back to that person. After the study, US SAILING adopted the procedure to spot the person in the water as before, but do a crash tack (Quick Stop) to kill the speed of the boat and to stay very close to the overboard crew. This maneuver is standard operating procedure nowadays on cruising boats.

Further testing was done with shorthanded crews, such as a husband and wife sailing together. With the husband overboard, it was difficult for the wife to do the Quick Stop alone and get her husband back on board. The testing resulted in the *Seattle Sling* (because the testing was done off of Seattle, Washington). The commercial version is called the *LifeSling*, pictured in Chapter 9.

WHAT TO DO WHEN YOU GO AGROUND

In Chapter 7 you learned the basic procedures for getting unstuck if you don't have a motor. This section covers groundings on larger, heavier cruising boats, with the help of an engine. Most sailors who cruise extensively have been aground at one time or another, with little or no danger to crew or boat. Running aground only becomes risky if you fetch up on a lee shore with the wind and sea pushing you farther aground on a rocky bottom. If you are thoroughly stuck, aren't experiencing heavy sea conditions, and there are no rocks, just wait for the tide to come in and lift you off.

Many marinas are located up narrow creeks with shifting bottoms, where running aground is a common occurrence. But some sailors go aground because they do not look at the chart carefully enough. Don't assume that the farther you are from shore, the deeper the water is. Get in the habit of looking at the chart, particularly when you see a buoy. A buoy could mark a spot that is surrounded by water that is 100 feet deep, or it could mark a nearby rock or shoal that is only a couple of feet under the surface. Most sailors may assume a buoy well away from shore is in deep water, but don't make that assumption.

On one of our flotilla cruises in the Virgin Islands, we were anchored in a quiet harbor behind a reef. A 35-foot cruising boat out beyond the reef in a 20- to 25-knot breeze seemed to be having trouble, spotted our snug little harbor, and headed right for us without looking at the chart, we later learned. The boat ended up on the reef where it was pounded for several hours before it could be towed off, resulting in thousands of dollars' worth of damage. Many good harbors are only good because they are protected by a reef that has a narrow opening somewhere along it. Yet the water looks the same as deep water if you're heading into the sun, so you must watch the chart carefully.

If you run aground and the tide is going out, the first few minutes are crucial. A cruising boat has little power in reverse so don't waste precious time trying to back off. Put the helm hard over so the boat turns toward deep water and rev the engine in forward gear. If

Figure 15-5. All crew on boom when aground in 1979 pre-Fastnet Race

your sails are up, trim them in tight to heel the boat and lessen its draft. Adjust the sails to catch the wind and help rotate the boat. Rock the boat by having the crew lean way out over one side, hanging onto shrouds. In Figure 15-5, taken in one of the short races around the Isle of Wight prior to the 1979 Fastnet Race, crew members are sitting on the boom to get us off a sand bar: we found ourselves embarrassingly marooned when we cut too close in a race.

If none of these tips work, quickly take the anchor out in the dinghy and drop it in deep water. Then pull the boat off by using the powerful jibsheet winches. You can also use the bow of your dinghy to push against the sailboat's bow like a tugboat does when docking a ship. Surprisingly, this is a very effective way to rotate the bow toward deeper water.

If you are still hard aground, you need to heel the boat more. Carry the anchor out in the dinghy straight abeam from the middle of the boat and drop it. At this point there's little pressure in the anchor line. Have the crew in the dinghy work back along the line and make an overhand loop in the anchor line about 30 feet from the boat, then come back to the boat, get a halyard and attach it to the loop. Winch on the halyard to pull the mast over, heeling the boat and hopefully breaking it free. Do not do this with a main halyard from a fractional rig, where the jibstay does not run to the top of the mast; the mast does not have enough support for that sort of strain and could break. If there is a powerboat nearby, an easier way to get off is to ask them to pull the halyard for you.

If you are not in a dangerous situation, all the above-mentioned efforts fail, and no other boat is around to pull you off, you may have to settle down and wait for the tide to come in again. If you go aground near high tide on the East Coast of the United States, your wait will be close to 12 hours and you will be almost high and dry at low tide. Make sure all hatches and hatch boards are closed so water cannot get into the boat as the tide comes back in.

If you are in a rocky area in high winds in U.S. waters and the boat might be threatened, call a rescue operator like SeaTow or BoatTow U.S. on your VHF or cell phone. Both of these organizations charge for their services, but they are highly skilled at towing. You may be offered help by a passing power or sailboat. If so and you accept, to avoid a possible salvage claim on your boat, pass them *your* tow line rather than take theirs. Make sure your tow line is tied securely to a cleat in the bow with a fair lead (not over a bow pulpit or around the anchor if stowed on deck). Ask them to go slow until there is strain on the line and pay out that line so it can't catch in their prop. When free, signal them to stop and release your line, then gather it in at the bow and get underway.

TIPS FOR GETTING OFF WITHOUT A TOW

- Act fast in the first few minutes
- Turn toward deep water, back the way you came
- Rev engine in forward gear
- Trim sails in tight to heel the boat
- Rock the boat
- Take the anchor out in the dinghy to deep water and use the jibsheet winches to pull the boat forward
- Use the dinghy as a push-boat against the sailboat's bow
- Take the anchor out abeam attach the halyard and wind the halyard winch to heel the boat
- If you are still stuck, make sure no water can get into the boat, settle down, and wait for the tide to come in
- If in danger, call SeaTow or BoatTow U.S.

WHAT TO DO IF STEERING FAILS

There is a mechanical system below deck that turns the rudder when you turn the wheel of a cruising boat. The main part of this system is called the *steering quadrant* and it should be inspected periodically to check for wear and tear that could ultimately cause failure.

Be careful not to store anything in the quadrant area that might fall or jam into the steering when the boat heels. While attempting to dock, a way-

TO STEER BY SAILS ALONE

◆ To fall off, ease main and trim jib
◆ To head up or tack, trim main and ease jib
◆ To sail off the wind, trim staysail or jib tight amidships and ease main in and out

ward can of oil or tool could limit your maneuverability—which could prove to be an embarrassing and potentially dangerous situation.

Your boat should have an *emergency tiller*. This is generally a strong pipe with a fitting on the end, which fastens to the top of the rudder post through a plate-covered opening near the steering pedestal. If your steering fails and you are in relatively shallow water, head into the wind by steering with your sails and anchor immediately. Then make your repairs at leisure. In deep water you will have to steer by the sails for a while until you either fix the steering, or insert the emergency tiller. Practice using the emergency tiller on a nice, quiet day to avoid lost time when you need it.

If you lose your rudder, you have to steer using just your sails. If you practice sailing a boat without touching the wheel, losing your steering is not a disaster. Review the instructions in Chapter 5, then practice steering without your rudder as often as you can.

During one of our Offshore Cruising Club flotilla charters in Greece, our cruise leader, Rob Eberle, noticed one of the boats appeared to be in trouble and was sailing toward shallow water off a point of land. He immediately got one of the crew members on the radio, a fairly recent graduate of the Learn to Sail course, who replied and said they had lost their steering. Rob asked if she remembered how to tack a boat without using the rudder. She said, "Yes, luff the jib and trim the main," to which Rob replied, "Do it! Now!" The boat tacked and sailed away from the shallow water.

A COLLISION CAN RUIN YOUR DAY

Proper vigilance and knowing the right-of-way rules are your best defense against a possible collision. Just as a car has blind spots, so too does a cruising boat—particularly to leeward, behind the sails. If you are steering, assign a crew member to be your lookout and to constantly check under the

Figure 15-6. Results of a collision in Antigua Race Week

mainsail and jib to leeward to see if there are any boats or obstructions you might hit.

During Antigua Race Week several years ago, we were on starboard tack aboard a 72-foot racer built from state-of-the-art carbon fiber when a heavy 80-foot aluminum maxi-racer on port tack barreled into us. There were at least 20 people on that boat, which was heeling so much the helmsman couldn't steer away (off the wind). No one was on the mainsheet to spill the air out of the sails and let him change course. Luckily there were no major injuries, but the boat was badly damaged. Carbon fiber shatters easily and the impact cracked the hull along its entire port side.

So what's the message here? It is easy to be lulled into complacency on the water when everything is so peaceful and quiet. But if you are sailing at 6 knots and another boat that looks far away—say, 2 miles away—is approaching you at 6 knots, you both could collide in 10 minutes if you are on a collision course. So every few minutes, sweep the horizon for other boats.

In Chapter 8 you learned the basic right-of-way rules regarding sail and power boats. Now is a good time to reread that chapter, as the rules are the same regardless of the size and type of boat you sail.

Offshore instructors use this simple ditty to explain who has right-of-way: "New reels catch fish so purchase some." The sidebar explains how to use this handy memory jogger, listed in order of who takes precedence. Each lower vessel gives right of way to any vessel above it in the pecking order.

PECKING ORDER

New Reels Catch Fish So Purchase Some:

New = **N**.U.C. (**N**ot Under Command due to exceptional circumstances)
Reels = **R**.A.M. (**R**estricted in Ability to Maneuver)
Catch = **C**.B.D. (**C**onstrained By Draft)
Fish = **F**ishing (trawling, not trolling)
So = **S**ail (under sail alone, not powering)
Purchase = **P**ower
Some = **S**eaplane

SAILING AT NIGHT AND IN RESTRICTED VISIBILITY

If you only intend to charter boats, you may never encounter night sailing; most charter companies prohibit night sailing for safety and insurance reasons. But night sailing is one of the most satisfying aspects of cruising—if you know what you are doing. Picture yourself in light winds, sailing toward a distant shore as a brilliant moon above cuts a path over the shimmering sea. Phosphorescence streaks by as your hull plows through the black water below. It doesn't get any better than this!

If you are accustomed to city and suburban loom, you might think night sailing at sea is always in pitch-black darkness. Out on the water, even with total cloud cover, visibility is pretty good. On some moonlit nights you can see perfectly for miles, as if you were wearing dark sunglasses in daylight.

In certain parts of the country—such as Long Island Sound between the Connecticut and New York shores—there are so many navigation lights it is virtually impossible to get lost at night if you follow the chart carefully and steer an accurate compass course. When you spot a light, count the number of seconds between flashes: "One thousand and one, one thousand and two, one thousand and three . . ." until it flashes again. This should give you the number of seconds between flashes.

Counting is better than trying to read a stopwatch, which might require a flashlight or going below to see the dial. That moment when you turn on the light has the same effect as looking straight at the camera when someone takes a flash photo of you. Night vision is impaired when lights are turned on topsides or below, making it difficult to get more sightings for a short time.

HOW TO READ NAVIGATION LIGHTS

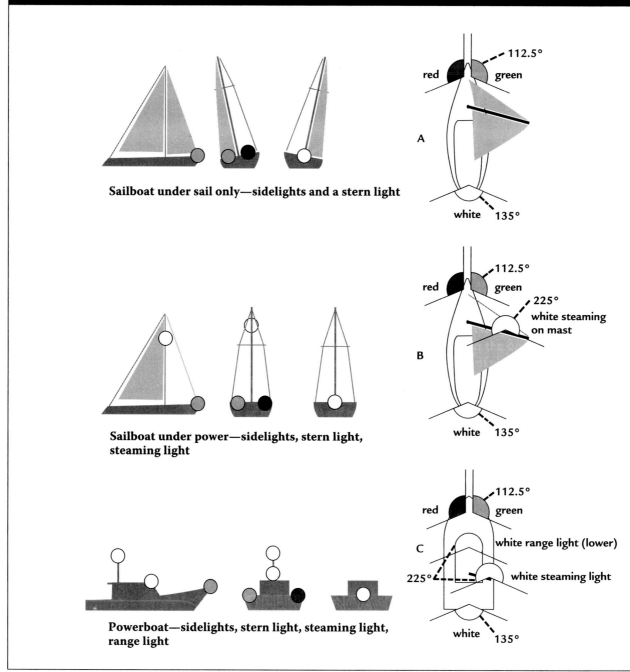

Sailboat under sail only—sidelights and a stern light

A
red | 112.5°
green
white 135°

Sailboat under power—sidelights, stern light, steaming light

B
red | 112.5°
green | 225°
white steaming on mast
white 135°

Powerboat—sidelights, stern light, steaming light, range light

C
red | 112.5°
green
white range light (lower)
225° white steaming light
white 135°

That's why a lot of cruising boats have a red light in the navigation area (which doesn't disrupt night vision).

Never give the crew on lookout duty the characteristics of the light you want to find. If you say you are looking for a four–second white flashing light just off the starboard bow, your spotter might see a light and accept it as the one you specified. When a light is spotted, ask the crew member to call out its characteristics to avoid any chance for error.

The possibility of a collision is a major danger in night sailing. That's why it is imperative that you have the ability to read navigation lights, which must be on between sunset and sunrise or in restricted visibility. Almost all vessels carry red and green sidelights. These are

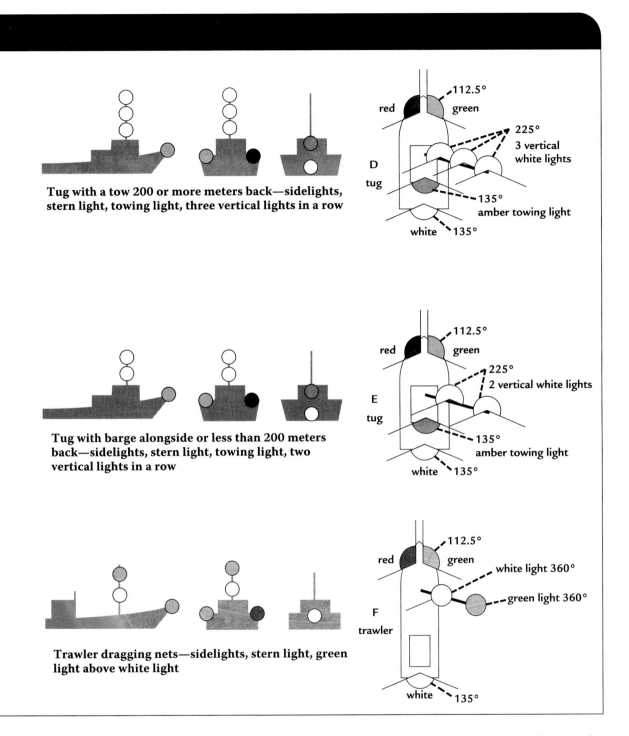

Tug with a tow 200 or more meters back—sidelights, stern light, towing light, three vertical lights in a row

D
tug

112.5°
red
green
225°
3 vertical white lights
135°
amber towing light
white 135°

Tug with barge alongside or less than 200 meters back—sidelights, stern light, towing light, two vertical lights in a row

E
tug

112.5°
red
green
225°
2 vertical white lights
135°
amber towing light
white 135°

Trawler dragging nets—sidelights, stern light, green light above white light

F
trawler

112.5°
red
green
white light 360°
green light 360°
white 135°

ten point lights and can be seen from dead ahead to two points abaft the beam. The red light, always on the port side of any boat, can be remembered by the following phrase: *port wine is red*. The green light is on the starboard side.

Cruising boats are equipped with a number of navigation lights. When you are sailing, and not using any auxiliary power, you must show your sidelights and a white stern light only. If you are under power, regardless of whether your sails are up or not, you must also have your steaming light on the mast turned on. Larger powerboats display a steaming light and a higher range light. The relationship between these two lights tells you which way the boat is turning.

CLOSE ENCOUNTERS AT NIGHT

- Know how to read lights
- Determine if you are on a collision course
- Decide who has the right-of-way
- Alter course if you don't have the right-of-way
- Shine a spotlight on your sails
- Point a spotlight at the approaching boat
- Use binoculars if the lights are confusing

TIPS FOR FOCUSING BINOCULARS

- Cover right lens; adjust focus for left eye with center focus adjustment
- Cover left lens; adjust focus for right eye with focus ring on right eyepiece

Some special lights are very important to know. Below you will read about a few of the many possibilities you could encounter in an area busy with nighttime traffic. Study the U.S. Coast Guard *Navigation Rules* for the rest.

If you see three vertical lights in a row, you can be sure it's a tug with a tow. The tow should have sidelights and a stern light, but they are often very weak and hard to see. Be sure you know where the tow is. If you pass behind the tug, you may hit the towline—or worse yet, hit the barge.

When you see two vertical lights, the barge is either alongside the tug or less than 200 meters astern. This situation poses much less of a threat since you can quite easily spot the last barge in the line.

A green light above a white light indicates a trawler dragging nets. This boat has right-of-way over sailboats when it's dragging, so be careful to avoid it.

Reading lights involves determining the course, speed, and type of boat you are seeing. Until you have this experience, you should consider having someone else aboard at night who can determine if you are on a collision course, if you have right-of-way, and whether or not you need to make a course change.

When it looks like there may be a close call developing, and the other vessel may not be aware of your existence, play a spotlight over your sails for several minutes to attract attention. This works well in good visibility, but it is next to useless in bad weather when you most need to be seen. In low visibility, shine the spotlight right at the wheelhouse of the other vessel. From this vantage point, the battery-operated spotlight will look like a pinprick of light, if seen at all. It certainly won't blind anyone, which you obviously want to avoid; but it will make them aware you are out there.

Your binoculars, which you use so frequently during daylight, can also be very useful at dusk or at night. On a night sail in Long Island Sound, we were converging with a number of commercial boats and it was hard to tell exactly what they were doing. The lights were confusing and seemed close together. Using binoculars, it became clear that we could cross one tug towing a barge and then safely sail between that tug and another tug towing a barge to windward of it.

In another situation, we were converging at dusk with a ship that was lit up like a Christmas tree. We could not pick up the sidelights and had no idea what our converging angle was. A check with the binoculars showed the boat to be a large sailing schooner, obviously with a generator going because of all those lights. We easily set a course to avoid it.

SOUND SIGNALS FOR FOG

- Sailboat under sail alone—1 prolonged, 2 short blasts at least every 2 minutes
- Sailboat using an engine—1 prolonged blast at least every 2 minutes

Last, you should always have aboard a signaling device, such as a horn or a bell, to identify your type of boat when sailing in low visibility conditions like fog. A *prolonged blast* means a blast of a 4- to 6-second duration. A *short blast* means a blast of about a 1-second duration. If you are sailing without any auxiliary power, your signal is *1 prolonged, 2 short at least every 2 minutes.* If you are a using your motor to *make way* (move through the water), your signal is *1 prolonged at least every 2 minutes.*

TEST YOURSELF

Safety and Health Tips

To test your knowledge of safety and health issues aboard a cruising boat, answer the following questions.

1. Name at least three ways to avoid being seasick.
2. Why do you attach a downhaul to a bosun's chair?
3. Describe how to get off if you go aground.
4. What is an emergency tiller?
5. What color is the sidelight on the starboard side of a vessel?
6. What do three vertical lights on another boat tell you at night?
7. What are the sound signals required for sailing in restricted visibility?

16 NAVIGATION
KNOWING WHERE YOU ARE AND WHERE YOU ARE GOING

Coastal navigation, called *piloting*, is done by transferring your actual position to an easily readable picture on a nautical chart. Nautical charts are produced by NOAA (National Oceanic and Atmospheric Administration) in the United States and by other national authorities around the world. Before you go on a cruise, make sure you have all the nautical charts available to cover the area you intend to explore. You can buy these at marine supply stores in paper and, in some cases, in electronic form.

BECOMING A NAVIGATOR

Charts are your road maps of the world's waterways. But while they are the nautical equivalent to a car driver's road map, nautical charts differ in one major way. There are no roads or highways to follow, and you have to figure out your own route for getting from one point to the next.

That said, charts have a lot of information you can use to help you find your way. They mark the location of the lights and buoys you see on the water, landmarks, depths, locations of nearby dangers—such as rocks, reefs, shoals, riptides, and more. You will use your chart to find a route with enough water depth for your boat's draft. (If you don't know your boat's draft, find out before you set sail!)

When you are cruising, you are continually navigating. Many cruis-

"In the beginning, it was difficult to do the chart plotting below while underway. Our instructor pinned the chart onto his drawing board with laundry clips so the wind couldn't blow and tear it apart, and I could do the plotting outside. After the big passage to St. Martin, I managed navigating below while the boat was moving."
CLAUDIA LOGOTHETIS (35), DREIEICH, GERMANY

Figure 16-1. Navigating on deck

ing boats have a comfortable nav station below, with a bench area large enough to spread out a chart, storage under the lid for navigation tools and charts you are not using, and a comfortable seat. The wall space surrounding this area has room for your VHF radio telephone and all kinds of electronic equipment cruising sailors like. Even if you don't have a dedicated nav station on your boat, you should store all your tools and charts below and use the main saloon table or a counter to chart your course out of the weather and wind.

Getting used to navigating below, however, comes with getting your sea legs. Since you are concentrating on small print and calculations in a confined area, you may find it easier to start by bringing the charts and tools on deck. The last thing you want is to lose any of these necessary aids overboard, so on deck always hold the chart and tools. If you put a chart down, place it under a cushion or winch handle to keep the wind from blowing it away, and put your dividers and parallel rulers in a cubby.

Figure 16-2. Navigating below

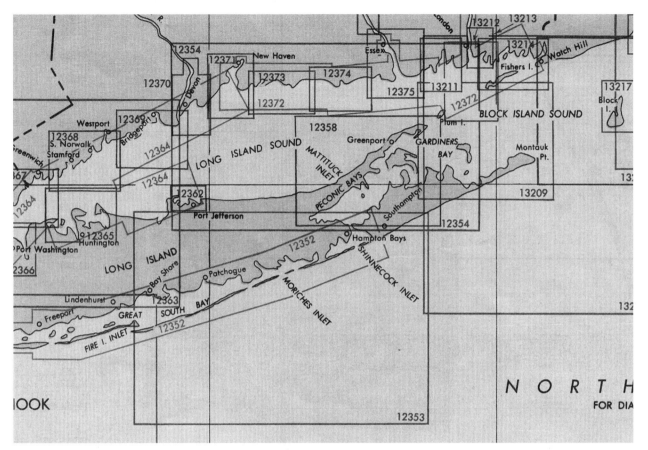

Figure 16-3. Identifying chart numbers

HOW TO USE CHARTS

The area a chart covers and the number identifying that chart are listed in a nautical chart catalog. A section of this catalog is shown in Figure 16-3. In this instance, if you plan to sail in central Long Island Sound, chart 12354 covers this area.

For very small boats, the Small Craft Series of charts published by NOAA is handy. These chart booklets are prefolded and compact, and you don't need a large, flat surface to spread out on. Because one Small Craft Series booklet covers the same area that a number of single charts cover, they are also more economical to purchase. However, Small Craft Series booklets don't give you the big picture of the area, and you may find it difficult to continue to the next adjoining chart when you run off the edge of the first. The less-distinct gray outline in the catalog section shown here is numbered 12372. This is the available Small Craft chart for the same area.

Charts come in many scales. Chart 12375, for example, covers only a small portion of chart 12354, yet it blows this area up to about the same size as 12354. Since 12375 enlarges a small area, it is called a *large-scale* chart. You should use large-scale charts whenever precision and accuracy are necessary—for example, when entering a harbor or negotiating a narrow passage. For planning purposes, however, a smaller-scale chart that covers a larger area is easier to use.

TOOLS FOR NAVIGATION

- ◆ Charts are your road map
- ◆ Parallel rulers plot your course
- ◆ Dividers measure distance

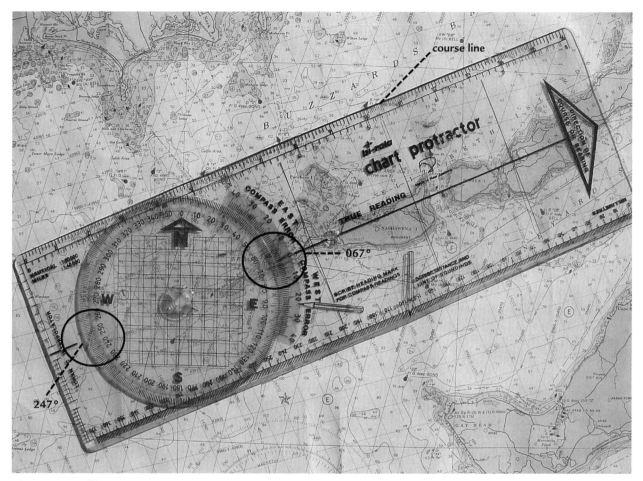

Figure 16-4. Chart protractor

The most common charts are those with scales of 1:80,000, 1:40,000, and 1:20,000. One foot on a 1:80,000 chart is equivalent to 80,000 feet on land, or roughly 13 nautical miles. On a 1:20,000 chart, 1 foot equals 20,000 feet, or about 3.3 nautical miles. Obviously there is less detail when you crowd 13 miles into a foot of chart space as opposed to 3.3 miles in the same space. The smaller the numbers, the larger the scale—and vice versa.

Take the time to review Chapter 8 for the basics of navigation. Remember: parallel rulers and dividers are the traditional tools used when working with charts. Parallel rulers move a course from your position to the compass rose, or a bearing from the rose to the landmark you sighted. Dividers measure distance. These two tools, plus a pencil compass and pencils with erasers, are all you really need.

If you charter in Europe, instead of parallel rulers you may find a *protractor*—a clear plastic rectangle with a compass rose in the middle—in your bareboat. To use a protractor, lay one edge on the desired course and slide the center over a meridian of longitude. The reading on the compass rose will be your true course. On the chart shown here (Figure 16-4), the course between the bell and whistle buoy is 067° or 247°, depending on which direction you are sailing. Remember to correct for variation (see below).

WHERE YOU CAN AND CANNOT SAIL

Depth of water is usually given in feet at mean low water. Extremely low water could mean depths of 4 or 5 feet less than shown on the chart, so take that into account. Along the East Coast of the United States, tides are usually semi-diurnal; which means two high tides and two low tides in a 24-hour period. The tide height changes about 25 percent during the first and last two hours of a tide, and about 50 percent during the middle two hours. For example, if you are in an area with a

6-foot tide range, during the first two hours the depth will drop 1.5 feet; during the next two it will drop 3 feet; and during the last two, 1.5 feet. Take this into consideration if you have to cross a sandbar or a shoal that you know is too shallow for your boat at low tide, yet has deep-enough water at certain times during the tidal fall. For a closer approximation, use the Rule of Twelfths. Take the range of tide (the change in feet between high and low water) and divide by 12. One-twelfth of the range rises the first hour, two-twelfths in the second hour, three-twelfths in the third, three-twelfths in the fourth, two-twelfths in the fifth, and one-twelfth in the sixth hour.

The United States Government compiles regional *Tide Tables*, which give the predicted times of high and low water and heights of the tide. On some charts the depths—*soundings*—may be in meters or fathoms. Check each chart for an explanation of how soundings are given. Also shown on charts are depth *contour lines*, which connect areas of equal depth. When using a *depth sounder*—an electronic device used to measure the distance to the bottom—contour lines become very useful. For instance, if contour lines are roughly parallel to the shore, you can stay a safe distance offshore by following a contour line on the chart of a certain depth. To do this, read your depth finder often and edge closer to shore if the readings get deeper, farther from shore if they get shallower.

The beige part of a chart indicates dry land. Objects that can be helpful in obtaining a *fix*—your position on a chart—include tanks, towers, conspicuous buildings, spires, and other landmarks that are located and marked in this beige area.

Constantly check where you are and record your position in a log. Identify other landmarks in the area to make sure you are zeroing in on the right one. One of the boats on our Tahiti cruise was steering for a church—only to find out it was the wrong church. Atolls in Tahiti can only be entered through very narrow passages in dangerous reefs. Because they were keeping track, they discovered their mistake before it became a real problem.

UNDERSTANDING VARIATION AND DEVIATION

Variation was introduced in Chapter 8. In this chapter, you will get a deeper understanding of how it is determined. Variation is the *angle* between the geographic

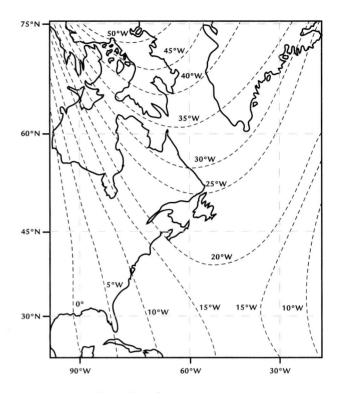

Figure 16-5. Variation chart

meridian (a line passing through both geographic poles) and the local magnetic meridian (a line passing through both magnetic poles). The compass on your boat points to the magnetic north pole. At any given point, this is a certain number of degrees to the west or east of true north, which points to the geographic north pole. In a few spots on earth, there is no variation and your magnetic compass will in effect point to true north. Every chart has the number of degrees of variation written on it for the area it covers.

Variation charts (Figure 16-5) show how much variation exists at different locations. If you are sailing between Cuba and the Florida Keys, the variation is 5° west. As you learned earlier, a compass rose is printed on most charts. The outer circle gives you the true north direction, the inner circle gives you magnetic.

You can find the variation in a given chart locale by reading the angular difference between these two circles. Variation is also written at the center of the compass rose along with the annual rate of change. For example: "VAR 14° 00'W (1989) ANNUAL INCREASE 4' tells you the variation for that area (in 1989) was 14 degrees, zero minutes west with an observed increase of four minutes per year. This means you have to apply the annual rate according to the date and age of the chart. Although it usually doesn't amount to much, a careful navigator will at least be aware of the annual increase or decrease in variation in a particular area.

Deviation, which was also introduced in Chapter 8, is the compass error induced by metal and electrical wiring on the boat. The deviation of your boat's compass can be determined by a professional compass adjuster. Using magnets, an adjuster *swings* your compass to reduce the error caused by the magnetic pull of metal on the boat. Because deviation is rarely totally eliminated, the adjuster will make a deviation table, that shows your compass deviation for various boat headings. If this residual deviation is small enough to be of little concern (1°–2°), you can assume your compass error is equal to variation alone and take all your bearings and courses in magnetic readings, using the inner circle of the compass rose.

You can determine and correct your deviation without an adjuster in a less formal manner. Position your boat next to a charted navigation aid, such as a buoy, draw a line on your chart toward magnetic north from the buoy and note which landmark the line passes through in the distance. When you point your boat at that landmark and read your compass, the difference from the north is deviation. Adjust the magnets on the side of your compass to reduce the deviation by one-half. Then head east, determine the deviation in that direction, and adjust the magnets on the front and back of the compass to reduce it by one-half. Continue the exercise heading south, then west; then repeat the process all over again until most of the deviation is gone.

Variation and deviation errors are expressed as either easterly or westerly: if easterly, the compass needle points east of true north; if westerly, the compass needle points west of true north. You can combine these to get a net compass error. For example, if the variation is 10° east and the deviation is 2° west, subtract 2 from 10 to get a net compass error of 8° east. If the variation is 8° west and deviation is 1° west, add the two to get a net error of 9° west.

If you know your compass heading, just add any easterly combined compass errors to obtain your true heading. Use the acronym CADET (Compass Add East for True) and all the rest falls into place logically. If you add easterly errors, subtract westerly errors. If you have a true course from the chart and you want to know what compass course to steer, reverse the procedure: subtract easterly errors, add westerly errors.

To obtain an *LOP* (line of position), take a bearing and adjust for deviation and variation. Suppose the compass bearing you took on a lighthouse is 276°. You know your deviation is 1° east and your variation is 7° east. If the chart does not have a magnetic compass rose on it, only a true one: Add 8° to 276° to get a true bearing of 284° and plot this on the chart.

After you determine your position, set a new course for your boat. Walk the parallel rulers over to the true compass rose and determine that your new true course is 093°. What course will you want to steer using your compass aboard? To find this, remember you are going from true to compass—not compass to true, as in the acronym CADET. So subtract your compass error (variation and deviation combined) of 8° east from 093° and the answer is 085°.

Another popular phrase used to adjust for compass error is: "TV Makes Dull Children." Note the words vertically stacked in the middle of the sidebar on page 200: True, Variation, Magnetic, Deviation, Compass. Using CADET,

TO DETERMINE TRUE HEADING

CADET = **C**ompass **Add** **E**ast for **T**rue

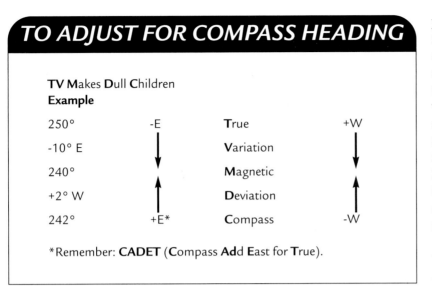

TO ADJUST FOR COMPASS HEADING

TV Makes **D**ull **C**hildren
Example

250°	-E	True	+W
-10° E	↓	Variation	↓
240°		Magnetic	
+2° W	↑	Deviation	↑
242°	+E*	Compass	-W

*Remember: **CADET** (**C**ompass **A**dd **E**ast for **T**rue).

you know to add east when going from compass to true, so draw an arrow and write "+E" below it. For example, if the true course is 250°, variation is 10° east and deviation is 2° west, what are the magnetic and compass courses? Moving down from true, subtract east and get 240° for magnetic; then add west to get 242° compass course. To make it easier, you might want to fill in the rest of the adjusting formulas as in the right-hand side of the box.

WHAT IS DEAD RECKONING?

Dead reckoning (DR) is the process of estimating where you are by applying your course and distance from a previously determined position. There are a number of theories as to how dead reckoning got its name. The most popular is that *dead* means exact, as in a *dead shot* or *dead ahead*. Dead reckoning, therefore, is as exact a reckoning of position as can be obtained solely by estimates of time, speed, and distance.

Navigation on a cruising boat is aided by various electronic helpers not available on a small daysailer. For instance, along with a depth finder and compass, you may have a log for measuring distance traveled, a speedometer, a GPS that can measure the speed and effect of current, and a radar. Nevertheless, the basic concepts mentioned in Chapter 8 apply whether you are sailing a daysailer or a cruising boat.

The DR Plot

Starting from a known position, you plot your course to your next destination and draw a line from your position to that destination, then move it to the compass rose with parallel rulers to determine your compass course. After you have traveled awhile, plot the distance you covered on the course you were steering. Mark it on the chart as your DR position, along with the time of day. Use the 24-hour clock when navigating and add 12 hours to any P.M. time. For example, in Figure 16-6, 1515 DR is 3:15 P.M. When the hour is only one digit, always put a zero in front of the hour: use 0930 for 9:30 A.M.

Courses are always written in three digits. On the same figure, the course between 1515 DR and 1615 DR is 093° C. If you wrote 93 someone could mistake a line or a smudge and read 193 or 293. Follow the course numbers with an *M* (for magnetic) or *T* (for true) or *C* (for compass). Professional mariners work in true, and most bearings and courses written on charts are in true; but it is perfectly okay for you to work with the magnetic compass rose.

You should know two of three variables when you try to determine your position. If you start at a known location and keep track of your speed and time run in a particular direction, you can easily figure out the distance traveled.

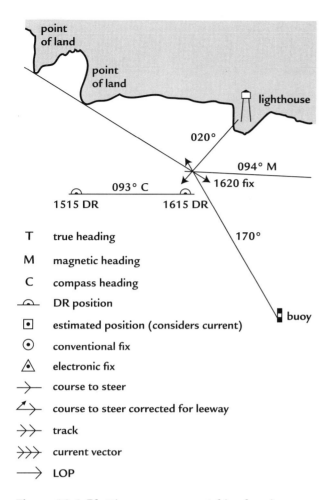

point of land

point of land

lighthouse

020°

094° M

093° C

1620 fix

1515 DR

1615 DR

170°

T	true heading
M	magnetic heading
C	compass heading
⌒	DR position
⊡	estimated position (considers current)
⊙	conventional fix
△	electronic fix
→—	course to steer
↗→	course to steer corrected for leeway
→→	track
→→→	current vector
—→	LOP

buoy

Figure 16-6. Plotting your course, taking bearings, and the symbols to use on a chart

Measure the distance from the first location in the direction you have been sailing and determine the second location. For instance, your known position at 1515 hours (3:15 P.M.) is noted on the diagram. You sail one hour on a 093° compass heading. You draw a 093° course line from the 1515 DR and, if you are sailing at 6 knots, measure 6 nautical miles on your chart with your dividers to determine your 1615 DR position. Your speed, 6 knots, multiplied by the time, one hour, gives you the distance.

There are simple *speed-time-distance* equations. To get speed, divide distance by time. To get distance, multiply speed by time. To get time divide distance by speed. As an aid, use these formulas: imagine a street named D Street, but the sign for that street looks like $\frac{D}{ST}$. Now put your thumb over the variable you want to find and what remains is the formula to find it. For instance, if you want speed, put your thumb over the S (speed)

and divide D (distance) by T (time): $\frac{D}{T}$. To find distance, multiply speed by time. To find time, divide distance by speed.

In order to work with minutes instead of hours, most navigators multiply distance by 60 to get 60 times D, divided by ST. The formulas then become $S = 60\frac{D}{T}$, $T = 60\frac{D}{S}$, and $D = 60\frac{S}{T}$.

Confirming and Correcting the DR Plot

Dead-reckoned positions are only estimates. A DR plot does not account for leeway (from the wind) or set (from the current, if present), nor is your estimate of boat speed through the water likely to be exact. Sailboats, in particular, are subject to the vagaries of the wind; it is very difficult to set a particular course and speed in order to end up at a desired destination on a given schedule. That's why long-distance cruising sailors rarely make plans to meet guests on a remote island on a specific day, much less at a specific time.

You can *try* to adjust your DR plot for current. Set an initial course and determine your *ETA*—estimated time of arrival—based on the speed you are making through the water adjusted for current, which gives your speed and course over the bottom. But if the wind dies, you won't make the speed you based your calculations on and will spend a longer time in the current—which requires a further course adjustment.

If the wind shifts, your speed may change, because you are now on a different point of sail and either traveling faster or slower—even if the wind velocity doesn't change. The wind may shift further so you no longer *lay* your course—are not headed toward your original destination—and now you have to *beat* (make a series of tacks) to get there. In short, you are constantly updating your position as you sail along and are forever changing the course to your destination. If you don't keep careful track of your boat's DR (dead reckoning) plot, you will get lost.

For all these reasons, the process of coastal navigation—what we call piloting—requires you to confirm and correct your DR position with a true fix at every available opportunity. If you have a functioning GPS receiver, this is no problem at all. But if you don't—and ideally, even if you do—you should take bearings on buoys and landmarks at every opportunity to obtain a fix. Let's see how this works.

To continue the plotting exercise (Figure 16-6), you update your position an hour later at 1615 and find on the chart three good landmarks or navigational aids to take bearings on. A lighthouse marked on the chart bears 020°, a buoy bears 170°, and a point of land has just obscured another point of land behind it. (Use the third type of bearing whenever you can because it is less subject to errors caused by compass swings or parallel rulers slipping on the chart. Simply watch for two islands or points of land to come into line. Note the time on your chart, locate these objects, and line them up with a straight edge. Draw a line touching both points of land to determine your bearing. This simple, very accurate and fast procedure requires no compass.) Now plot all three bearings as on the diagram.

Each bearing is a line of position to the object. Where two or more LOPs cross, you have a fix. Plot the bearings on the chart and get a small triangle. If you are lucky, you may get all three lines to cross exactly at the same spot as in Figure 16-6; but a small triangle is an accurate-enough position for a fix. Just mark a dot representing your position in the middle of the triangle, note the time, and plot a new course to your destination, in this case 094° M.

If you have a log that reads the number of miles you have been sailing, note the log reading on the chart at the time of the fix. If you have a depth sounder, check the depth of the water at the time of the fix and compare it to the depth shown on the chart for that location to help confirm the accuracy of your fix. Use the depth sounder for all DR plots too.

HOW TO AVOID HAZARDS

In Figure 16-7, you continue along the coast and see a point of land with a lighthouse and some rocks. You want to be sure you will be able to avoid them. There are various ways of determining your distance off.

One is to use a *sextant*, which usually measures the angle of a star or the sun above the horizon. In this case you measure the angle from the base of the lighthouse to its top and then consult tables to determine your distance from the lighthouse. Another is to use a *range finder*, which directly measures distance from an object. A third is *radar*, which shows the position of an object relative to your boat on a screen. When you start cruising you should have at least one of these instruments aboard.

In the first case, you must know the height of the object. If it is a navigational light, its height is usually written on the chart or at least listed in the government-printed light list, which cruisers carry aboard. With this information in hand, describe an arc with a pencil compass that includes the rocks and hazards. In this case, it is about half a mile. Mark it down as a danger range of 0.5 NM and make sure your range finder readings keep you outside this distance from the object.

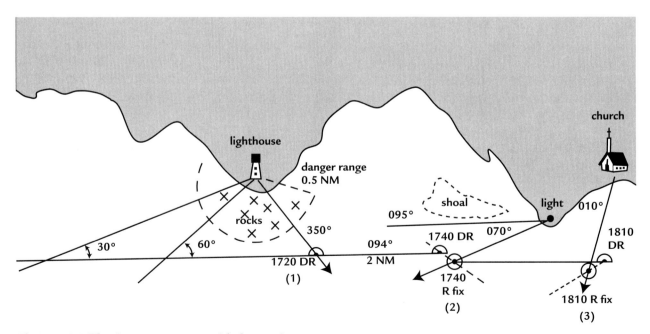

Figure 16-7. Plotting a course to avoid obstructions

If you don't have a means to measure your distance off, there are other ways to stay clear of the rocks. Keep careful track of your course and speed. Plot a bearing on a landmark like the lighthouse in Figure 16-7. If you are sailing at 6 knots and it has been 5 minutes between two bearings, you will have sailed half a nautical mile. After 5 minutes of sailing, take and plot a second bearing. Place your dividers so the points are half a mile apart. Set your parallel rulers on the compass course of your boat's heading and run them across the two bearings until the dividers show the bearings to be half a mile apart. Then draw your course line and see if you clear the rocks.

If you have been sailing against a current you won't have sailed half a mile in 5 minutes and could very well be closer to shore than you estimated. If you are in a *fair* current—flowing the direction you are going—the opposite is true. This procedure is not shown on the diagram. However, the diagram does show the *doubling the angle* method sometimes used to determine distance off an object. A bearing is taken relative to the bow of the boat, called a *relative bearing*. In this case, it is 30°. When that bearing doubles to 60°, the distance you sailed between the two sightings equals the distance to the object from your boat when you took the second bearing.

You can do the same thing using bow-and-beam bearings. First take a bearing when the object is 45° off the bow of your boat. Then, when the object is abeam—90° from the boat—the distance run from the time you took the first bearing equals the distance to the object when abeam.

Continuing on your cruise along the shore (Figure 16-7), take a DR position (1) at 1720 after sailing an hour from the previous fix. Then combine it with a bearing on the lighthouse of 350° M, but remember it isn't a fix because it is only one LOP, not two or more.

Farther along, you see a light on the next point. You know there is a shoal that you must stay seaward of, so draw a line on the chart from the light to point that just clears the shoal. This line turns out to be 095° and is called the *danger bearing*. Any bearing you subsequently take of the light that is 094° or lower keeps you clear of the shoal. If you take a bearing and it's 096° or higher, you are inshore of the 095° danger bearing and could possibly hit the shoal.

You are still sailing at a speed of 6 knots and 20 minutes later, at 1740, you take a bearing on the light and find it bears 070° (2). You know you sailed on a course of 094° over 2 nautical miles in 20 minutes. But your DR doesn't cross with the new bearing. Advance your first bearing 2 miles so it runs through the 1740 DR and is parallel (350°) to the first bearing, the dotted line in the diagram. The point where it intersects your bearing on the second object is called a *running fix*. Mark it as "1740 R fix" and continue your 094° heading from that new fix.

Half an hour (3 nautical miles) later at 1810, you take a bearing on a church ashore and find it to be 010° (3). Your 1810 DR doesn't coincide with the bearing. Advance your second bearing (070°) 3 miles to the 1810 DR (the dotted lines) and the point it crosses the bearing on the church is your 1810 running fix.

OTHER TIPS FOR NAVIGATING

Since the lubber line of the compass is in line with your boat's bow, a simple and accurate bearing can be taken by just pointing the boat at a landmark or buoy. This works well even if you have to alter your course slightly to place the object dead ahead. Here are some other ways to get a fix as you cruise.

Bearing and depth sounder. Sailing along some coasts the depth contours are fairly steep and roughly parallel to the coast. By combining a visual bearing that is relatively perpendicular to the shore with a depth sounding that is roughly parallel to the shore, you can get an approximate fix.

Bearing and distance. Take a bearing on a landmark on the chart and measure the distance from it with a range finder. The bearing is a line of position, and the distance from where it crosses that bearing gives you a fix.

Visual bearing and distance off determined by contour heights. All charts show the topography of land masses. Numbers and topographical contours show the height and steepness of hills. Until you get used to looking closely at contours on a chart, many sections of the shoreline may look like many others. When the contour lines are close together, indicating a steep slope, it is quite often easy to spot the hill it represents. The heights of the peaks are usually marked on the chart. Of two nearby summits, one may be 400 feet high and the other, 600 feet high. When you look at the shore, the perspective of the two summits to one another can give you a good idea of your geographical relationship to them. Use the known height of the peak with a distance-measuring device to get the distance off. Then cross the bearing line of position at that distance to get a fix.

Always be skeptical of your work. Once a fix is plotted, check by looking around to see if it makes sense. According to your position, do nearby objects appear in the proper perspective? Is that island really on your starboard bow as your fix shows? If the fix indicates a large change of course that seems strange, as if you had been in a current or making excessive leeway, take the bearings over again and replot the fix to confirm your position.

Read the number on the buoy. Nothing beats reading the number right off a buoy, if it is close enough, in order to verify that it is the right one. In fog, low visibility, and current, buoys that seem to confirm your position often turn out to be the wrong ones on closer inspection. If you don't check the number and otherwise confirm your position, you might make a course alteration on the assumption that your navigation is correct—and you could end up in trouble.

Confirm what you see with another fix. Remember that buoys for two harbors may look alike and be numbered the same. You could be entering the wrong harbor if you are way off. If you aren't sure, quickly plot a second fix to check the first and then another if necessary. With practice you will gain confidence in your work and catch mistakes before they can place you in danger.

Use binoculars on charts. If you find reading small print on charts difficult, a great little trick is to turn a pair of binoculars upside-down, put the eye end very close to the print, and look through the wrong end of one side. The print will be magnified many times.

To quickly figure a reciprocal course. Add 200 and subtract 20. For example, to get the reciprocal course of 147°, add 200 to get 347° and subtract 20 to get 327°.

Turn chart to match direction. If you are sailing south through a channel marked with a number of buoys, turn the chart upside-down so the chart course is aimed the same direction as your bow. This makes it easier to keep track of buoys as you pass them.

Make chart folds big enough. If you take a large-scale chart on deck because you are following a channel close to land, be sure to have enough of it unfolded to navigate properly. We have watched sailors steering for a point of land thinking they had it pinpointed on the chart, when actually they were steering for land that was under the next fold of the chart.

Go slow. There rarely is harm in throttling back on the engine and making a circle if you are powering into

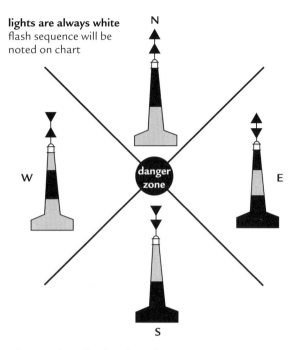

Figure 16-8. Cardinal marks

a strange harbor and unsure of your location, moorings, or docks. It is far better to stop and get your bearings than to charge blindly ahead.

Keep an accurate logbook. A ship's logbook is your diary, a record of your navigation. Rather than plotting all the time, you should record your boat's course and speed in the log every hour. Whether you are close to land, on short trips or out at sea, every hour is sufficient. You might be skeptical about recording a course so often when you have been swinging 20° in following seas and surging from 5 to 10 knots. Just make your best judgment of the average for the period. You will be amazed at how accurate the results are when you finally get a fix, even after 10 or 12 hours of averaging. If you have an electronic log aboard that records nautical miles covered, write down the miles run in the logbook every hour to back up your speed estimate. When you decide to update your boat's position, you can either plot each log entry or average them together. Averaging will give a fairly accurate course, but not distance. The plot is always recorded on the chart with time.

Outside the United States and Caribbean, Red-Right-Returning is reversed. In Europe, red buoys are on your port side when entering harbors and green buoys are to starboard. This makes more sense than our system, because it coincides with navigation lights on boats (red on the port side).

Marks commonly used in Europe. Starboard channel marks are more conical shaped than port channel marks, just as are cans and nuns in the States. Figure 16-8 shows *cardinal* marks, which you will find in Europe. These indicate direction (north, south, east, or west) from the mark where the best navigable water lies. Note the north mark has both arrows pointing up or north, the arrows on the south mark both point down or south. One east arrow points north and one points south. On the west mark the arrows point at each other. Stay to the east of an east mark, to the west of a west mark, north of a north mark, and south of a south mark. If you don't use these often enough to memorize them, keep the diagram handy when sailing overseas.

NAVIGATING IN CURRENT

Current occurs in areas where there are tidal depth changes. Current velocity can be a large percentage of your boat's speed and is a major factor when navigating. Current speed is called *drift* and the direction of its flow is called *set*. You may be averaging 5 knots, while sailing in a current that is 40 percent (2 knots) of your speed. If the direction of that current is toward the west—a 2-knot westerly current—you are experiencing a 2-knot drift and a westerly set.

Current velocity changes with the state of the tide. At low or high water, the current is *slack*, not moving. One hour after slack, the speed is at one-third of its maximum, as determined from the current tables; at two hours, it is two-thirds of maximum; at three hours, it is at max. Current slows down from maximum at the same rate. This *Rule of Thirds* only works with 6-hour tides from low to high, or vice versa, and should not be confused with the earlier rule regarding height of tides.

The *Tidal Current Tables* compiled by the U.S. Government (and published commercially) give the maximum flood and ebb current and the time when current changes direction. *Tidal Current Charts* are printed for twelve bodies of water on the East Coast and West Coast. These tables and charts are also combined in two must-have annual publications: *Eldridge Tide and Pilot Book*, which covers the northeast coast of the U.S., and *Reed's Nautical Almanac*, which is available in East Coast, West Coast, and Caribbean editions. Both are available at marine stores that sell charts. Suppose you are cruising (as shown in Figure 16-9) where the current is 2 knots in a direction of 270° T. You find you are at point A sailing on a course of 360° T at a

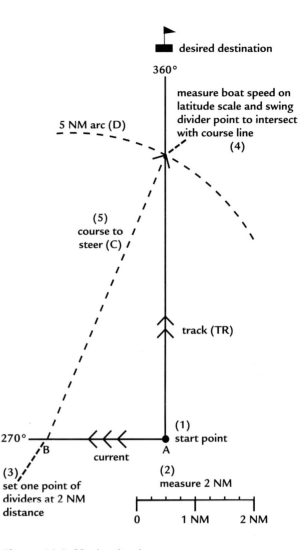

Figure 16-9. Navigating in current

speed through the water of 5 knots. To find your course to steer, taking current into account, first draw line AB 2 nautical miles long, indicating the effect the current will have on the boat in 1 hour. Next spread the arms of a pencil compass or dividers to indicate a 5 NM distance. With one tip on B, the pencil compass describes an arc that intersects the track line. Line BD is the course to steer. Line AD is your progress over the bottom toward your destination in 1 hour, with speed *made good* in knots. If the current velocity or direction changes over the period of time it takes you to reach your destination, you can use an average current for your calculations.

This diagram can be drawn right on the chart. Point A may be a buoy for instance. It can also be drawn directly on the compass rose. Draw a line representing

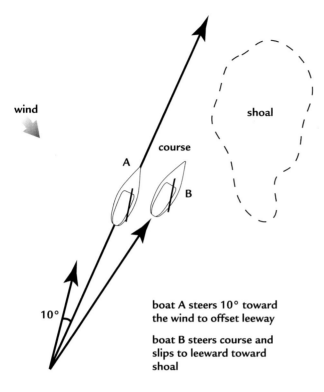

wind

shoal

course

A

B

10°

boat A steers 10° toward
the wind to offset leeway

boat B steers course and
slips to leeward toward
shoal

Figure 16-10. Plotting a course to adjust for leeway

your desired course, 360°, on the compass rose. Draw another line, 270°, representing the current and follow the same procedure as above. (The standard plotting symbols for courses on a chart are shown in Figure 16-6.)

Leeway is the side-slipping a sailboat does in heavy winds. In normal sailing conditions it doesn't amount to more than a few degrees and is generally ignored. In strong wind conditions with a shallow-draft boat or high topsides, leeway can be a factor. If your boat is making 10° leeway, draw a small arrow 10° toward the wind on the course-to-steer line and that is the new, corrected course you should steer.

When your DR includes allowances for current and leeway, the result is called an *estimated position* and you should mark "EP" on the chart with the time. Some navigators even draw two separate plots, one DR and one EP, until a fix can be obtained.

SATELLITE NAVIGATION

Wilderness adventurers and sailors alike depend on GPS (global positioning system) receivers for navigating. Satellites used for GPS are maintained by the Department of Defense, and because the signals are publicly accessible, errors referred to as Selective Availability

(SA) have been introduced for security reasons. GPS units come in many sizes and vary in price. The most popular are the size of a cell phone and are battery operated. Pricier models correct for the government-induced errors; but even without this correction, GPS units are highly accurate and dependable.

Using a GPS you can pinpoint your position with a direct reading of latitude and longitude. Before a unit can be used it must be told its approximate position in relation to the GPS satellites continuously circling the globe. Without knowing its location, the receiver may take 5 minutes or more to find your current position. To speed up the process, you must initialize your receiver—enter the approximate latitude, longitude, date, and time of where you currently are. Newer models will do this automatically, or you may choose to enter the approximate coordinates. They also include an electronic compass that has to be calibrated in a few simple steps.

If your unit is already initialized, just turn it on as directed. When the receiver is tracking three or more satellites it will compute a position fix. For step-by-step procedures, refer to the manual that comes with your unit. Many current GPS units, even those that are handheld, have installable charts.

To chart a course using a GPS unit, you select and store *waypoints*—the location of the various buoys and objects along the way—to determine the compass course you need to take for each leg. These are then connected to form the legs of your course. Your unit will have several screens to help you do this quickly and accurately.

One screen gives the bearing and distance to a mark or destination, and, if you are moving, your heading and speed. A course-deviation indicator gives you a picture of your position relative to your planned course, a scale showing how far left or right of the course you are, and the course you need to steer to get to that mark.

Other screens can point to the direction of your destination on a compass indicator, give the bearing and distance to that destination, the time to go before you get there, and show a plotted course line that provides a graphic picture of your course and tracking error.

As noted above, a GPS can give you a range and bearing to a destination at any time if you just plug in the latitude and longitude of your destination at the outset. It can also give you constant updates on your boat's *cross-track error* (the distance you are to one side or the other of your intended track), your speed made good over the bottom (not through the water) toward your destination, and your ETA (estimated time of arrival).

So what's wrong with getting all that good information? The original course needs to be plotted carefully on your chart initially to make sure it doesn't pass across shoal areas, through buoys, or even over land; and then replotted later when your GPS shows a different course. Leeway, current, and wind direction can all affect course changes. If you forget the original course and constantly adjust your heading according to readings on your GPS without checking your chart, you may end up on the rocks.

GPS tends to make navigators lazy. If the unit malfunctions and you haven't been piloting the old-fashioned way, you are not only lost but have reduced your ability to navigate because of lack of practice. GPS units rely on batteries, and signals can be obstructed. You don't want to be caught out there, depending solely on a GPS unit when the screen suddenly goes dead. Use the GPS as a backup to traditional piloting.

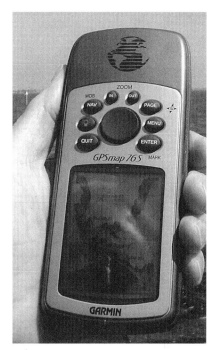

Figure 16-11. GPS receiver

TEST YOURSELF

Navigating

Test your knowledge of navigation by answering the questions below.

1. If you want to get your true course from your compass course, do you add or subtract westerly errors?
2. What is *dead reckoning*?
3. How do you say 9 P.M. in a 24-hour format?
4. If you know your speed and time, how do you calculate distance?
5. What is a *danger bearing*?
6. What percent does the tidal height change in the first two hours of a semi-diurnal tide? What percent the second two hours?
7. What are *soundings*?
8. Explain how to use CADET.
9. Describe a DR plot.
10. If you know time and distance, how do you calculate speed?
11. Describe *doubling the angle*.
12. Describe *leeway* and how it affects your course.
13. When entering a harbor or port in the U.S. or Europe, is the buoy system the same?
14. Describe how to enter a harbor using the phrase Red-Right-Returning.
15. Describe three good ways to get a fix.

17 CREATURE COMFORTS AND OTHER TIPS FOR CRUISING

Cruising boats are different from daysailers because they are really like a small home. Your boat will have running water, toilets that flush (though not exactly like they do at home), showers below and on deck, lights, and many more comforts that make the cruising experience enjoyable. But none of these features are plugged into a network or system that replenishes the supply automatically. You have to think about the resources you are using, plan ahead, and conserve when necessary. This chapter includes hints to help you plan a successful, comfortable cruise.

"I wanted to sail after going boating with my best friend, and my dad wanted to get a cruiser he could live on after retirement. I have done a month of cruising on an Island Packet 35 my family recently bought, and now we are going every weekend. We are going to sail along the East Coast for a while and maybe take some long-distance trips over the summer. Sailing makes me happy and relaxed and all worries fade away."

**JOSEPH YUN (13),
BERKELEY HEIGHTS, NJ**

YOUR DINGHY

When you are cruising, your dinghy is your car—your transportation from a mooring or anchor to dining out and exploring ashore. Dinghies come in many shapes and sizes. Cruising boat owners often opt for inflatable dinghies with portable hard flooring because they are relatively lightweight; but in prolonged sun, they tend to deteriorate over time.

Charter agencies try to use dinghies that are light enough to be easily handled, yet large and stable enough to take the whole crew ashore in one trip. Regardless of the type you choose, there are certain rules that make the use of a dinghy both safe and comfortable.

Figure 17-1. Cruising comfortably in the British Virgin Islands

Load the dinghy carefully. Step one person at a time, into the center of the boat, and sit down out of the way before the next person gets in. When boarding from the deck of a cruising boat, place a ladder (if you have one) over the side, then bring the dinghy alongside. The dinghy will rise and fall in swells, so wait until it is at the highest position before you step in.

When you see waves breaking on shore don't try to ride the dinghy all the way in. Get out of the dinghy just short of the surf and either anchor the dinghy there or walk it in. Pull it well up on the beach and anchor it, or tie it to a tree. That way, when the tide comes in, your precious taxi can't be swept away while you're gone.

Don't swim after a dinghy that is drifting away. With any amount of wind, the dinghy will probably drift faster than you can swim. If you are on an anchored cruising boat, quickly untie the bitter end of the anchor line, tie a fender to it, and throw the whole thing overboard. (Tie it well or you may lose your anchor and the complete anchor rode.) Then go and retrieve your dinghy. After you return with the dinghy, just pick up the fender and your anchor. This technique is much faster and less hassle than raising the anchor in hot pursuit of a wayward dinghy.

More dinghies are lost at cocktail parties than at any other time. When you arrive at the host boat, you will find several other dinghies hanging off the stern. We recommend tying your dinghy to a stanchion with a bowline rather than cleating it with all the others. Often there are two or three dinghy *painters* (the bow line of a dinghy) tied to the same cleat. The first happy sailor to leave the party uncleats the others to free his painter, then attempts to retie them with one hand while holding his own in the other—perhaps missing a painter or two. When you go to board your dinghy, darkness has fallen and—surprise!—your dinghy is nowhere to be seen. If you are cruising in the Caribbean, it is probably somewhere between your harbor and Central America. Lots of luck finding it.

Figure 17-2. Climbing aboard from a dinghy

DINGHY CARE

- Avoid cleats used by other dinghies when visiting other boats
- Use a bowline and tie it yourself
- Snub the painter in close or tie it alongside when you are anchoring and docking
- Tow on the back side of waves
- Use a second line from the dinghy to the boat as a backup when towing
- Take off the oars and motor in heavy weather

Figure 17-3. Dinghy is towed on the backside of a wave, bow up with safety line

When you leave a mooring, anchorage, or other congested area under power, your dinghy should be snubbed in close to the boat. This way, you avoid any chance of wrapping the painter around your propeller until you get your sails up and are no longer using your engine.

As you get into open water and try to let the painter out, you might find a lot of strain on the line. First tie the bitter end of the painter to a stanchion with a bowline, so no matter what happens you can't lose the dinghy completely. Uncleat the painter, leaving a 360° loop around the base of the cleat. Then ease the line. The friction of the loop should make it easy to hold onto even as the dinghy is pulled at speed.

When the proper amount of line is out, cleat it; but leave the bowline on the stanchion. It doesn't do any harm and might come in handy. In heavy seas, the dinghy should ride on the back of the third wave astern, bow up. You don't want it to scoot down the face of the wave and possibly into the stern of your boat.

When you tow your dinghy in moderate to heavy seas, double up on the towlines. Use one as a primary painter, the other as a safety line tied to another fitting on the dinghy and led to a different cleat on the boat. You should take the oarlocks, oars, and outboard off the dinghy. If you don't, at least make sure they are well secured.

In bad sea conditions or on a long passage, particularly at night, don't tow the dinghy at all—as it can swamp and break the towline. Instead, hoist it aboard with the main halyard and a three-part bridle attached to the bow and two corners of the dinghy transom. Then lash the dinghy upside-down on the cabintop or foredeck. One or two crew can do this job. You will rest a lot easier knowing your dinghy is secure.

USE OF WATER ABOARD

Many cruising boats carry hundreds of gallons of water. The water tanks are positioned in low areas of the boat, to keep weight down low and keep the boat balanced. Flow is controlled by valve handles, positioned in the line running from the tank, and a pressure pump, which is used to get water to the faucets. Normally, you use one tank at a time, turning the used tank off and the new tank on as needed. You should work off of one tank at a time to avoid losing all your water into the bilge if a hose leak develops.

Start using the tank farthest forward. Weight in the bow is undesirable and pitching is reduced when the forward water tank is empty. If you hear the pressure pump running continuously after you turn off a faucet, the tank is empty or getting low. Normally a water pump runs a short time to build up pressure and then turns itself off automatically.

To prime a full tank, open its valve and turn on a faucet. The pressure pump will run as water spurts out until air is bled out. You may have to turn on several faucets to get all the air out of the system, then close them one by one as each gets a steady flow of water. After you close all the faucets, the pump will continue to run, then turn itself off after adequate pressure is restored.

On a cruise of a week or more, especially with more than two or three sailors aboard, conserve water to avoid having to find a place to refill tanks during your cruise. Before you leave—whether you are chartering, on your own boat, or a friend's—make sure you top off all your tanks.

Although you can drink the tank water in some regions, it is safer to stock up on bottled water for drinking and use tank water for cooking, cleaning, and showering.

When showering, turn on the water just long enough to get wet, turn it off, lather up, then quickly rinse. If you are in a warm climate with clean water, you might enjoy bathing in the sea first, then rinsing off with fresh water from the shower on deck. Dishwashing detergents like Joy lather well in salt water. Wash your hair while swimming, too. This uses far less water and keeps hair out of the sump below decks. If showering below, be sure to drain the sump under the shower floor before you get underway.

If your galley has two side-by-side sinks, stop both sinks to wash dishes. Fill one with soapy water for

Figure 17-4. Freshwater shower on deck

TIPS FOR WATER USAGE

- Use one water tank at a time; keep others closed off
- Start with the forward tank
- To prime a full tank, open faucets until spurts stop
- Top off tanks before leaving
- When showering, get wet, turn off water, lather up, rinse
- Turn off the water pump at night and when leaving the boat for prolonged periods

SAFE AND HAPPY GRILLING

- Grill only at anchor, never at a dock
- Tie the dinghy far from the grill
- For easy cleaning, line the grill with aluminum foil
- Precook foods like chicken that take longer to cook
- Dump ashes before you get underway

washing and the other with clear water for rinsing. If you are low on water, you can wash the dishes in a bucket of salt water, assuming the harbor is clean, and rinse well with fresh water. Salt water residue retains moisture and stainless silverware can start to pit if not rinsed well. Many boats have a salt water spigot with a foot-operated pump in the galley.

At night many sailors turn off the noisy water pump to avoid waking everybody else up when someone gets up and opens a faucet. Fresh water is still available with the switch off, as most cruising boats have a quieter manual or foot operated backup pump to use at night or when conserving water.

Turn off the water pump switch when leaving the boat for long periods of time. If a leak develops while you are away and one or more of the tanks empties into the bilge, the water pump will run continuously in an attempt to build up pressure and eventually burn out. When on an extended cruise, be sure to bring an extra water pump.

COOKING ABOARD

In areas where there are few restaurants, dining aboard is a creative and joyful event. Most cruising boats carry a charcoal or gas grill that hangs over the stern, mounted to a corner of the *stern pulpit*—the rail across the stern. In warm climates you can cook many of your meals in the open air with the setting sun as your backdrop. A gas grill is cleaner and more efficient, but some believe charcoal flavoring is better. On a charter you are more likely to find charcoal.

Figure 17-5. Dining in the cockpit

If your dinghy is tied astern, move it to the opposite corner or along the other side so ashes and sparks can't fall into it. A charcoal grill should only be used at anchor when the boat lines up with the wind, causing smoke and sparks to drift harmlessly astern and away from the boat. Never use a charcoal grill at a dock, even if the wind direction is safe at first. A wind shift could blow sparks over the boat or onto adjacent boats.

To keep the grill clean for the next meal, line the bottom with aluminum foil before filling it with charcoal. With a wind blowing, it takes longer to use a grill aboard than ashore. If grilled chicken is on your menu, it helps to preboil it on the stove below before marinating it in a barbecue sauce.

The most common galley stoves on cruising boats are fueled by CNG (compressed natural gas) or LPG (liquefied petroleum gas). Most charter companies in the United States and the Caribbean use CNG because it is a safer, more efficient fuel and lighter than air. If a leak in the system occurs, CNG dissipates. Propane, on the other hand, will drop to the lowest part of the bilge and just stay there—leaving your boat prone to an explosion from a spark from the starter motor or someone inadvertently lighting a cigarette. European boats use propane, so if you smell gas, avoid any action that could make a spark.

Gas is normally carried in two tanks mounted on deck near or at the stern. When you run out of gas, unscrew the gas line from the empty tank and screw it onto the full tank. The threads are *backward* from normal threads—in this case, left is tight and right is loose. Never switch tanks when the deck barbecue is in use. A charter boat was lost that way.

Your boat should have a solenoid switch to turn the fuel off in the line that runs from the tank to the stove. After you have finished cooking and before you turn off the stove, switch off the solenoid to burn excess fuel out of the line. When the flames go out, then turn off the burners.

New cruising boats have good refrigeration. Holding plates, which are kept cold by your batteries or by running the engine periodically, are the source of cold. Many onboard refrigerators are top-opening boxes set in the galley countertop. When storing provisions, plan your menus ahead. Put the ingredients for the last meal on the bottom and work your way up to the ingredients you'll use on your first day out. If you have to start digging with the lid or door open, cold air will quickly escape. For that reason, replace cold drinks as they are used so you don't have to add a lot of warm ones when you run out. The lid of a top-loading refrigerator is heavy. If your boat does not have a hook on the bulkhead that you can latch the lid to when open, rig a line or hook to keep it from falling on your head. Of course, don't hold it open for long or valuable cold air will escape quickly.

Marine refrigerators often have a freezer compartment and retain cold through cooling and freezing plates. Any frost buildup on those plates acts as insulation between the two compartments and reduces the effectiveness of the freezer. If this occurs, run the engine less. Avoid putting perishables against the plates. Lettuce, for instance, will get freezer burn.

Cardboard boxes used to carry groceries can introduce unwanted passengers, such as insects. Empty the boxes and leave them ashore. If fruits and vegetables are in plastic bags, get rid of the bags in warm climates to

STOVE SAFETY

- Use CNG for fuel if possible
- When transferring from one tank to another, screw hose counterclockwise
- Before using the stove, open the tank valve, then switch the solenoid on
- To light a burner or oven, push the knob in and turn to max, light burner or oven coil while holding knob in for 30 seconds, release knob, turn to desired flame level
- To turn off a stove or oven, switch the solenoid off to let excess gas burn out, then turn off knobs (and the flame)
- Close the valve at the tank

REFRIGERATING PROVISIONS

- Stow provisions in reverse order of use
- Replace cold drinks as used
- Keep the refrigerator cold by running the engine or through charged batteries
- Open doors as little as possible; close quickly
- If frost builds up, don't charge as much
- Use an ice bucket at cocktail hour
- Get rid of cartons carrying food to avoid pests
- Remove fruits and vegetables from plastic produce bags

Figure 17-6. Cooking below

keep the food from rotting. Use an ice bucket at cocktail time, so you aren't constantly opening the freezer compartment to get ice for your drinks.

Cooking down below at anchor is just like cooking in a small kitchen at home—if you are in a quiet anchorage. Cooking while you are underway in choppy seas, when the boat heels, can be a challenge. If you are planning to sail all day on a tight reach or close-hauled, consider making up sandwiches before you get going. Place them in the refrigerator in a bag you can grab easily so you can simply bring them on deck at lunchtime. Likewise, if you have an icebox or cooler in the cockpit, you may want to fill it now with cold drinks before the sail.

MARINE TOILETS

The toilet on a boat is called a *head*, but sailors tend to use the same term for the closet that contains the head, sink, and shower. One simple rule to make on a cruising boat is to keep the door to the head hooked open, unless it's in use. This allows fresh air to circulate and lets everyone know just by looking below whether the head is occupied or not.

Only two items are flushed down the head: toilet paper and what you ate. Anything else can clog it up, including paper towels and sanitary napkins. If a clog occurs, here's the rule: whoever clogs it, cleans it! You only need to go through this messy job once to be a believer—and an enforcer—for life. If you clog the head on a charter and ask for help from the charter company, or bring the boat back with a clogged head, you might have to pay a fee. It's best to learn how to do this yourself.

A marine toilet can be either manually or electrically flushed. The latter is more common on very large sailboats and powerboats. Water exits and enters through a looped tube. If there is a high loop in the line, the seacocks may be left open when sailing. If not, they should be kept closed and opened only when the head is in use. If you have any doubts, keep the fittings closed to avoid water filling the bowl—and eventually your bilge—while underway.

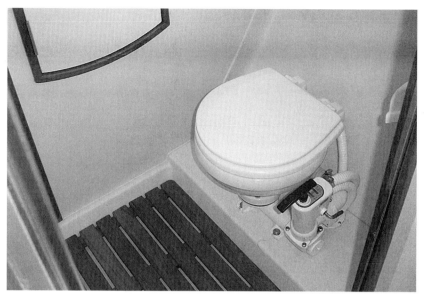

Figure 17-7. Marine toilet (aka the head)

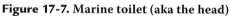

If the toilet on your boat is manually operated, like the one shown in Figure 17-7, water is pumped in and out with a lever—in this case, the black handle. First make sure all the seacocks are open, then pump clean water into the bowl. When you are finished, pump until the bowl is flushed clean; then keep on pumping at least 10 to 15 more strokes to flush any sewage right through the system, which travels either out the hull or into a holding tank. Before heading back up on deck, push the valve lever forward and pump the bowl dry. When the boat heels, if there is water in the bowl, it can spill over the lip onto the floor of the boat. As a courtesy to all aboard, wipe away any splatter or residue in the bowl with toilet paper and flush again. Small and poorly ventilated, heads have a tendency to smell if not kept clean.

Match sulfur makes an excellent deodorant, so keep a box of safety matches for odoriferous moments. Be sure to pour some water on the dead match before tossing it in the wastebasket. Never flush it down the toilet.

In most areas of the United States, holding tanks are required and pumped out at specified marinas. But in the Caribbean, there are few (if any) pump-out stations at this writing. In these areas the head pumps sewage directly overboard. Plan when and where you use the head. You may be sailing in beautiful tropical waters and decide to anchor in a quiet cove for lunch. While most of the crew dive off the stern for a refreshing swim, one crew member, who has been holding it all morning, may decide to use the head. Needless to say, those in the water are not pleased when "pollution" starts drifting their way. It sounds so obvious to make a rule that you don't use the head when friends are swimming. But first-time charterers sometimes forget, or they equate the boat's head with a home toilet that carries waste away.

As of 1980, all boats in the United States are supposed to have an MSD (marine sanitation device) like a Macerator. But not all boats do, particularly boats built before 1980. At this writing, holding tanks, not just Macerators, are required in many states and some states enforce the *no waste* rules requiring you to pump waste into a holding tank on the boat, then empty it

TIPS FOR USING THE HEAD

- Keep the door open when not in use to circulate air
- Flush only toilet paper and what you consume
- If you cause a clog, you unclog it
- Keep seacocks closed when not in use
- Pump water into the bowl before use; pump clean, then pump 15 more times to flush waste out through the plumbing
- Clean up any residue in the bowl; flush again
- Use safety matches to get rid of odors
- Never use the head when swimmers are around if you don't have a holding tank

GARBAGE TIPS

- Keep a supply of heavy-ply garbage bags aboard
- Store full bags, tied securely, in a deck locker or dinghy towed astern
- Take bags ashore to proper receptacles
- Never throw plastics overboard
- Plastic soda- and beer-can six-pack rings kill birds and fish

ashore in designated pump-out stations. Not all marinas have pump-out stations. Eventually the bugs will be worked out and good systems will be invented. For now, discharge rules are handled on a regional or local level, so adhere to the rules in your cruising area. If you are on a charter, ask about local laws and customs before you set sail.

DEALING WITH GARBAGE

There was a time when sailors dumped all their garbage overboard and thought nothing of it. But that was before plastics, which can float around for centuries before decomposing.

In December 1988, the first international agreement to clean up the oceans went into effect when the United States ratified Public Law 100-200. Under the MARPOL (marine pollution) Protocol, Annex V it is illegal for any vessel to dump plastic anywhere in the ocean. Violators can be fined up to $50,000. It is also illegal to dump garbage (victual waste), paper, rags, glass, metal, bottles, crockery, and similar refuse inside of 12 miles from the nearest land.

Most charter companies and countries where chartering is common adhere strongly to this protocol. It is in their best interest, and yours too, to keep their waters pristine so charterers can continue to enjoy the beauty of the area for years to come. Make sure you have sufficient garbage bags before you set sail. When they fill up, put them in an empty *lazarette* (deck locker) or tow your garbage astern in the dinghy. Then take the bags ashore to locations that accept them.

Be wary of kids who offer to take your garbage for a fee. We paid a couple of young boys in Bequia when they offered to relieve us of our several days' burden—and then watched as they rowed out to the middle of the harbor and innocently dumped it all overboard.

SAFETY BELOW

You should have several charged fire extinguishers in easily accessible niches, but not adjacent to a stove or engine that could catch fire. If you are chartering, learn where they are located before you depart. Your boat should also have two easy ways to get on deck in a hurry, in case a fire blocks one passageway.

A below-deck hazard that happens more frequently than fire is scalding. A friend of ours was boiling water underway and had not thought that conditions warranted releasing the pins to allow the stove to gimbal—to allow it to swing and stay level when the boat is moving. The wake from a passing powerboat caused the pot of boiling water to spill on his bare arm, leaving deep burn scars. Always let the stove gimbal when in use and secure pots with the clamps provided. In rough seas, some sailors don foul-weather gear in the galley. This can be uncomfortably hot and a lot like wearing a helmet in your car in case you have an accident: the inconvenience outweighs the chance something will happen. A good gimballed stove properly used will solve any problems. If it is too rough for anything to stay on the stove, even with pot holder clamps that fasten to the stove-top rail, you won't be cooking anyway.

When pouring or spooning hot liquid from one receptacle to another, take a tip from airplane crew. Never pour into a cup that someone else is holding. One person should always hold both pot and cup, so the left hand literally knows what the right is doing.

Slipping is another below-deck hazard, which usually occurs when the cabin sole is wet. Make a rule that anyone wearing wet clothing, such as boots and foul-weather gear, should remove it and stow it in an area near the companionway before moving about the cabin. If the sole does get wet, wipe it dry as soon as possible. Bare feet also add to your chances of slipping, so wear deck shoes at all times. Injuries occur when a sailboat lurches suddenly. Be *boat wise* and know just where the ceiling handrails are, particularly in the area of the companionway.

TIPS FOR SWIMMING AND FISHING

If you plan to cruise in warm waters and swim off your boat, a swimming ladder off the stern, a stern lazarette for snorkels and fins, and a deck shower for a freshwater rinse will meet all your needs.

Be careful about swimming where there are many outboard runabouts. We were anchored stern-to with a line tied to a tree ashore in Turkey, and a group of us were happily swimming off the bow of our boat. A large Zodiac with a 50-horsepower outboard engine came out from between two boats at full bore and never saw us. Fortunately no one was hurt. But be aware that in most parts of the world, small powerboats dashing back and forth in harbors use only two speeds: stop and full speed ahead.

Some say it is not a good idea to wear shiny, glittery items such as watches or jewelry in water where barracuda live. Although we have never been bothered by barracuda while swimming, we know of a woman who was attacked while sleeping on a beach with her feet dangling in the water. We wear watches when swimming; she had no jewelry on her ankles or toes. Maybe barracuda just know who is tastier.

Near a rocky beach or shore, watch out for sea urchins with black spines that can penetrate your skin and break off like splinters. Meat tenderizer poured liberally on the puncture tends to cut down swelling and pain. If you don't have meat tenderizer, lime juice works well too.

Shell collectors cruising in the Pacific or Indian oceans must be careful when handling cone-shaped shells with a textile (not solid) pattern and bright red proboscis. If you pick one up, avoid the open end (the head). Wear gloves since the proboscis of some species can reach the back of the shell. At least four species are known to cause heart failure.

Jellyfish are usually fairly harmless, but the sting results in an uncomfortable welt. Avoid Portuguese man-of-war jellyfish with a pretty semi-circular sail on the surface of the water and tentacles that hang down. Use vinegar or lime juice to neutralize a jellyfish sting.

Stingrays and skates are not aggressive. But many species have a barbed spine that is painful if you step on it. If you can't see the bottom, wear foot protection and always shuffle in the sand in shallow water, rather than walk.

If you do get a venomous sting from fish or mollusks, clean and flush the puncture wound immediately. Urine, which is also effective on fire

BELOW-DECK SAFETY

- Place fire extinguishers where accessible
- When boiling water, gimbal the stove
- Secure pots on the stove with clamps
- Hold both receptacles when pouring something hot from one cup to another
- Stow wet clothing in a locker near the companionway
- Wipe up any wet areas on cabin sole
- Wear deck shoes
- Use handrails when moving about below

SWIMMING AND FISHING TIPS

- Don't swim in areas with heavy powerboat activity
- Carry money in an air-tight film canister when swimming to shore
- Wear booties on reefs or rocky shores
- If a sea urchin spine gets you, rub with meat tenderizer or lime juice
- Don't eat fish you catch off a reef
- Avoid shellfish during a *red tide* episode
- Use vinegar, lime juice, or urine on jellyfish and other marine-life burns
- Shuffle when walking in shallow water

coral abrasions, is surprisingly sterile and can be used if no clean water is handy.

If you fish from your boat (most long-distance cruising sailors do to augment provisions), in open water everything is fair game. But be wary of fishing in crowded harbors and on reefs, and read up on the area or ask locals what is safe to eat, or not.

This final tip has more to do with having fun ashore, as opposed to safety. If you want to swim to a beach bar or restaurant, store your money in one of those little canisters that hold film. They are completely watertight and can be tucked in your bathing suit pocket or bodice.

COMMUNICATING BETWEEN BOATS

If you are going to cruise in areas where a cell phone doesn't work, you should have a VHF (very high frequency) marine radiotelephone aboard. The first contact channel is normally channel 16. After your contact responds, immediately agree on another channel and switch to it to continue. Choose one of the ship-to-ship channels: 09, 12, 13, 14, 65, 66, 68, and 73.

On channel 16, which is also the official international emergency channel, always listen first before transmitting so you don't interrupt an emergency conversation. Don't converse on it—even though you'll find it is often clogged by extraneous chatter that obscures true emergency calls.

Mayday is a top priority distress call for life-threatening situations aboard, so don't use it lightly. If you ever have to make a Mayday call to the Coast Guard, be ready to give them the following information: your boat

Figure 17-8. VHF radio

type, number of crew aboard, your location in latitude-longitude coordinates, and the nature of your emergency.

Pan-Pan is an urgent message relating to the safety of a ship or person. *Sécurité* relates to navigation safety or important weather warnings.

To set up your radio for calling or receiving, turn the ON-OFF volume switch up high and the *squelch* knob up (clockwise) until you hear an awful blast of static noise. Then turn the squelch knob down just enough to quiet the static. Often the inability to communicate with another radiotelephone is caused by the squelch knob turned down too far. Make sure it is as high as possible without static noise.

Remember that your conversations can be heard by other boats with radios on, so don't say anything embarrassing or off-color, and don't use profane language (it's a federal offense).

Years ago we were anchored in a Connecticut harbor when a sailboat anchored ahead of us with two people aboard—a man and an incredibly beautiful woman in a bikini. While enjoying cocktails and a glorious sunset, with our radio on below, we heard the yacht ahead of us call the marine operator and contact a private home. The conversation went something like this: "Honey, I can't get home tonight. I'm totally fogged in. I'll get back as soon as possible tomorrow." We were looking right at the name of the boat, given over the radio, and absolutely no fog.

USING A VHF RADIO

- Turn volume and squelch buttons to high
- Power squelch back until static just disappears
- Listen before transmitting
- Contact on channel 16, then switch to another channel to talk
- Mayday—only for life-threatening situations
- Pan-Pan—for safety issues related to boat or person
- Sécurité—for threatening navigation or weather situations
- Anyone with a VHF on in the vicinity can hear your conversation
- Broadcasting profane language is a federal offense

TEST YOURSELF

Safety and Life Onboard
To test your knowledge of life onboard and some of the safety issues you'll encounter, answer the following questions.

1. How does propane differ from CNG?
2. After using the stove below, how do you shut down the flame and flow of fuel?
3. What's the most efficient way to load a refrigerator?
4. Describe the law regarding plastic tossed overboard.
5. What's the safest way to serve coffee, soup, or other hot liquids?
6. Describe when to use Mayday, Pan-Pan, and Sécurité calls on a VHF radio.

18 CRUISE READY!

Everything you learned in this book has prepared you to start cruising. All you need now is some hands-on experience and the desire to see the world under sail.

The vast majority of new sailors consider bareboat chartering as the first step to big-boat sailing. It's a hassle-free way to get into cruising, without having to own a boat.

ABOUT BAREBOAT CHARTERING

A bareboat charter does not mean the boat is "bare." It will come fully equipped with everything you need to sail and live aboard comfortably—including electronic aids, linens, cooking and dining utensils, even all your meals if you like.

Bareboat chartering means cruising on your own without a professional captain and crew to help you. Like renting a car, you are responsible for the boat and must prove to the charter company that you have the skills and experience to take one of their yachts out on your own. To rent a car you need a driver's license. To charter a sailboat you may need proof, such as the US SAILING certification at the Basic Cruising and Bareboat Cruising levels.

In any case, the charter company will ask you for a resume of your experience, specifically: sizes of boats you have sailed; how much skippering experience you have; your navigation and anchoring proficiency. Proof of the certification you get in a US SAILING course is widely accepted as a standard of certain skill levels by sailboat charter and rental companies. It simply eases the qualification process. Be wary of any company that doesn't ask about your sailing experience. Those that do are more apt to provide boats in the best condition.

Although some countries in Europe require their citizens to possess licenses for chartering, there are no such rules that affect U.S. citizens—regard-

Figure 18-1. A charter boat at anchor in Tonga

less of where you charter. US SAILING certification, which starts at the Basic Keelboat level you studied in the first part of this book, provides a log book where you can document the courses you take and the miles and places you sail. All of these certifications, coupled with good navigation and anchoring skills, are usually your passport to successful, fun-filled bareboating.

"Taking your course on a Hunter 466 is of much benefit. It truly gives you the feeling of what it's like to take the helm of a vessel this size and displacement."

**GABRIEL EMANUELLI (40),
MIRAMAR, FL**

This book has given you the knowledge to comfortably charter a yacht that may be worth $200,000 or more. Charter companies are of course very careful about determining if you are capable of taking on such a responsibility. By reading this book, you've already taken the first step. You already have a comprehensive store of knowledge under your belt. Now, you just need to apply it to bigger boats and get the on-water experience to move quickly to chartering or cruising on your own.

Chartering Flotilla-Style

Signing up for a group charter organized and supervised by expert sailors is a great way to get your cruising feet wet, so to speak. After you take the on-water portion of the Fast Track to Cruising course, you can start cruising without having any big boat experience by signing up for a flotilla charter. A flotilla is a fleet of small ships (in this case charter yachts) led by an expert on a lead vessel.

Figure 18-2. An Offshore Sailing Club flotilla cruise in Greece

US SAILING CERTIFICATION

Many sailors seek certification to verify and advance their skills. US SAILING—the National Governing Body (NGB) of sailing under the U.S. Amateur Sports Act—has created and maintained the definitive national standards for sailing instruction and continues to develop highly successful training and certification programs for young and adult sailors. When you gain US SAILING certification at the Basic Keelboat, Basic Cruising, and Bareboat Cruising levels, you know you are truly ready to cruise.

"I took occasional lessons from a local captain in Galveston Bay, later took coastal navigation, and then Offshore's Coastal Passagemaking. I chartered with my family and participated in cruises in Maine and Antigua. On the last flotilla I was assigned a skipper and met my future wife there. She was assigned as my navigator!"

JAMES PRICE (57) WITH ILSE, CAPE ELIZABETH, ME

A flotilla cruise is also a way to meet others who share a desire to cruise. Over our more than 40 years of teaching, many marriages and lasting friendships have resulted from contacts made on flotilla cruises. In 1972, shortly after the concept evolved of making a fleet of self-hire cruising sailboats available for competent individual sailors, we chartered four identical boats and took a group of graduates to The Moorings in the British Virgin Islands for a week of cruising. This was the first commercially organized flotilla charter in those islands, and turned out to be a valuable learning experience for new sailors. Now, sailing magazines, a few other sailing schools, and charter companies offer similar group cruises on a regular basis.

Most of those who participate on a flotilla cruise each year either don't yet have enough time logged on larger sailboats to charter on their own, or (if they *do* have the skills) don't have friends or family to go with them. So, flotilla cruises are an experience builder, a way to meet other sailors, and make for an enjoyable vacation.

When you charter on your own, you have to make all the arrangements, plan the itinerary and provisions (with the help of the charter company) and take responsibility for the boat and those with you. All these details and responsibilities lie on the shoulders of the firm that sets up a flotilla cruise and you just need to get yourself to the point of embarkation and back. It's a lot like vacationing on a cruise ship in that you pack and unpack only once. But a sailboat cruise is all hands-on and only sailing clothes are needed. On a flotilla, you actively participate in the sailing; steering and trimming; learning to navigate and handle a larger boat; and at the same time learning how bareboat charters work.

Can anyone participate, even those that don't have any sailing know-how? In some cases, yes, but to really be part of the crew it's best to have at least the basic knowledge provided in the learn-to-sail section of this book.

The World Is Your Oyster

Around the United States, you can take advantage of charter opportunities along the coast of Maine, in New England, the Chesapeake, San Juan Islands and Gulf Islands of the North Pacific, Apostle Islands, Sea of Cortez (Baja California), and the Florida Keys. But the most popular areas are those in the warmer waters of the Caribbean. These places will most likely be your first choice for a charter, especially the British Virgin Islands, the Bahamas,

Figure 18-3. Enjoying a flotilla cruise in Greece

Figure 18-4. A lagoon in Tonga in the South Pacific

Figure 18-5. Sailing the Caribbean

Belize, Honduras, Guadeloupe, and many more islands of the West Indies and Lesser Antilles. In these islands, the water is always warm, the breezes are moderate and constant, and sailing to windward on a bright sunny day gives you a real high.

Check out websites for charter companies like The Moorings (www.moorings.com) and Sunsail (www.sunsail.com). They are full of information about each area where their fleets are available. The best weather windows, layouts of the available boats, suggested itineraries, and all the details you should know to make your cruise seamless are covered thoroughly.

Offshore's cruising club has taken new sailors to many of the best charter areas in the world: the Greek Islands; along the coasts of Turkey and France; around the islands of Tahiti and Tonga in the South Pacific; in the Whitsunday Islands of Australia; New Zealand's Bay of Islands; the Balearic Islands of Spain; the Croatian coast; and around Corsica. Every day takes you to places where cruise ships cannot go, like the magical lagoons of the Kingdom of Tonga. Every year charter companies open a new base somewhere in the world to explore.

Comprehensive cruising guides cover almost every area of the world. Cruising Guide Publications (Dunedin, Florida) publishes books for the

> *"I've daysailed a few times on rentals and with friends, crewed for a friend on a passage from Key West to Belize, and am leaving this week to return to the BVIs for a bareboat charter."*
> **CHRIS CLEMENS (37), DENVER, CO**

Caribbean and other destinations. Don Street is an indefatigable author of Caribbean cruising guides. Roger Duncan and John Ware's *A Cruising Guide to the New England Coast* is the Down East bible. H. M. Denham has written excellent guides for Greece and the Aegean. Imray, Laurie, Norie & Wilson, Ltd. has excellent guides for the Mediterranean, covering Spain, Portugal, France, Italy, Turkey, Greece, and Croatia. You can usually obtain these and other guides through stores and websites that specialize in nautical charts, marine books, and sundries.

Climates and Prevailing Conditions

Many guidebooks also include information on average rainfall and the local winds—such as their force and direction, and the average number of days each month sailors might experience a bora in Croatia, mistral along the French Riviera, sirocco in southern Itlay, meltemi in Greece, or other regional winds with mystical names you'd rather read about than encounter! But just as important is the wealth of information available in these guides on local customs, places to anchor, historical sites, and great dining and shopping ashore.

Pilot charts are another good source for wind information. These are printed for each month of the year for various areas of the world, like the pilot chart of the Mediterranean shown in Figure 18-6. To find out what wind conditions you might expect for your cruise, look at the wind rose. Like a feathered arrow, the arrows on a wind rose fly with the wind, and the tails indicate the direction from which the wind is blowing. The length of the arrow shaft—measured from the outside of the circle to the end of the visible shaft, using the scale on the chart—gives the percentage of the total number of observations the wind blows from that direction.

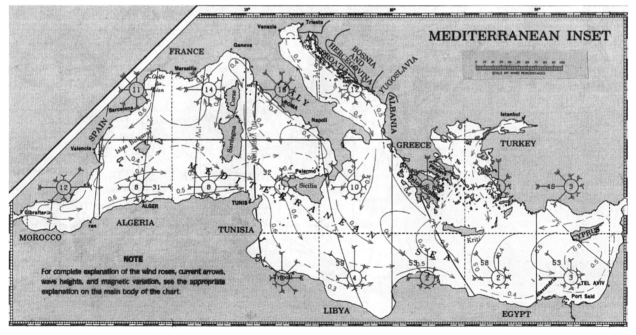

Figure 18-6. Pilot chart of the Mediterranean

CONVERTING BEAUFORT SCALE TO KNOTS

There are thirteen forces (0–12) in the Beaufort scale. To convert Beaufort force to knots, simply remember: *three-four-five*. Multiply the first four force levels (0–3) by three; the second four (4–7) by four; and the next four (8–11) by five.

For example: force 6 X 4 = 24 knots, which falls in the middle of the force 6 range (22–27 knots); force 10 X 5 = 50 knots, which falls in the middle of the force 10 range (48–55 knots); force 12 is 64 knots and over.

In Europe, wind strength is measured by force on the Beaufort scale. In the accompanying table, force is equated to knots of wind speed. A force 3 wind, for example, is 7 to 10 knots. You can also estimate the knot equivalents of the Beaufort scale without this chart, by using a simple calculation (see the sidebar).

Beaufort Wind Scale

Beaufort Force	Wind Speed (knots)
0	under 1
1	1–3
2	4–6
3	7–10
4	11–16
5	17–21
6	22–27
7	28–33
8	34–40
9	41–47
10	48–55
11	56–63
12	64 and over

On a pilot chart, average wind force is shown by the number of feathers on the arrows. For instance, the wind rose south of Cyprus on the pilot chart for May 2001 shows that 3 percent of the time the wind is predicted to be calm, and 53 percent of the time the wind is predicted to be force 3 from the northwest. The number in the center of the circle gives the percentage of calms for the month. The other number is the strongest wind strength trend. Pilot charts also give information about the frequency of storms and fog, the height of waves, the local air and water temperature, and the ocean current, among other things.

Itinerary

This wind information in the guidebooks will be valuable as you plan your charter itinerary. If you are returning the sailboat to the same location you started from, you can't afford to get too far away—particularly if you're sailing downwind and will have to head back upwind to return your boat. Figure roughly a 5-knot average speed and 3 to 6 hours of sailing a day, which satisfies most sailors where there is a lot to see ashore. This keeps the daily distances between ports in the 15- to 30-nautical mile range.

Remember, the joy of cruising is sightseeing by water. You take your hotel room with you—instead of having to pack and unpack every night as you move from hotel to hotel and get in your rental car or board a bus, train, or plane to reach a

"My wife, Kay, and I ride a Harley Davidson, so we are used to the 'freedom' involved with both motorcycles and sailing! With sailing, we can meet more new people, see more of nature and other cultures."

TOM HEINEN (62), TALALA, OK

Figure 18-7. Catamarans are popular charter boats because they heel less than a monohull.

new destination! When you are cruising, allow enough time to enjoy the history, the food, and the customs of each port you visit. If you would rather go out and pound 12 hours to windward, save it for a windy day at home.

Charter companies offer *monohulls* (single-hulled cruising boats, usually sloops) and *catamarans* (a boat with two parallel hulls). Hands-on live-aboard course training is also available at Offshore on either type boat. Many charterers like the catamaran because it traditionally has a spacious main saloon with broad visibility and hardly heels at all, even when going to windward.

Given a certain prevailing wind direction, particularly on a monohull, you might want to schedule easy reaches the first day or two so everybody can unwind and get their sea legs. Next work your way upwind in fairly short hops. Save the long stretches for reaches and runs; when you get to the farthest upwind point from the charter base in the time allotted, start back downwind.

Check-in time at the end of the cruise is usually before noon, so plan on spending the last night within about 5 miles of the charter base. This allows you time to clean the boat before heading in. Returning a charter boat in as clean, or cleaner, condition than you received it is good sailing etiquette and will probably save you money. Some charter companies charge an extra cleaning fee if a boat is left particularly dirty.

Checking In/Checking Out

Most charter companies require a refundable security deposit or purchase of nonrefundable security insurance to cover potential damage to the boat and equipment, as well as items lost during the cruise. While "normal wear and tear" is not considered a loss, always be prudent and careful when using equipment aboard.

When you board your chartered sailboat, you will be given a list of items and equipment you are responsible for. Check it carefully and make sure everything on that list is on the boat. Then look over the boat carefully for any pre-existing damage—such as bent stanchions or scratches and chips, the way you would when renting a car. You should also find the boat's various through-hull fittings so you can quickly close a valve if a hose or a hose clamp breaks. And don't forget to find the location of life vests, flares, the emergency tiller, fire extinguisher, and the first-aid kit.

Every charter company in the world will conduct a checkout before you board. This usually includes instruction on how to operate equipment on the boat, plus guidance on navigating in the area. In the navigation briefing, you should learn which areas on the chart to avoid and the best approach to take when entering different harbors. Generally speaking, Caribbean companies believe that if you can find a harbor each day and stay there all night after you found it, your cruise will be a success. Europeans assume you have all that basic knowledge, and they are more concerned that you don't mess up the boat because of unfamiliarity with its operation.

After a navigation and boat checkout, and before you get underway, you need to stow your gear and provisions. In the Caribbean, you may opt to cook aboard most of the time. In areas like the Greek Islands and the Côte d'Azur, you will surely want to dine ashore almost every night. If you opt for your boat to be provisioned when you arrive, the charter company will probably put perishables in the refrigerator but leave the rest for you to put away. Regardless, you should stow everything yourself for several reasons. You want to check off what you are supposed to have, both your food and consumables (toilet paper, paper towels, and the like). It's also important to know where everything is, so you can find items when you need them.

When you are cruising, make sure you tie up your dinghy carefully wherever you go. When you're sailing, take care of the outboard that comes with it. These two items are costly and, in some cases, you can be held totally responsible for major damage or *disappearance*. This is a nice way to say: watch out for theft in remote areas. And always check your knots when you tie up the dinghy for the night.

WHAT TO PACK FOR YOUR CRUISE

Always pack your gear in a soft duffel. There are no storage places on a boat for hard luggage. If you are going to cruise in warm waters, pack light. If you intend to check your duffel on a plane, carry a smaller one aboard with your documents and passport (if needed), a pair of shorts, a shirt, underwear, swim suit, toilet kit, medica-

tions, and valuables. Many island airports are remote and luggage can be delayed or lost. After you start the cruise, it is a major inconvenience to get back to the airport.

If you wear eyeglasses, an extra pair could come in handy. When sailing, eyeglass straps are a must. Be sure to bring any prescription drugs you need, as well as over-the-counter remedies for common travel problems. If you are taking any medication, check with your doctor to make sure you can be out in the sun. Tetracycline, for instance, can cause nausea—just like seasickness; and it doesn't react well with prolonged time in the sun.

A good sun lotion is vital in any climate, with an SPF (sun protection factor) of at least 15—particularly if you are fair-skinned or haven't been exposed to sun much recently. Test the lotion beforehand to make sure you are not allergic to PABA, which is used in many lotions.

Bring sailing gloves to avoid rope burn and blisters, which take a long time to heal in saltwater exposure.

Don't forget your camera and extra memory chips or film. If you have to buy color film in a foreign country, it can be very expensive and the type you want may not be readily available. Bring more than you think you may use. The vistas and colors in most sailing areas are a photographer's dream.

Check with the charter company to find out if your boat has a cassette or CD player and, if so, bring your favorite music. Although you may find a hand bearing compass and binoculars aboard, they may not be of the highest caliber. You might want to bring your own, along with a GPS to practice your navigation. Charts are normally provided on all bareboat cruising charters. In most cases, charter companies will also provide a cruising guide for the area, but be sure to confirm this ahead of time. If a cruising guide is not provided, consider bringing your own.

The great pleasures of warm weather cruising involve swimming and snorkeling. Where reefs are clear and colorful fish are plentiful, charter companies usually provide masks, snorkels, and fins. Sometimes, though, the masks the company provides don't fit a small, narrow face or over eyeglasses, and the company's masks see a lot of use. You may want to bring your own.

Zip-locking bags are included on our checklist of what to pack for a one-week cruise because they come in handy for storing leftover food and for separating wet and dirty clothing in your luggage on your way home.

Figure 18-8. Dressed comfortably for cold-water sailing

ONE-WEEK WARM WEATHER CHECKLIST

- ❏ 2 pair shorts
- ❏ 2 swimsuits
- ❏ 1 pair long pants
- ❏ underwear to last the week
- ❏ 2 knit shirts
- ❏ short sleeve T-shirt (you'll buy others in most places)
- ❏ long sleeve T-shirt
- ❏ belt
- ❏ light windbreaker
- ❏ sailing gloves
- ❏ visor or hat with lanyard with clips
- ❏ toilet kit and medicines
- ❏ 1 pair boat shoes
- ❏ 1 pair sandals for shore
- ❏ 1 pair reef shoes for wading
- ❏ socks (optional)
- ❏ camera, memory chips, film, lens cleaners
- ❏ eyeglasses and sunglasses with straps
- ❏ paperbacks
- ❏ passport, visa (if necessary)
- ❏ air tickets
- ❏ cash, credit cards, and traveler's checks
- ❏ sunscreen
- ❏ zip-locking bags
- ❏ favorite spices
- ❏ beer can insulator
- ❏ hand bearing compass
- ❏ binoculars
- ❏ GPS
- ❏ snorkel and mask
- ❏ cassette tapes or CDs

If you like to cook, the boats are well provisioned—but don't expect a wide assortment of spices in the galley. You may want to bring some of your favorite spices with you. If you are sailing in the "spice islands" of the Caribbean, such as around Grenada, you will find plenty in the markets ashore. You can find out what is available by checking with the charter company in advance.

Electric razors and hair dryers that use 120 volt electricity are not practical on a charter boat. Some boats do have inverters that change DC to AC current, but you may want to ask before you pack things you can't use aboard. The wind and sun in a warm climate work just as well as a hair dryer, and brushing on deck keeps hair from accumulating below.

Cruising in a colder climate presents different needs for clothing and gear. Bring a good suit of foul-weather gear, warm socks, two pairs of boat shoes, a pair of sailing boots (if you're sailing in northern regions), a heavy jacket, sweater and sweatshirts, and long-sleeved or turtleneck shirts. Swimming in Maine and the San Juan Islands off Seattle is not for the faint of heart; but daytime sun can be warm enough for wearing a bathing suit, shorts, and a T-shirt.

CUSTOMS AND CURRENCY ABROAD

Some sailors forget when they visit a small country that the customs and immigration officials are not used to our fast-paced lifestyles. Being polite and respectful is important—even if you feel you are being provoked.

If you don't have a passport, you may as well get one now. With everything that is happening in the world, this is the only sure way to get back into the United States—even from countries that don't yet require one.

If you need foreign currency, you can buy a trip-pack in many major cities before leaving, but you will pay a premium. In most airports abroad, you can exchange dollars while waiting for your bags to be unloaded. In the Caribbean, the U.S. dollar is broadly accepted. Credit cards can be used almost everywhere, even in the Galapagos, but some areas don't honor all of them.

If you are going to an area or country with higher inflation, don't exchange too many dollars at any one time. During our last cruise of the Dalmatian Coast (now Croatia), we got 10 percent more for our traveler's checks at the official government exchange rate at the end of our two-week visit than at the beginning. Unless you are sailing in a country that belongs to the European Union and uses the Euro for currency, try to use up all your foreign currency before you leave. If you plan to return someday with your unused currency, it might be worthless or no longer in circulation.

If you dabble with drugs at home, don't even think of taking them on any cruise. Offshore Sailing School instructors and cruise leaders are directed to kick any person taking drugs off the boat. The reason is simple. All bareboat charter contracts have clauses to the effect that if the boat is used for illegal purposes, the charterer is totally responsible for whatever happens to the boat. Insurance is voided, making the deductible irrelevant.

If local authorities board your boat and impound it under the U.S. zero-tolerance policies, the charter company will go after you for the full price of the boat—which can be well over $200,000. Even if the authorities give the boat back, you are responsible for legal fees, repair of the boat (in searching for additional drugs the interior is often demolished), storage fees when impounded, and loss of charter revenues to the charter company.

All this could result from smoking one joint of marijuana or just having the residue of some marijuana in your toilet kit. Even in the beautiful, civilized British Virgin Islands, drugs are a quick way to a long jail term.

CRUISING COURTESY

The advice below relates to accepted etiquette among sailors. These are not regulations, just common courtesies and will make you seem like an experienced sailor if you adhere to them.

Always ask permission of someone aboard before setting foot on their boat. Wear rubber-soled shoes or sneakers, or take your street shoes off before you board. Street shoes can scratch the deck, black soles leave marks, and no one wants someone else's dirt aboard.

If you find your boat on the outside of a raft-up—where many boats can be berthed side-by-side—you'll have to walk across the inside boats to get ashore. Cross the other boats forward of the mast rather than across the cockpit, where you might interfere with the privacy of those below decks. However, at night when everyone seems to be asleep, avoid walking over cabin areas.

When sailing, stay well clear of any boats that are racing, even if you have the right-of-way. The same holds true of powerboats that are trolling for fish.

If you fly an ensign, raise the flag at 0800 and lower it at sunset. Depending on the latitude of where you are cruising and the time of year, sunset can be at cocktail hour or long after you went to bed. When we were in Norway for a wonderful big boat regatta (in which the late King Olaf participated), our ensign was lowered with great ceremony long after midnight. The yacht ensign or national flag is raised first, followed by the yacht club burgee and owner's private signal. They are all lowered in reverse order.

Most important are the little courtesies extended to others aboard. There is nothing more infuriating than a crew member who won't do their share of the "dirty work"—washing salt spray off the decks, cleaning up after a meal, cooking, changing sails, and the many other tasks involved in cruising. Anyone who expects to be waited on had better go on a cruise ship.

Always tie off your halyards at night to keep them from slapping against the mast—even if you settle down for the night in a dead calm. Halyards make an awful racket on your boat and can disturb the peace of an entire anchorage. And if the wind pipes up while you are sleeping, you'll find yourself waking up from the clamor and getting out of your bunk to tie them off, in the dark.

Again, if you anchor later than another boat and find yourself swinging too close, you need to move, not them. If you were there first, they should move.

Always keep your boat shipshape. Whether you charter, borrow, or own your own, a clean and neat boat makes the cruising experience not only more fun, but ultimately a lot safer. Have pride in your abilities and your knowledge of proper seamanship. We hope we have instilled that pride in you, and hope you will carry it on with you as you embark on the Fast Track to Cruising!

BEYOND CHARTERING

If you plan to buy a boat and go cruising, there are many options. You can buy a used boat, new boat, or enter a time-share plan. You can invest in a boat used by a charter company that gives you an annual return or charter time, or a combination of the two, and ultimately the boat itself in three to five years.

Some sailors own a cruising boat just for weekend use and an occasional vacation with family or around home. For this type of sailing any size cruising boat with accommodations (berths) for two or more below is just fine. You don't need a boat with beefed up sails, hull and rigging particularly built for extended ocean conditions. You don't need a lot of extra gear. In this case, easy sailing and recreational characteristics like a big cockpit and expansive living space below are often the deciding factor.

One of the first areas East Coast cruisers with more time start to explore is along the coast to Maine and then down the ICW (Intracoastal Waterway) to Florida and across to the Bahamas. Many sailors do these routes every year, spending summers in northeast waters and winters in the Abaco or Exuma Islands of the Bahamas. On the West Coast with fewer harbors and cruising areas, many sailors head to the Pacific Northwest or down to Mexico.

FIGURE 18-9. A big cockpit makes cruising with friends more fun

Figure 18-10. Cruising along the coast of Maine

Figure 18-11. Rigorous conditions on a long-distance passage

Perhaps you are planning a summer sabbatical or a shorter getaway of a few weeks, a month, maybe three longer outings each summer interspersed with weekend or evening sails; then put your boat *on the hard* (out of the water) in a marina for the winter. Sailing and cruising magazines have semi-annual editions devoted to launching your boat in the spring and taking it out of the water in the fall each year.

The ultimate dream—to live aboard and explore near or distant lands—belongs to many but often not actually lived until retirement. The preparation for this lifestyle is much longer and the decisions far greater. Where you plan to cruise, how long, and with how many impact the type and size boat you choose and the equipment you put aboard.

Whether you buy a new or used boat depends on your pocketbook and goals. Most cruising-boat hulls are now molded in fiberglass, which doesn't deteriorate or require the upkeep of wood. So when shopping for a used boat, you might want to focus on those that require not much more than buffing the hull and cleaning and painting the bottom each year. Because fiberglass doesn't self-destruct there are a plethora of used-boat choices on the market. Just go to a seaside or lake area and start visiting the marinas, boat brokers, and dealers (who take used sailboats in trade for new boat sales).

Some hulls are aluminum, ferro-cement, carbon fiber, or steel although these are far less common among cruising sailors. Aluminum and steel are strong but require attention for electrolysis in salt water. Carbon fiber is also strong and very light, but is also costly and hard to repair. Ferro-cement, once the choice of backyard builders, is very heavy.

Heavy is not necessarily better when contemplating long-distance cruising. The design and how well a boat is built is much more important. A marine surveyor should always be employed to give you an unbiased evaluation of a used boat you are considering; there are no warranties if something structural or mechanical occurs after you take possession.

The best place to start looking for a new cruising boat is at an all-sail boat show. The industry association, Sail America, produces five all-sail shows: in St. Petersburg, Florida, in November; Philadelphia and Chicago in late January, early February; Miami in mid-February; and Oakland, California, in April. The United States Sailboat Show in Annapolis, Maryland, each October is the granddaddy of them all—with cruising boats ranging from 30 to 80 feet or more, all in the water, and many smaller sailboats on land. At any sailboat or power-sail combination show, you'll find booths for suppliers of gear and equipment, and services ranging from marinas to charter companies and sailing schools. All of these shows also provide free seminars and more in-depth classroom programs at modest fees.

Magazines like *SAIL*, *Cruising World*, *Blue Water Sailing*, *Sailing* and *Latitudes & Attitudes* publish monthly how-to columns, boat reviews, and informative articles on where and when to cruise. You'll also find advertisements in these magazines for most of the sailboat manufacturers in the world and brokerage sections for used boats. Their websites are even more informative and up-to-date.

Experienced cruising couples like John Neal and Amanda Swan Neal (www.mahina.com) offer weekend offshore cruising seminars for people considering or planning long-distance ocean cruising on their own sailboats. They also take sailors on passages (for a fee of course), providing first-hand instruction and invaluable experience. Lin and Larry Pardey (www.landpardey.com) also give seminars across the United States, including memories from 38 years and over 175,000 miles of voyaging under sail. Both the Neals and the Pardeys are popular speakers at boat shows. Many sailing schools (including ours) offer advanced courses for those considering cruising over longer distances, like the US SAILING Coastal Passagemaking course—a rigorous one-week training program that certifies the student at the Coastal Passagemaking level.

So pick up one of the magazines listed above, start going to sailboat shows and all the educational opportunities they provide, and soon you'll embark on that cruising lifestyle; new friends, new adventures, a whole new way of looking at yourself and the world. Just for a moment, re-read the foreword by Bernadette Bernon and say to yourself: "I can do that too! It's time to go cruising."

There's no better lifestyle than cruising!

SEVEN-DAY STUDY PROGRAM

The Fast Track to Cruising program covered in this book can be completed in seven days if approached in the context of a rigorous instructional setting. Spend three days learning the basics in Chapters 1 through 8 and four days learning to cruise in Chapters 9 through 18. Occasionally you should go back to the earlier chapters to refresh yourself on important concepts. When you are finished, you will be ready to bareboat charter or cruise on your own or a friend's boat.

If you're learning on your own, outside a concentrated instructional program, proceed at your leisure, taking as long as you like to master the material in this book. Remember, learning is half the fun.

In this section, we present you with the tests that those who actually participate in Offshore Sailing School's Fast Track to Cruising® program take each day before setting out on the water. The answers to these questions are covered in this book.

Day One

1. What is LOA?
2. What is the primary purpose of standing rigging?
3. Which point of sail is 90° off the wind?
4. If you are in irons, how do you sail away on port tack?
5. If you are on starboard tack, which side is the boom on?
6. Which knot is used to make a loop in the end of a line?

7. What's the name of the line used to raise the sails?
8. What is a series of tacks to get to an upwind destination called?
9. In order to tack, do you push the tiller toward or away from the mainsail?
10. Name the three corners of a sail.
11. Name the edges between the three corners of a sail.
12. What is the difference between stays and shrouds?
13. What are topsides?
14. What is the difference between standing and running rigging?
15. What are telltales?
16. What are the commands for tacking and jibing?
17. What does hardening up mean?
18. What is by the lee?

Day Two

1. What is the fastest point of sail in light air?
2. Describe a header and a lift.
3. Describe the difference between a veering and a backing wind.
4. What is apparent wind?
5. What two functions does the keel of a sailboat perform?
6. What are some of the reasons you may be experiencing excessive weather helm?
7. What does a cunningham do?

8. What is your main concern when sailing downwind?
9. Is a full sail more or less powerful than a flat sail?
10. Is apparent wind always stronger than the true wind?
11. What happens to apparent wind in a puff?
12. If you head slowly into the wind and the top telltale on the jib starts to flutter on the windward side before the lower two, what does this mean and how do you correct it?
13. What should you do first if a person falls overboard?
14. What is your first maneuver when you do a Quick Stop Recovery of a crew overboard?

Day Three

1. What is the best approach when attempting a mooring shoot?
2. Does the stand-on vessel or the give-way vessel have right-of-way?
3. What scope should you use to anchor your boat overnight in normal conditions?
4. What is the same tack right-of-way rule for sailboats?
5. What is the opposite tack right-of-way rule for sailboats?
6. If a sailboat with sails up is motoring, is it a sailboat or a powerboat?
7. When should you consider reefing the mainsail?
8. What is the overtaking rule?

Day Four

1. If you put a cruising boat in reverse, with rudder amidships and a right-hand propeller, will the stern tend to go to port or to starboard?
2. When springing the bow off the dock, do you use the forward or aft spring line? Do you put the engine in forward or reverse?
3. Why pump the bilge before leaving the dock?
4. What percent of maximum rpm should you cruise under power?
5. What is the main boom topping lift and what must you remember about it after the mainsail is raised?
6. Is the leeward genoa sheet released completely during a jibe? If so, why? If not, why not?
7. Why do you slide the main companionway hatch closed when raising the mainsail?

8. When meeting a powerboat in a narrow channel, which is the preferred method of passing?
9. How does luff tension control draft?
10. When does a jib trimmer cast off a sheet during a tack? Why is this important?
11. Why is it important to pause in neutral when shifting between forward and reverse?
12. What are the dangers of backing the stern into heavy seas?
13. Which spring line is used when springing out the stern?
14. Describe a back-and-fill turn.
15. A boat with lee helm will turn in which direction?
16. After starting the engine, is the key left in the "ON" position or turned to the "OFF" position? Why is this important?
17. List the daily checks performed on the engine before getting underway.

Day Five

1. If, on a light-air day, the jib starts to luff, but the skipper hasn't altered course, what two reasons could there be?
2. What concern do you have when sailing wing and wing?
3. If you're powering into a dock or mooring too fast, what should you do?
4. Briefly describe how you would set up your sail plan for light winds and choppy seas.
5. List the situations when the dinghy painter should be brought up tight to prevent it from fouling.
6. Why is it a bad idea to motorsail in heavy weather?
7. Why do most marine diesel engines have a mechanically operated fuel pump that can also be operated by hand?
8. Explain how to determine the recommended scope of an anchor rode for an average overnight anchorage.
9. What is a special anchorage?
10. Describe the characteristics of an anchor light.
11. What is a tripline as it relates to anchoring?
12. How can you determine if your anchor is dragging?
13. What are two primary considerations in your approach when picking up a mooring ball?

Day 6

1. Describe the steps to effectively heave-to.
2. List in sequential order nine steps taken to jiffy or slab reef the mainsail.
3. What is a leech cord and what does it do?
4. On which point(s) of sail is the boom vang used to control the shape of the leech?
5. If close reaching and a person falls overboard, outline the steps taken for recovery.
6. What are some ways to minimize the amount of heel in heavy weather?
7. What is a preventer? When is it used?
8. List steps to depower sails.
9. What sound signals does a sailboat use in limited visibility such as fog?
10. Name two international distress signals.
11. Why would you attach a downhaul to a bosun's chair?
12. What are some of the steps you can take if your anchor is dragging?
13. What is the danger zone of a powerboat?
14. What is the purpose of a length of chain between the anchor and the rode?
15. What information must you be prepared to give the U.S. Coast Guard if you call Mayday on your VHF?
16. What do three vertical lights on another boat mean to you at night?
17. What hours are navigation lights required?
18. On which side of the bow do you find a red navigation light?
19. How do you heel the boat if you go aground and why?
20. Describe an emergency tiller and its use.
21. How do you use the land behind a converging boat to determine whether they are on a collision course?
22. Why should you go forward on the windward side of your boat in heavy winds?
23. How do you determine if you are on a collision course with another vessel?
24. What is the best way to treat a victim of hypothermia?

Day 7

1. What is the log reading that is entered in the ship's log?
2. What does a round black shape on the bow of a vessel mean to you?
3. What does the Rule of Twelfths apply to?
4. Can compass deviation be determined from the compass rose on your chart?
5. Will a Type III PFD keep an unconscious person's face out of the water?
6. List the three colors that a NOAA chart uses to indicate depth. List from shallowest to deepest.
7. What does a magenta diamond shape or circle shape mean on a charted navigational aid?
8. What is leeway and how do you allow for it in navigation?
9. Describe set and drift.
10. What does the acronym CADET stand for?
11. How do you use the phrase TV Makes Dull Children in navigation?
12. Which water tank should you use first when cruising?
13. What is the international law regarding the discarding of plastic overboard?
14. What is the function of the solenoid switch in the cooking system?
15. What is the difference between propane and CNG?
16. What is a good VHF channel to use to talk to another vessel?

TIPS AND CHECKLISTS

Getting Underway

1. When you board, step in the middle of the boat—on the floorboards if the boat is a tippy one—while holding onto the shrouds, if possible.
2. If the jib is not rigged on a furling headstay—hank on the jib tack first, feeding it between your legs for control and checking along the foot for twists.
3. If jibsheets are not attached—tie them on with bowlines to the jib clew, lead them back to the cockpit winches through proper blocks, and tie stop knots in each free end.
4. If the jib halyard is not already attached—attach it to the grommet in the head of the jib; first look up and check for twists around a shroud, spreader, or another halyard.
5. If the mainsail is not flaked along the boom—feed the mainsail foot into groove on the boom; attach the tack at the gooseneck and the clew to the outhaul; pull the foot tight with the clew outhaul.
6. If battens are not in their pockets—start with the lowest one; make sure the most flexible batten is placed in the highest position; make sure all battens are pushed down into the pocket and under the flap at the leech, so they can't fly out when the sail luffs.
7. Before raising the sail—follow along the mainsail luff to remove twists; feed the luff into the groove in the mast, starting at the head; attach main halyard.
8. To raise the main—first make sure the main-sheet is completely free to run, vang and cunningham are loose, and the halyard is not fouled around shroud, a spreader, or another halyard.
9. Main is being raised—hold the boom up by hand and make sure the leech isn't caught under a spreader.
10. After the sail is raised and the luff is tight—cleat and coil the main halyard and finish with a half hitch (but don't use a half hitch on sheets).
11. Raise and secure the jib, or unroll it if you have roller furling.
12. To get underway—untie the mooring line and hold onto it while backing the jib to the desired tack, then drop the mooring.
13. Don't cleat the mainsheet on a small boat in a breeze.
14. When checking sail trim, adjust the jib first—ease it until it luffs, then trim in; do the same with the main.

Leaving a Dock

1. Assign jobs to your crew.
2. Double up docklines so they can be released from the boat.
3. Check the wind and current.
4. Prepare the sails and anchor for quick use.
5. Spring the bow or stern out.
6. Use prop walk to your advantage.
7. After leaving, stow lines and fenders.

Safety Precautions when Sailing and/or Powering

1. When raising and lowering sails, close hatches that can be hidden by sails so no one can fall through.
2. Don't stand in the bight of genoa or spinnaker sheet—if a turning block fails, released pressure throws parts like missiles.
3. Use winches properly to avoid catching fingers.
4. Don't stand to leeward of the boom or goose-neck; if either fail, they fly to leeward.
5. Don't stand or sit where you can get hit by the traveler car or tangled in the mainsheet in a fly-ing jibe.
6. Be aware in case you suddenly run aground or hit a rock; people aboard will pitch forward.
7. Check frequently to leeward of the jib for ap-proaching traffic and possible collisions.
8. Don't work near a running engine when its cover is off.
9. Keep fingers away from the anchor windlass when raising or lowering the anchor.
10. Wear shoes—sailing barefoot can cause falls and stubbed or broken toes.
11. Use stove clamps when cooking hot soup, boil-ing water, stews, or other foods that can spill un-derway or in a busy anchorage.
12. Keep engine in neutral when around swimmers, or if lines are over the side.

Tacking

1. Sight abeam to windward to estimate direction of your next tack.
2. Sight aft of abeam to windward to avoid tacking into the path of another boat.
3. Release the jibsheet when there is a large luff in the jib.
4. Watch to make sure the jibsheets don't hang up on edges of hatches or vents.
5. Turn slowly and not past 90° while the genoa is being trimmed in.
6. If trimmers are having a tough time winching the sail in, give them a small luff.

Cruise Preparation

Traveling
1. Pack light and use duffels.
2. Carry an emergency kit on the plane in case of lost baggage.

3. Take a valid passport and check if a visa is needed for cruises outside the United States.
4. No illegal drugs!
5. Take medication, sun lotion, sailing gloves, eyeglass straps, and camera.

Itinerary
1. Check pilot charts for average wind strength and direction.
2. Take a cruising guide for the area.
3. Take it easy the first day or two.
4. Get upwind early in the cruise.

Predeparture Checklist for a Cruising Boat

- ❏ Turn on the house battery.
- ❏ Turn on the DC main breaker.
- ❏ Flip instrument switch on.
- ❏ Flip radio switch on.
- ❏ Air conditioning systems off; dock power breaker off.
- ❏ Disconnect shore power cord—shore end first, then boat end; coil on deck or stow.
- ❏ Check bilge for excess water and test the bilge pump.
- ❏ Check raw-water intake strainer.
- ❏ Open seacocks for raw-water intake.
- ❏ Check fuel level, freshwater tanks levels; top off if needed.
- ❏ Check engine—oil level, transmission fluid level, freshwater coolant level, belt tensions.
- ❏ Unlock steering-wheel brake.
- ❏ Turn on engine battery; check water level in battery once a week, and top off if needed.
- ❏ Check that engine kill switch is at running position.
- ❏ Start engine with the throttle in neutral; preheat if necessary.
- ❏ Check to make sure salt water is exiting from ex-haust; turn off engine and troubleshoot if not.
- ❏ Check gauges—battery (12+), oil (55–65), water (150°–180°)
- ❏ Turn radio on to channel 16.
- ❏ Remove sail cover and attach halyard; make sure halyards and sheets are clear and ready to run.
- ❏ Check that anchor is ready to use.
- ❏ Prepare docklines for departure.

GLOSSARY

Here you'll find definitions for many of the terms we used in this book.

abeam—at right angles to the boat

accidental jibe—an unexpected boom swing. See also **jibe.**

aft—at, near, or toward the stern

aground—touching the bottom

aloft—up in the rigging

anchor—heavy object lowered in the water to keep boat from drifting

anchor rode—chain, rope, or both used to attach anchor to boat

angle of attack—angle of boat's centerline to water flow

angle of incidence—angle of sails to the apparent wind

apparent wind—the vector wind caused by the true wind in combination with the boat's forward motion; the wind you feel

aspect ratio—relation of height to width

astern—behind the boat

athwartship—across the boat

back (a sail)—to push a sail to windward (against the wind)

back an anchor—put two anchors in line attached to each other by a short length of chain

backing wind—wind direction shifting counterclockwise, such as W to SW

backstay—wire from upper part of mast aft to deck; a component of standing rigging

backwind—wind off the jib hitting the lee side of the main

balance—to neutralize forces so boat sails on a straight course with little helm

ballast—weight in keel used to increase stability

batten—a slat inserted in the leech of a sail

batten pocket—pocket for battens in the leech of a sail

beam—the widest part of the boat

beam reach—sailing with the wind abeam

bearing—the angle to an object

beat—a series of tacks

Bernoulli's Principle—as velocity of air increases air pressure decreases. Air picks up speed as it flows behind the jib and mainsail. The reduction in air pressure creates lift, causing the sails to pull the boat forward.

berths—bunks for sleeping aboard

bilge—low area of boat where liquids collect before being pumped out

bimini—awning over cockpit

bitter end—the end of a line

blanketed—deprived of wind in the sails by another boat or large object to windward

blocks—pulleys that sheets run through

boom—horizontal spar that supports foot of sail

boom vang—device to keep the boom from lifting

bow—forward end of the boat

bow line—a docking line from the bow to the shore

bowline—a common knot used by sailors to form a loop (pronounced *bolin*)

bow wave—the initial wave created by the bow breaking the water

breast line—single line from middle of boat to opposite piling

broad reach—sailing between a beam reach and a run; sailing with the wind on the quarter

buoys—floating marks

by the lee—wind on same side of the boat as boom when running

cabin sole—floor of cabin

camber—belly of a sail

can—odd-numbered navigational buoy, usually green

capsize—to overturn a boat

catamaran—a boat with two parallel hulls

centerboard—a board or plate raised and lowered on a pivot pin to reduce leeway

centerboard trunk—housing for the centerboard

centerline—an imaginary line down the middle of the boat from bow to stern

center of buoyancy (CB)—The point around which the forces pushing upward to keep a boat afloat are concentrated. The CB will be located somewhere on the for-and-aft centerline of a well-trimmed boat at rest, but as the boat heels and its wetted surface changes, the CB moves to leeward, thus resisting further heeling. See also **center of gravity.**

center of effort (CE)—The theoretical point in a boat's sail plan at which the wind's pressure is focused. The fore-and-aft relationship between the CE and the center of lateral resistance (CLR) determines a boat's helm balance. See also **center of lateral resistance.**

center of gravity (CG)—The geometric center through which all weights in a boat act vertically downward. If you could suspend a boat from its CG, it would hang perfectly level. In a keelboat the CG is located deep in the hull, giving it "ballast stability." The relationship between the CG and the center of buoyancy (CB) creates a "righting arm" that causes the boat to favor an upright position. As the boat heels and the CB moves farther leeward from the CG, the righting arm grows in strength, thus resisting further heeling. (See discussion on page 70.)

center of lateral resistance (CLR)—The imaginary vertical line through a boat's underwater profile that divides the underwater area into two equal halves, forward and aft. The CLR is like the axis of a weather vane. If you were strong enough to place your forefinger on a boat's CLR and push it sideways, it would yield without pivoting. The relationship between the CLR and the center of effort (CE) dictates the boat's tendency to either round up into the wind or fall off. Simply put, if the CE is located aft of the CLR, the boat will have weather helm—it will pivot toward the wind. If the CE is forward of the CLR, the boat will have lee helm. (See discussion on page 64–66.)

chart—nautical map

chock—guide on deck for docklines or anchor rode to pass through

chord—straight-line distance from luff to leech on a sail

cleat—device to secure a line

clew—the aft corner of a sail

close-hauled—sailing as close as possible to the wind

close-reach—sailing between close-hauled and a beam reach

cockpit—a recessed area in the aft deck to accommodate crew

collision course—one in which the relative bearing on another boat doesn't change and boats are converging

come about—to change tacks with the bow turning through the wind; to tack

companionway—passageway from cockpit to interior cabins below

compass—magnetic card that points to magnetic north

contour lines—lines on a chart that connect all areas of equal depth and height

cotter pin—a split pin separated and bent when inserted to keep clevis pins and turnbuckles from backing out

cringle—a reinforced hole sewn or pressed into a sail through which a line can be passed

cubbies—lockers used to store food and personal effects

cunningham—device to tension the luff of a mainsail

current—water flowing in a definite direction

Dacron—synthetic material used in sail manufacture

daggerboard—centerboard that retracts vertically rather than pivots

danger zone—on a motorboat, the area from dead ahead to two points aft of starboard beam; another motorboat converging from this direction has right of way

daysailer—small sailboat

depth sounder—electronic instrument that reads depth of water

deviation—compass error caused by metal aboard the boat

dinghy—a small rowboat used to get to shore from mooring. Can also be stepped for sailing

displacement—total weight of the boat

dividers—two metal legs hinged at top for measuring chart distance

dock—a landing pier, wharf, or float

dog—the act of fastening down hatches

dogs—wing nuts that fasten hatches when closed

douse—quickly lowering sails

downwind—sailing with the wind pushing from behind

draft—distance from waterline to boat's lowest part

draft (of a sail)—as seen from above, the distance from the straight-line chord between a sail's luff and leech to the deepest point of the sail's curve, or camber

ease—to let out, as in a sheet

fairlead—a fitting through which a line passes, changing the line's direction

fall off—to turn the boat away from the wind

feathering—to sail so close to the wind that sails luff periodically

fin—a type of keel

flake—preparing or coiling a rope or a sail such that it will pay out without tangling

foot (of sail)—bottom edge of a sail

footing—increasing speed by falling off slightly

foredeck—the deck forward of the mast or foremast

forestay—any wire that runs from foredeck up to mast for setting a jib and supporting the mast

forward—toward the bow

fouled—tangled

fractional rig—forestay runs from bow to at least three-quarters up the mast, but not to the top

freeboard—distance from deck to the water

furl—to fold a lowered sail and secure it

galley—cooking area (kitchen) in a cruising boat

gennaker—asymmetrical, light-weight reaching jib

genoa—jib whose clew overlaps the mast

gimbal—swinging mechanism that allows a stove to stay level with horizon when the boat heels

give-way vessel—when two boats meet, the one expected to alter course and/or speed to prevent a collision

gooseneck—swivel fitting attaching the boom to mast

gust—a sudden increase in wind velocity, also called a puff

half-hitch—knot used to tie line to an object

halyard—wire or line that pulls the sail up

hank—a fastener by which a sail is attached to a stay

hard alee—command of execution when tacking

hard aground—boat is stuck on the bottom

harden up—turn the boat toward the wind

harness—heavy nylon straps joined by stainless clip and tether, worn over shoulders and around waist in heavy weather

hatches—hinged doors on top of cabin

head—marine toilet; often used to refer to entire bathroom aboard

head (of sail)—the top corner of the sail

header—wind shift toward the bow

headstay—the foremost stay from bow to top of mast

headway/steerageway—forward motion, enough to steer effectively

heeling—when a sailboat leans to the lee

horseshoe life preserver—U-shaped floatable collar mounted on stern to toss overboard if someone in water needs help

hull—body of boat

hull speed—boat's theoretical maximum speed

in irons/in stays—head to wind and dead in the water

initial stability—resistance to heeling up to about 12°

jacklines—wire rigged from bow to stern along both sides of deck to clip harness tether into in heavy weather

jib—foresail carried on the jibstay

jib hanks—snaps to connect jib to stay

jib lead—adjustable fairlead for jibsheets, determines angle of jibsheet to the clew

jibe—to change tacks downwind

jibe ho—command of execution when jibing

jibsheet—line tied to clew of jib or genoa that adjusts sail in and out

jibstay—wire from bow to mast (but not to masthead)

jiffy reef—reef in the mainsail that is tied rather than rolled

kedge off—use anchor to pull boat off a shoal

keel—vertical fin under boat with weight for stability

knockdown—boat is blown over such that both mast and keel lie at waterline

knot—one nautical mile per hour

knotmeter—measures speed in knots

latitude—see **parallels of latitude**

lazarette—storage compartment usually located under cockpit seat bench

leech—the trailing edge of a sail

leech cord—small line running up inside leech to reduce flutter

lee helm—bow turns to leeward when tiller is released

leeward—in the direction opposite from which the wind is blowing (pronounced *looward*)

leeway—side-slipping to leeward

length at waterline (LWL)—distance between points where bow and stern touch the water at rest

length overall (LOA)—distance from the tip of bow to end of stern

lifelines—safety wires running the length of the deck

LifeSling—floatable device thrown to person in distress in water

lift—wind shift toward the stern

locker—storage area found under settees, behind cushions, and on deck

longitude—see **meridians of longitude**

lower shrouds—shrouds that lead from base of spreaders to deck

luff—spill wind out of a sail

luff (of a sail)—the leading edge of the sail

lull—sudden reduction in wind velocity

magnetic north—direction indicated by north-seeking magnetic compass

main—short for mainsail

main halyard—line that raises and lowers the mainsail

main saloon—living area in a cruising boat, where seats and dining table are found

mainsail—sail hoisted along after edge of mainmast (pronounced *mainsl*)

mast—vertical spar supporting sails

mast step—plate that holds bottom of mast in place

masthead—top of mast

masthead fly—device at top of mast to indicate wind direction

masthead rig—jibstay runs from top of mast to bow of boat

meridians of longitude—measures angle to east and west of Greenwich, England

messenger—light line used to feed heavier line or blocks to areas not easily reached

mooring—a permanent buoy to which one ties a boat

nav station—designated area for navigation below, usually has flat area for working on charts with storage for charts, navigation aids, and mounted electronics

neutral helm—no tug on the tiller; no weather or lee helm

no-go zone—area between close-hauled and directly into wind where boat cannot sail and is dead in the water, in irons

nun—even-numbered conical navigation buoy, usually red

outhaul—line attached to clew of sail on a boom that adjusts foot tension

overhaul—to pull the slack out of a sheet to trim a sail

overpowered—excessive heeling in comparison to forward drive

painter—tow line permanently secured at bow of dinghy

parallel ruler—draws parallel lines to transfer course or bearing on a chart

parallels of latitude—measures angle north or south of the equator

pinch—to sail too close to the wind to maintain speed

pitching—precipitous rising and falling of the bow on steep seas

planing—exceeding theoretical hull speed by skimming the water

play—to adjust trim in and out constantly

point—to sail close to the wind

point (on a compass)—one of 32 divisions of the compass (11.25°)

points of sail—close-hauled, reaching, and running; describe relationship between wind direction and boat's heading

port side—the boat's left side

port tack—sailing with the main boom on starboard side

portholes—cabin windows that can be opened

portlights—cabin windows that cannot be opened

positive stability—self-righting if turned over

prepare to jibe—command of preparation when jibing

preventer—a line tied to a boom to prevent an accidental jibe

projected area—the actual hull or sail area exposed to the water or wind

puff—a gust of wind, see **gust**

quarter—portion of the boat between the beam and the stern

quarter wave—wave following boat at angle to stern quarter

Quick Stop Method—to pick up person overboard by turning through the wind to back the jib

reach—sailing with the wind across the boat

ready about—command of preparation when tacking

reef—to shorten or reduce size of sail

reeve—to pass a line through a fitting

rigging—all the wire and rope on a boat

roach—convex area of sail lying aft of a straight line from head to clew when viewed from the side

roller-furling jib—headsail that rolls up vertically

rolling hitch—a knot that can be used to hold tension when tied to another line

rope clutches—leads for halyards with levers that act as a brake

rudder—underwater fin turned by tiller or wheel to steer the boat

rudderpost—metal tube or bar that turns the rudder, connects rudder to tiller or steering quadrant

run—sailing with the wind from behind the boat

running rigging—all lines, tackles, etc., that adjust the sails

sail ties—nylon or rope strips used to tie up mainsail when stored on boom

schooner—boat with two or more masts, with aft mast the tallest of the two

scope—relation of length of anchor line used to depth of water

scull—moving the rudder back and forth like a flipper to propel the boat

seacocks—valves that open and close the through-hull fittings

sentinel—a weight placed on anchor rode to reduce angle line makes with bottom

set—describes a sail that is raised and full of wind

settees—bench-like seats in cruising boats

sheets—lines attached to clew of sails to adjust trim

ship (water)—to take on seawater into the cockpit or dinghy

shooting—to turn directly into the wind

shrouds—wires running abeam from masthead to the deck that hold up the mast

sloop—single-masted vessel with a jib

slot effect—tendency of jib to make mainsail more effective

snub—to place one wrap around a cleat or winch to absorb much of its pull

soundings—depths on a chart in meters, fathoms, or feet

spar—general term for mast, boom, pole, etc.

spinnaker—a light parachute-like sail for sailing downwind

spinnaker pole—spar to position tack of spinnaker

spinnaker sheet—line to clew of spinnaker opposite the pole

spreader—struts that spread the angle shrouds make with the mast

spring lines—docklines that keep the boat parallel to the dock

stall—inability of wind to stay attached to lee side of sail

stand-on vessel—when two boats meet, the boat that's expected to maintain its course and speed unless risk of collision exists

standing rigging—all the fixed rigging that holds up masts (shrouds and stays)

starboard side—the boat's right side

starboard tack—sailing with the main boom on port side

stays—wires from the mast to the bow and stern that keep the mast from falling forward or aft

staysail—small jib tacked between mast and headstay

steerageway—enough speed to steer effectively

stem—forward edge of the bow

stern—extreme after end of a vessel

stern line—docking line used to hold stern of boat to dock

sump—catch area or low point in the bilge below floorboards, where water drains

surfing—sliding down the face of a wave

tabling—edging on the leech of a sail

tack—to change tacks with the bow passing through the wind

tack (of boat)—see **port tack** and **starboard tack**

tack (of sail)—forward lower corner

tail—to pull a line behind a winch

tail (of a line)—free end of a line

telltales—wool or other light strips of material placed on shrouds or sail to show wind direction or flow

tiller—arm fitted to rudderpost to steer by

topping lift—support line or wire from masthead to end of main boom, used to hold boom upright when sail is not set

topsides—the sides of the hull above the waterline; also used when describing going from below to deck

transom—the usually flat portion of the stern running across the boat

traveler—track running athwartship to change mainsail's angle

trim (fore and aft)—the attitude of the boat, bow up or bow down

trim (sail)—to pull in, to adjust the set

true north—direction to the geographical north pole

true wind—the wind as felt when stationary

turnbuckle—a fitting, adjustable in length, that attaches bottom of shrouds and stays to chainplates

ultimate stability—ability of boat to resist turning over

upper shrouds—shrouds that lead to masthead

variation—local difference in degrees between true and magnetic north

veering—wind direction shifting clockwise, such as S to SW

warp—threads that run lengthwise in sailcloth

weather helm—tendency of boat to head into the wind when helm is released

weigh anchor—to raise the anchor aboard

winch—a drum with gears and handle to assist pulling in lines under strain

windlass—electric winch mounted in deck locker in bow, used to raise anchor and chain

windward—in the direction from which the wind is blowing

wing and wing—sailing downwind with jib on one side and main on opposite side

INDEX